D1248096

How to Work Without Losing Your Mind

'An invaluable guide to surviving professional life. Cate Sevilla is insightful, inventive and so supportive' Viv Groskop, author of *How to Own the Room*

'A brutally honest, beautifully practical guide for anyone reassessing their priorities in work and life. This book is a masterclass in swerving burnouts and resetting boundaries' Lucy Clayton, co-author of *How to Go to Work*

'Explored with huge heart and unending empathy, I implore every millennial and gen Z woman to read this, whether they're at the start of their career or its zenith' Laura Jane Williams, author of *Our Stop*

'A timely and provocative book that is at once empathetic about the challenges work presents and empowering on how to overcome them' Bruce Daisley, author of *The Joy of Work*

'Entertaining and practical; moving and funny; and, most importantly, a helping hand from someone who's been through it' Emma Gannon, *Sunday Times* bestselling author of *The Multi-Hyphen Method*

'A frank, funny and kind guide on how to turn a job into a career' Ailbhe Malone, editor, *Strategist UK*

'A thought-provoking and practical guide to the ever-evolving world of work, Cate Sevilla's words feel particularly comforting and clarifying during these uncertain times' Yomi Adegoke, co-author of the bestselling *Slay in Your Lane*

'Oh, how I wish I'd had this book ten years ago! Cate gives both the sympathetic hug and the firm shake by the shoulders that so many of us need to navigate the world of work right now. It's hilarious and helpful with so many on-point insights that you'll wonder if she's been reading your Slack messages (she hasn't)' Lauren Bravo, author of *How to Break Up with Fast Fashion*

'It's funny and smart and incisive and smashes every narrative we're fed as workers (and women). And it's way beyond being an essential book on work culture; it's an essential feminist text. The women who read this – employees, managers, wherever they are in the structure – will be changed by it. It's nothing short of radical' Terri White, editor, *Empire*

'Fearless and funny! If you feel like work is getting or letting you down Cate is here to give you a hug and offer you practical advice. All of our careers are now full of change and uncertainty and Cate's book will help you to take control and look after rather than lose your mind!' Sarah Ellis, co-author of *The Squiggly Career*

'I wish I'd read it before ever entering an office, and I one hundred per cent hope anyone who ever has to manage me reads it' Flo Perry, author of *How to Have Feminist Sex*

'This is a genuinely useful, smart, thoughtful and beautifully written exploration of a subject that affects us all, but we know so little about. I do not use this word lightly (or much at all if I can help it) but Cate's brilliant book is genuinely EMPOWERING' Daisy Buchanan, author of *How to be a Grown Up* and *The Sisterhood*

'I can't think of a better time than the darkness of a covid winter to sit down with this wonderful book and re-assess your relationship to work. Cate Sevilla has a wisdom about the working world that is rare in its depth and sensitivity. She can teach you how to fix a bad work situation or to spot when it's time to walk away. Her book will teach you how to survive at work without sacrificing your soul – from dealing with bad communication, awful managers and impending burnout, to setting boundaries and getting organized. Everyone who works has to read this book' Hannah Jewell, *Washington Post*

'This is the only professional handbook I want or need . . . Reading her book makes it feel like you're sat across from a friend you can tell anything to before leaving with multiple life-changing revelations – including how lucky you are to have Cate Sevilla in your life' Anne T. Donahue, author of *Nobody Cares*

How to Work Without Losing Your Mind

CATE SEVILLA

BUSINESS

PENGUIN BUSINESS

UK | USA | Canada | Ireland | Australia
India | New Zealand | South Africa

Penguin Business is part of the Penguin Random House group of companies
whose addresses can be found at global.penguinrandomhouse.com.

First published 2021
001

Copyright © Cate Sevilla, 2021

The moral right of the author has been asserted

Set in 12/14.75 pt Dante MT Std
Typeset by Jouve (UK), Milton Keynes
Printed and bound in Great Britain by Clays Ltd, Elcograf S.p.A.

The authorized representative in the EEA is Penguin Random House Ireland,
Morrison Chambers, 32 Nassau Street, Dublin D02 YH68

A CIP catalogue record for this book is available from the British Library

ISBN: 978–0–241–43966–1

Follow us on LinkedIn: https://www.linkedin.com/company/penguin-connect/

www.greenpenguin.co.uk

Penguin Random House is committed to a
sustainable future for our business, our readers
and our planet. This book is made from Forest
Stewardship Council® certified paper.

For my husband and my therapist.
I couldn't have done this without you.

Contents

Introduction

In the early months of 2020, when many of us were still battling new year's resolutions and very much still believing that '2020 would be our year!', it turned out that – globally, collectively, if not completely universally – 2020 would very much *not* be our year. At least not in the way we had hoped. Rather than a year filled with exciting travel or finally going to Glastonbury, 2020 became a year filled with uncertainty and loss, unprecedented change and new beginnings that none of us asked for or wanted. To put it lightly, the majority of 2020 was fucking awful.

Covid-19 changed all of our lives in ways that we will be trying to comprehend for a long time. The grief, from loss not just of life per se but also of normality and life as we knew it, came in waves. At times it felt like a tsunami. For many of us, this was made most apparent in our working lives. Work, for those lucky enough to have it – whether a '9 to 5', steady freelance gigs or enough paid hours to pay the rent – was what gave our days, weeks and lives structure – the takeaway coffee on the way to the station, the podcasts listened to on our daily commute, the faces of colleagues seen day in and day out, the misery of train delays on the way home. The global pandemic blew all of this to smithereens. People worldwide lost their jobs in incomprehensible numbers.

The world of work has been changed in unprecedented ways. People who had never worked from home before were suddenly doing it every day. People who previously had no idea what Zoom was were suddenly using it several times a day for important meetings (and the occasional pub quiz). Suddenly we were all that guy on the BBC whose wife and child burst into the room while he was Skyping a report on BBC News. Those of us who had previously been told that it was impossible for us to do our jobs remotely or part-time from home were shown that, well, that wasn't exactly true.

For all the parts of work that have changed, altered or shifted – there is one element that has stayed the same, and has often been amplified: STRESS.

Bosses are still maddening. Colleagues are still profoundly irritating. Balancing family and work is still daunting. And how to progress in our careers without burning out is still a huge question that so many of us are searching for an answer to. More than ever, we are wondering how to work without losing our minds – and that is exactly what I'm here to help with.

Hello, fellow loo-crier

I imagine you might have purchased this book after spending the better part of your working day huddled in a bathroom – whether in a stall at work or hiding in the family bathroom at home – while ugly-crying into the sleeve of your cardigan. Or maybe because you've found yourself lying awake each night for hours on end, replaying enraging emails and Slack conversations with your work nemesis in your head instead of counting sheep (or listening to a sleep story read by Matthew McConaughey). Perhaps you're not crying much at all and are just great at compartmentalizing your rage and are TOTALLY FINE but kinda also might spontaneously combust in your next meeting with your boss. Either way, I get it, and I've got you.

Even if you're not a crier, work stress is no joke. Difficulties with our boss or anger at our colleagues are often dismissed as petty problems that we 'shouldn't let get to us'. That these problems should stay tucked away in our desk drawer and be forgotten about, much like random pens and packets of Post-it notes we unnecessarily hoard from the stationery cupboard.

We're taught that our problems at work don't count as *problems* out in the real world, and that they should stay at work, just like our problems at home should *stay* at home. '*Don't bring your work home with you!*' Or '*Check your personal problems at the door!*' This traditional separation of 'work' and 'life' is also particularly confusing if you work from home – where, exactly, are those problems supposed to live? We're essentially told to exist as split beings. That we should have impenetrable skin and never take anything personally while remaining personable at all times. That burnout is an inevitable symptom of ambition, hard work and achievement – rather than being what it is: an unnecessary by-product of toxic working cultures and unhealthy management styles. That we should never get tired or ill. Shockingly, there are very few people who can actually function like this. And if you're struggling to play along with this absurd, impossible narrative, it can get real lonely, real fast. Not only can work stress isolate you from your colleagues, but the stress and anxiety you're feeling at work can also start to isolate you from your friends, your partner and your family.

Personally, I have spent an unimaginable amount of my work life with a pounding heart, sweaty palms, churning guts and an anxious rage coursing through my veins. I've endured many meetings with my hands hidden under a table, my mouth and face trying their best to appear pleasant while I dig my fingernails into my palms and the voice inside my head screams, *'OH MY GOD FUCK OFFFFFF!'* I've fantasized about escaping meetings by launching myself out of boardroom windows, like a corporate Lara Croft flipping through the air and landing safely outside on my awaiting Triumph, my middle finger raised in salute at my boss as I ride off into the sunset, never to be seen again. I've wandered the halls of large office buildings, staring helplessly at the colourless carpet, overwhelmed by stress and loneliness. I've ugly-cried in so many office loos they might warrant their own walking tour of London. (DM me if you're interested.)

Throughout my career, in times of stress, I've spent a lot of time reading many different business books and inspirational quotes from inspirational business women, hoping for some answers, hoping that someone will tell me what to do next, and how to do it. The problem is, with very rare exceptions, no matter how many times I read these quotes or watch their TED Talks or even purchase their books, with all due respect, I just never know what the fuck they're on about. I mean . . .

'Empathetic instincts, when coupled with operating rigor, drive a leadership style in which everybody wins.'
Fran Rauer, *The Myth of the Nice Girl*

'We must raise both the ceiling and the floor.'
Sheryl Sandberg, *Lean In*

'I'm a workaholic and I don't believe in "no". If I'm not sleeping, nobody's sleeping.'
Beyoncé Knowles

Whenever I read this sort of stuff my face literally turns into the 'calculating lady' meme. There's a lot of chat about ceilings (and floors) and nonsensical methodologies and general smugness about being a supposed boss lady. Never mind the shameless bragging about waking up at ridiculous o'clock to bang out an hour-long workout and an hour-long meditation session, plus a quick conference call with the Japan office before everyone else has even had breakfast.* Narratives like this give me insurmountable anxiety, because the message seems to be that, in order to succeed, I would basically need to change everything about myself and the way that I work – and apparently never sleep. It all just leaves me feeling tired, confused and none the wiser than before.

Who I am and how I got here

I've lived in London for over fourteen years, but I was born and raised in California. I grew up in a small suburban town just south of Sacramento called Elk Grove. My existence as a teenager was very much like that of Saoirse Ronan's character in *Lady Bird*: I was in theatre and drama club, I worked at cafés, lusted after boys in bands, cried a lot, read a lot of books, dreamed of living in Paris and New York, dramatically sang along to the *Moulin Rouge* and *Chicago* soundtracks, ate a lot of Taco Bell and rarely did my homework.

Rather unexpectedly, but much to my delight, I moved to the UK when I was twenty years old and have been working in digital publishing ever since. (I moved to London in what is

---

* Which is, of course, a plant-based meal of something completely unsatisfying, like three peas and a ginger shot.

a very romantic modern-day love story involving a handsome British man, Myspace and a $1,000 mobile phone bill.)

After years of freelancing as an editor and journalist, I joined the corporate world in 2013. Since then, I've worked for some of the world's biggest tech and media companies – including Google, Microsoft and *BuzzFeed* – and start-ups both big and small. I was even the lone woman director for a tech start-up founded by Jeremy Clarkson, Richard Hammond and James May, which was *interesting* to say the least.

While a lot of the companies I've worked for and the job titles I've held sound exciting and impressive, to be honest, I've found most of it really, really difficult. I've been yelled at in meeting rooms named after biscuits. I've gone through weeks where it felt like the only purpose of my job was to toe the company line and make other women cry. I've been gaslit with poor performance reviews and felt pretty abandoned by HR. In addition to my own aforementioned loo-crying I've also tried powerposing before stressful meetings (sorry, Amy Cuddy, but it didn't help) and meditating in designated quiet rooms usually reserved for tech-bro power naps. I've also hid from my manager in those same quiet rooms watching episodes of *Nashville* on my laptop as a way of keeping myself sane.

Some of the more recent career drama I've dealt with was in early 2019, when only four months into my new role as editor-in-chief of the women's lifestyle website *The Pool*, I lost my damn job. I experienced a very surreal, very public ending to what I thought was my dream job when the company suddenly stopped paying its staff, as well as the company's suppliers and freelance contributors.

I've felt at first-hand what happens when your average work stress and anxiety crosses a line and starts to slowly eat away at your mental health. In one job in particular I spent several months regularly visiting our in-office wellness centre due to various confusing symptoms. I was then told by doctors and nurses and physios that all the physical weirdness I'd been experiencing was, annoyingly, the result of stress.

How to Work Without Losing Your Mind is a guide to navigating the real, messy side of work that no one says much about but a lot of people experience. I want you to know that you are not alone in this. This is why I feel it's so important for me to be honest and real about how difficult I've found many aspects of my career, because in the midst of it all, I could really have done with some great advice on how to handle everything. To hear: 'Yes, I've been there!' is one thing; to hear: 'Yes I've been there, and this is how I handled it' is even better. That is what this book is about and why I know it's needed: because *I* needed it! It's based on what I know, not on corporate or self-help-style bullshit. (Be warned, in addition to using a fair amount of profanity, I also use a lot of Harry Potter and *Sex and the City* references, because I am a basic, elder millennial.)

Whether you're in management at an office-based desk job, a shift worker in a retail environment, self-employed or someone who offers specialist services, this book is for you. If you've ever been left feeling paralysed with envy over someone who seems to be absolutely smashing it in their career – this book is for you. Even if you're self-employed – as I presently am once again – I'm sure it will resonate with you.

Womxn at work

While work stress is a relatable topic for everyone, regardless of gender, I feel strongly that there are particular problems that specifically impact the working lives of women that other business and career books don't (or can't or won't) address – such as envy between colleagues and how to cope with fertility issues at work. At the same time, I cover a lot of topics that are *universal* and not gender-specific at all, from dealing with difficult managers and mental health problems, to setting boundaries, to how to succeed without continuously burning out. It's written using both my own experiences as a cis woman in the workplace and the experiences of other self-identifying women and non-binary individuals, from HR professionals and therapists to technologists and creatives to self-employed people, because no two people's experience of work are exactly alike.

When I use the word 'woman' or 'women', my intended definition is *anyone who identifies as a woman*, which includes both cis and trans women. Many of the experiences the book will cover will also resonate with non-binary individuals. When I speak about parenting, I use the word 'mothers' for the women and people who have children who identify as such, whether or not they've physically given birth. I also use 'parents' more than I strictly use 'mothers', and at times I use them interchangeably. My intention is to be as inclusive as possible while still specifically addressing issues that I and many other women have faced.

The advice in these pages is designed to feel like a comforting hug followed by a sharp – *but loving* – slap across the face, followed by another comforting hug and rounded-off with a swift kick in the ass to send you on your way. Because when dealing with work this is what we need: comfort in the fact that we're not alone; a reality check that it's never the end of the world, and an injection of motivation to go out and get what we want.

In order to do that, we also need to understand the wider systems at play that impact the lives of women. These are multifaceted, but include the hierarchical and systemically patriarchal structures of businesses that hire and pay women unequally, the legislation that dismantles and suppresses women's rights, and society's own misogyny-fuelled infrastructures that keep people who identify as women out of positions of power and authority. All of these play a part in why our working culture and the state of work for women is as shitty as it is. So, before we go into the practicalities of dealing with the difficulties of work, we'll first look at how little has actually changed for women at work in the last fifty years.

We've come a ~~long way~~ moderate-but-insufficient distance, baby!

In a relatively short amount of time a lot has changed. In the 1950s, in many companies women weren't even allowed to enter boardrooms, so we know that the office culture and behaviour of *Mad Men* wasn't just fiction. It wasn't until 1947 that Cambridge University fully validated degrees for women,[1] and it's only been fifty and fifty-seven years respectively since both the United States and the United Kingdom passed their Equal Pay Acts. It wasn't until the 1970s that women on both sides of the pond could even access credit without a man's signature.[2]

From the outside looking in, today women are pretty lucky. In the US, the number of businesses owned by women increased by a whopping 68 per cent between 1997 and 2014.[3] There are more of us in leadership positions than ever before, and mothers being the 'breadwinners' of the household is increasingly the norm. Some of us are paid quite well, earning annual bonuses and shares in start-ups – something our mothers would have very rarely been offered.[4] We've also had the opportunity to work in exciting new industries in a time of massive technological innovation, and as a result, many of us have worked in swanky offices – with ridiculous facilities such as ping-pong tables, full gyms and napping pods – and are welcomed to attend a weekly happy hour where our employers give us free (warm) drinks and maybe even slices of (sad, cold) pizza.

We've come a long way from the experiences of our grandmothers, but even with great strides of progress, there are still massive inequalities to contend with. A fantastic cultural example of this is Greta Gerwig's 2019 adaptation of *Little Women*, first published in 1868. Gerwig points out: 'So much of the book is about money, and women, and art and money, and how do you make art if you don't have money?'[5] What this film perfectly highlights is just how many of women's financial and work-related struggles have shifted but not altogether changed in the 150 years since *Little Women* was written.

Hearing Amy March say on screen in 2020 that 'the world is hard on ambitious girls', and Jo March passionately proclaiming that women have 'minds and souls as well as hearts, and they've got ambition and talent as well as just beauty', and that she's sick of people saying that love is all a woman is fit for, was both illuminating and maddening. Because while it's no longer completely unorthodox to have a career instead of children, or even instead of a marriage, a woman with more ambition than domestic aspiration is still *other*. The world is still so very hard on us. Which, of course, was brilliantly exemplified in the dismissive reception of the film by Gerwig's male colleagues in the industry – a rejection made even clearer by the lack of nominations for *Little Women* in both screenwriting and (especially) directing categories during 2020's award season.

A political example of this, however, was US President

Donald Trump's strategic, Gileadesque* attempts to dismantle funds and organizations that were formed to guarantee women's access to safe, legal abortions, birth control and sex education. This was an attack aimed at stripping women of a basic human right: to be in control of one's body. Because if we're not in control of *our own bodies*, how can we ever expect true equality in society, never mind the workplace?

Despite the progress we've made even in a single generation, we can't afford to pretend to revel in a time where women are running the world, the way Beyoncé wanted. It's both depressing and rage-inducing. Yes, we can have credit cards (hooray for debt) and, yes, we can technically own companies and sit on boards. But it would be naive and, quite frankly, *silly* of us to give a celebratory Mary Tyler Moore beret-toss when we know that, actually, things are still unequal. We shouldn't exactly be *grateful* that we're no longer only relegated to secretary or assistant positions, or thrilled that we're even 'allowed' to be at work.

In fact, during the coronavirus pandemic, it became alarmingly clear that women are indeed the backbone of our economy and what keeps our societies functioning. The *New York Times* reported in April 2020 that while normally men make up the majority of the American workforce, during the pandemic when everything was stripped back to the bare necessities – one in three jobs held by a woman was designated as essential.[6] From nurses and pharmacy technicians to supermarket cashiers, the *New York Times* wrote that this 'unseen labor force' whose work is often 'underpaid and undervalued' is actually what 'keeps the country running and takes care of those most in need, whether or not there is a pandemic'. It's

---

* If you haven't read Margaret Atwood's *The Handmaid's Tale*, or watched the TV adaptation of it, you really, really should!

true that our foremothers had it much tougher than us for a bunch of different reasons – if they could even have 'it' at all. It's also true that men definitely have a tough time at work, for there are so many difficulties that we all share. But there are a myriad ways in which modern working is hellish specifically for millennial and Gen Z women. If you're a woman of colour, it gets even worse. If you have a physical disability, any mental health condition, if you have a neurological difference or if you're a member of the LGBT+ community, this all affects you even more, as your experience (and your pay) will be very different and far more challenging than it is for your average white male. (Those are the facts, don't @ me.)

And, as one of the great philosophers of our time, Peter Parker, once said, 'With great power comes great responsibility' (yes, I went there). The more 'freedom' women are said to have – at work, with their finances, with their bodies and minds – the more new problems we have, too. We are continually working against the grain, constantly met with obstacles and people who wished we had stayed at home and out of their way – even if these feelings are buried deep below the surface, lurking in the corners of their mind assuming the name of 'unconscious bias'. And with these new problems, we also have a fuck ton of new responsibilities.

Sure, we're not Gileadean handmaids, and *technically*, yes, we've never had it so good – but it's still pretty fucking bad.

Here's my shortlist of reasons why work is so shit for us – an actual shit list:

 no.1 We work for under-qualified, poorly trained managers who have negative impacts on our career trajectory and development, our ability to work effectively and our mental health.

no.2 Toxic work cultures that are lacking in boundaries – allowing egos, envy, mental health problems and drama to run rampant – and also promote unhealthy working habits that normalize burnout and extreme amounts of stress.

 no.3 Employees are lulled into a false sense of security by being told their company is 'family' and encouraged to 'bring their whole self to work' – and then punished for it.

 no.4 Women are still paid less than their male colleagues, and our overall working culture puts parents at a disadvantage and is particularly unsupportive of working mothers.

The system we exist in works against us, and can feel like it's been set up for us to fail. The working world merely tolerates women, rather than fully accepting us. We are let in the doors, which men insisted on holding open for us, and then treated as unequal.

At its heart, that is what this book is about: dealing with this shit list and changing our relationship with an oppressive, restrictive, broken system of modern working. It's about acknowledging what we can change and control, and the things we can't. It's about dealing with the external factors at work that can make things difficult, and working on some things within yourself, too. This is personal. What you want out of your work – and therefore out of your life – is all right there. The answer is all in *how* you work and *how* you deal with the shitstorm and stay sane. I believe there is always something you can do to create change no matter what you face, and that you must start with the changes within yourself – and I'm here to help you do that, starting now.

1

Power + Authority:

When your boss is the worst

Is the laptop absolutely necessary? :) :*

The bright yellow Post-it note was stuck down next to me on the meeting table. I sat there, sphincter clenched, trying my best to get my insurmountable amount of work done while in an unnecessary weekly meeting that I was unnecessarily obliged to attend. The note has been passed to me and written by my micromanager boss – rather indiscreetly.

I read it over and over again.

Is the laptop absolutely necessary? Happy face. Kiss.

Kiss?!

I had a lot of questions, but mainly I wondered what kind of a psychopath draws emoticons on a disciplinary note and includes *both* a happy face and a kiss? It was the kiss that threw me, like, was it meant to soften the blow of her acting like a controlling weirdo? She's taking the time to *hand draw an asterisk* in the middle of a meeting but *I'm* the one not paying attention? Not even when Berger broke up with Carrie on *Sex and the City* using a Post-it did he use an emoticon. *Even Berger* knew it wasn't the time or the place.

I clenched my jaw and bit my lip as I slowly lowered my laptop screen, like a tail being tucked between my legs. I felt small, and my cheeks grew hot. My chest burnt with an embarrassed rage. I felt like a child who had just been told off by a teacher. Which, for a perfectionist people-pleaser like me, was highly annoying both then and now. But even more annoying? Getting in trouble when I believed I hadn't done anything wrong. And this Post-it perfectly summed up my relationship with my then manager.

Is the laptop absolutely necessary? If you'd like this project finished on time then, *yes*, it is fucking *necessary. Happy face. Kiss (my ass).*

What I found particularly galling about this passive-aggressive Post-it was that my manager has spent countless meetings hunched over her laptop, clacking away on her email while the rest of the team stared helplessly at the dreaded 'roadmap' for whatever godforsaken quarter we were currently working our way through.

Was using a laptop in the middle of a meeting rude? It's not great, and it's not something I did before or after working at this company. It was a learned behaviour and part of the culture there – if you're exceptionally busy and have to be in a meeting, working on something else while you're in there is more or less accepted, unless it's specifically stated that everyone should be off their laptops. At Google, for example, and at other companies that have built a similar culture, your laptop remains on your person at all times. If you were to spend a bit of time observing Googlers at any of the company's international offices, you would see them scuttling around like manic ants, laptops clutched to their chests as they power walked from meeting to meeting, sometimes perching their MacBooks on filing cabinets to respond to an email, or even typing with one hand as they used the other to prop it up midair while in a packed lift.

Hours of back-to-back meetings were the norm, and getting your work done was something that was apparently meant to happen in romantic, stolen moments between cross-functional meetings, team catch-ups and the small, intimate two-person sessions that are referred to as 1:1s.* In between these back-to-back meetings, we'd grab free-yet-still-sad salads and lukewarm cans of Diet Coke, perhaps a tiny muffin or a weird protein bar made from dates, matcha and mange tout from the café, and then rush back to eat it in another meeting. We'd apologize in hushed tones if we dared need to leave a room for five minutes so we could quickly wee. No time for a poo! THERE WAS JUST NO TIME.

For some reason I had kept the note in my drawer at work instead of throwing it away, as some sort of evidence of the absurdity I was experiencing. I then kept it in a folder after I left that job, and when I found it again a year later, I posted a photo of it online. The response I received was both hilarious and affirming. Never had I had so many comments about anything (not even a cute selfie!). 'What the FUCK?' was the overall consensus, and my initial thought beyond 'I know, right?' was,

---

* Never do you refer to a meeting as a 2:3 or a 5:1, but sure, 1:1 it is.

'Oh man, that's not even the half of it.' But it perfectly represented my overall working experience with this person: confusion, passive aggression, absurdity and constant, unnecessary assertions of authority.

In my career I have had several managers. And, unfortunately, most of them weren't particularly good. Some were just a bit crap but otherwise generally harmless while others were intensely stressful and had a poor impact on my mental health and self-belief. I had one manager at Starbucks who constantly referred to how young I was, or what I was (or wasn't) eating. I've worked for many men who didn't know how to make eye contact with me, but were (mostly) respectful of my work and my time. But I've also been managed by controlling, unhinged and aggressive men – one of whom unfollowed me on Twitter an hour after I put my notice in and then tried to get out of paying me my notice period.

However, the worst manager I've ever had – the author of the Post-it note – in combination with her own boss, who is a completely other story – sent me to the edges of my own stress and sanity levels. The only positive that came from working with her was that she also ended up teaching me some invaluable lessons about my relationship with work, and my own wants and desires for my career. Those lessons weren't intentionally taught, but I learned and gained perspective from her all the same.

Having a 'bad' manager is one of the most challenging and common workplace situations one can face, and there have recently been many studies looking into the specific psychological effects of being bullied at work.[1] It's been said that people don't leave jobs, they leave managers,[2] and I think that this is almost always true. Well, it certainly has been for me.

What a bad manager looks and feels like

In speaking to many different women from different industries, it's become clear to me that poor management or having a difficult relationship with your manager is not a unique or location-specific situation.

When I spoke to Kate Hogan, an integrative therapist in London, she said that the biggest commonality she sees across all of her patients – 80 per cent women, ranging in age from late twenties to early forties – is that they struggle with their relationship with their bosses and feel they're 'unable to ask for what they need, unable to push back'. She says, 'It's the relational stuff, *not* being able to manage the amount of work that's going on.'

Another woman said that when she was working at a popular club in Leicester Square as a cocktail waitress, she was regularly harassed by 'disgusting' customers. 'One day I said to my boss that every night this one guy comes in and he's really harassing me, and my boss turned around to me and said, "Well, you're here to sell sex." Meanwhile I thought I was there to just serve drinks and tidy-up!' A thirty-one-year-old woman from California I spoke to had a similar experience with her manager. She says her manager's email response to a formal sexual harassment complaint she had made about a male colleague that included both evidence and witnesses was: 'What do you expect me to do with this?'

Feeling abandoned by your manager in times of need, and the acute disappointment that can arise when realizing that your manager doesn't actually have your back, is very jarring and can alter your entire perspective on both your job and the company that you're working for. It's particularly upsetting when you're already feeling stressed or anxious about something, and then your manager compounds the issue by being insensitive.

Maggy Van Eijk, the thirty-year-old author of *Remember This When You're Sad: Lessons Learned on the Road from Self-Harm to Self-Care*, shared her experience of telling her manager at a large broadcasting company in the UK that she was pregnant. 'When I first told my manager that I was pregnant, he said, "But you don't even have a boyfriend." When I said I did – which doesn't even really matter, but I did – he said, "You just don't seem like the type that has a boyfriend." I don't even know what that means.'

When I first heard this story, I was actually speechless. While I'm not surprised things like this take place, it's just shocking that this happened at quite a large corporation that has the means to train and develop its managers. Equally, anyone promoted to a management level should, at the very least, have the emotional intelligence and common sense to know instinctively that sensitive topics like pregnancy should be approached with great care.

Maggy agrees, 'He was not a people manager at all . . . I think he wanted the status but didn't want to actually manage people.' Yeah, no shit.

How bad managers behave

From my research and my own personal experiences, 'bad managers' all share pretty similar characteristics. Dr Gary Namie, director of the Workplace Bullying Institute, has created a definitive list of twenty-five bullying behaviours. You can find this list on *Forbes* website in the article 'How To Deal With a Bullying Boss',[3] but his list includes tactics such as:

- Abusing the evaluation process by lying about the person's performance.
- Ensuring failure of a person's project by not performing required tasks: sign-offs, taking calls, working with collaborators.
- Singling out and isolating one person from co-workers, either socially or physically.

A lot of these behaviours resonate with me, but I think 'bullying' is a term that has lost some of its nuance, as it's used quite freely on social media and can mean many different things to different people. For me, bullying is what happens when a situation crosses the line from being 'a bit difficult' or, for example, occasionally disagreeing with someone or butting heads, to your antagonist relentlessly and actively shaming and intimidating you. It's important to note, as well, that bullying doesn't always involve shouting and yelling or name-calling. You can be intimidating without raising your voice – you can shame someone without calling them names.

In my own working experience, and from the many different conversations with women that I conducted during the writing of this book, these are the top characteristics most 'bad managers' seem to have in common:

Overall lack of transparency and withholding of information

- This includes lack of transparency around their own workload and whereabouts.

Poor interpersonal skills and/or low emotional intelligence

- Has difficulty making eye contact.
- Struggles with basic levels of social politeness.

- Does not make the effort to connect with staff on a basic personal level ('How was your weekend? How is your new kitten?')
- Never makes time to speak to them 1:1.

Isolating themselves from the wider team both physically and emotionally

- Chooses to work in office or in meeting rooms away from the larger group.
- Regularly walks through the office without acknowledging the staff around them.
- Prefers mass emailing to transparent conversations in person, particularly when delivering difficult news.
- Never participates in team-building activities.
- Gives blatant and obvious preferential treatment to certain staff members.

Lack of respect for their staff's time or workload

- Contacts them out of hours.
- Constant bombardment of emails and instant messages.
- Every task is 'urgent' or an 'emergency' and has unrealistic deadlines.
- Is late for meetings, cancels meetings at the last minute, does not show up for meetings at all, constantly reschedules and moves 1:1 meetings.

Micromanagement

- Obsesses over arbitrary details.
- Must always know where you are.
- Constantly asks for updates on what you're working on.
- Tells you exactly how to complete tasks (perhaps while looking over your shoulder).

In some extreme cases, their behaviour can also include:

- Aggressive and threatening language; humiliation tactics.
- Dismissal of complaints.
- Retaliation when complaints are filed against them.

Withholding information and being hypercritical of insignificant details ranks pretty high on the list of irritations of the women I spoke with. Especially if the overly critical manager is usually never to be seen or heard from when you actually need something from them, and they just pop up to criticize something you've done.

Maggy explained how a manager's lack of accessibility can be troubling, 'You don't always have to be a super warm and open person, you can still be whoever you are, but you need to be accessible. [A direct report] needs to be their true self to you and complain if something is going on and give you feedback – it has to be a two-way street, as well, even if you're someone's superior.'

Working at big, international companies can come with many extras (free lunches; motorized standing desks; more rooms to hide and cry in), but that in itself can be tricky when you're being managed by people in another market or country. Maggy says, 'In a big global company, you can often tell that you're on the priority scale and that you're lower down, when a 1:1 keeps getting moved, or you're never asked to lead a meeting.' Managers might not realize it, but doing things like this signals to staff that they aren't a priority and that not everyone is treated equally.

As many of us working from home during the pandemic probably discovered, it's also tricky being managed by someone remotely. If you felt like your boss wanted you chained to your desk pre-pandemic, being hounded by them remotely might have felt strangely still more confining. Even if you've only ever worked in a job remotely, having a very hands-on manager who expects you to respond to every chat message, every phone call and every email within seconds is terribly stressful. Constantly fearing retaliation from your manager for being slow to respond to a message – because you're having a quick tea break, are on the loo, or have temporarily turned off Slack notifications so you can focus on your actual work – impacts focus, and even our ability to relax in non-working hours and days off. Disappointingly, a remote boss isn't always a chill boss.

Felicity, thirty-eight, who is in scientific communications in the UK, works at a big, international company and has had some pretty odd experiences with her team's senior vice president (SVP), who is based in the US. She tells me they only ever know he's in town because they'll suddenly pass him in the hallway, and he won't say hello or even make eye contact. *Oof!*

Worse still, the first meeting Felicity ever had in the same room as the SVP was when he was making Felicity and the rest of the team redundant. When she asked if they could have a meeting to explain why they didn't find her skills relevant for this new team they were creating, he agreed. But then at the last minute he rescheduled (via email, despite sitting on the next desk over) and then completely missed the rescheduled appointment. Even worse, he missed it because he was sitting in a glass meeting room, chatting on the phone. 'He couldn't even pop his head out and go, "So sorry, Felicity, I'm on a crisis call here, I promise I'll reschedule, I'm really sorry," ' she told me. 'He can't do that. He just sits there knowing I'm sat there looking at him thinking, *You do not care about me at all, and you don't care about my career at all either.*'

Such mismanagement and blatant disregard for people's

time is utterly disrespectful, something those in leadership positions must remember, regardless of how busy they are. If you are meeting someone who reports either to you or to a manager you manage – it's a big deal for them. Whether they intend to or not, managers who behave like this send a message of 'you are not important to me'. It also says: 'I'm totally shit at paying attention to my own diary!' which is so unprofessional. How can your staff prioritize time management when you clearly have no clue what's going on with your own schedule?

The manner in which managers speak to their staff is also crucial. Bullying may not always be so blatant and obvious as it is portrayed on TV and in films, but it's the underhand threats and micro-aggressions that can wear people down. Particularly when the issues being played out are nuanced – such as specific cultural stereotypes and understandings between people of colour.

Marianne, thirty-one, a queer, mixed-race woman, described the complex relationship she had with her direct manager while working as a teacher at a high school in northern California. When the school's administration team was restructured and she was given a new manager, she noted that 'of course, it was the only other person of colour in our admin who became my manager'. She told me that there are cultural issues between people of colour in the workplace that need to be talked about more. She cited as an example 'when the only person of colour that is in a position of power is the hardest on you, because you are the only person of colour in your department'. She says that her manager was harder on her than any of her white colleagues.

As a result, 'By the middle of the year, I'd been deemed "hyper aggressive", "outspoken", "assertive" and "intimidating".' Her manager repeatedly told Marianne that she had to put her head down and work because she'd been singled out as 'intimidating and aggressive' – but didn't mention by whom, or why. She explained that she finally had to point out to him that, 'as a brown man, you're telling the only brown woman in our department that she's "too loud" and "too aggressive"'. But rather than back down, her manager fully admitted that he didn't want her to make waves and deal with the splashback, saying to her: 'I just need you to do that for me until you get your tenure.' Marianne says that her manager basically threatened to not approve her tenure if she didn't put her head down and do exactly what he wanted her to do, i.e. not be so 'aggressive'.

Marianne's manager put her in a terrible position – if she were to complain and 'make waves', not only would that fit directly into the 'aggressive' and 'outspoken' behaviour he'd reprimanded her for, but he was also implying that her job was at risk if she didn't quiet down. The cultural ramifications and complexities here make it even more complicated and hurtful, and this ticks many boxes in the list of bullying and poor management behaviours discussed above.

When a manager actually admits to their crappy behaviour but ultimately shows that they're unafraid of the consequences because they're threatening you with an even greater consequence if you speak out – this is intimidation. This is bullying.

Your feelings are valid and real

Dealing with this kind of behaviour is isolating and stressful, and can unquestionably lead to tremendous amounts of anxiety, with huge implications for our mental health.

It is very easy to view something like the Post-it incident as unimportant and inconsequential because it's not as bad as the story your friend has about her boss screaming at her at an event in front of a client. But the feelings, the way those incidents made those involved feel – shame, embarrassment, frustration – are all valid and real, no matter how they came about.

Being fully aware of how your relationship with your boss is affecting you is extremely important. As therapist Kate Hogan explains, speaking with friends (if not a therapist or a career coach) helps to give an extra awareness to the idea that what you're experiencing at work is real, and not OK. She says, 'What often happens if we're in our own chaos, our own crises, is that we think there's something wrong with us, and often there *is* something that we can bring to the table to change what's going on, but quite often we take full responsibility and say, "I'm just not managing well," or, "I'm not handling my work situation well, it's not OK for me to bring this up because I should just get on with it, I should just suck it up, I'm privileged, I have this great job, I should be grateful."'

In comparison to some of the stories I've heard, my Post-it note anecdote can feel a bit, well, small. But, obviously, it wasn't about the Post-it. And there are so many different feelings you experience when you work for a difficult manager: it can trigger your own anxieties and fears in different ways from those of your colleagues. A bad boss for one person can be an extremely supportive and helpful boss for someone else.

How you feel, how dealing with a difficult manager impacts your life inside and outside work, *really* matters. Poor management should not always just be accepted as 'part of the job' or 'just how they are'. You shouldn't just have to 'suck it up' or 'not worry about it so much' or 'just get on with it' if you're finding that dealing with your difficult manager is negatively affecting your mental health, and ability to do your job.

In isolation, incidents like the Post-it don't seem that bad, but these micro-aggressions build up. Just as a glass of water doesn't seem that heavy at first, if you have to hold it for hours, days and sometimes years, this small burden, this constant low-level anxiety, becomes a weight heavier than we can bear.

How to deal with a difficult manager

There is no one-size-fits-all fix for your manager. The good news is that, while it may feel like your boss is a total psychopath, even if they display psychopathic traits, roughly only 1 per cent of the general population are actually psychopaths.* This may be reassuring, but still doesn't quite fix the problem.

When deciding how to tackle the issue of dealing with your difficult boss, we need to take a step back and assess what actually is going on.

I am not a medical professional, mental health professional or lawyer – but if you believe the treatment you're being subjected to at work is illegal, there are resources (which are listed in the back of this book) out there that can help you understand your rights as an employee, and which steps you should take next. However, if you believe your situation doesn't necessarily cross any legal lines but is still making your life miserable, let's start to figure out what you can do.

Dealing with a difficult manager isn't just hard because *they* themselves are difficult, but because in order to sort this

---

* www.forbes.com/sites/jackmccullough/2019/12/09/the-psychopathic-ceo/#6ecd5fb3791e

situation out, *you're* going to need to get comfortable with being uncomfortable.

You'll have to speak up for yourself and get involved in some awkward exchanges.

You'll need to exhibit patience and humility. You're going to have to listen mindfully to, and even empathize with, this person who's giving you such a hard time. You'll have to set boundaries and, crucially, learn how to manage upwards.

All of these things are rooted in the practice of having difficult conversations. Which, let's be honest, probably makes your bowels twitch as much as mine.

The (messy) art of (difficult) conversation

Having a difficult conversation with your manager or a colleague is never easy, but as the Fearless Queen Brené Brown, author of *Rising Strong*, says, we must choose courage over discomfort, and discomfort over resentment.[4] If you know that speaking to your manager about an issue that's been causing you a lot of anxiety and stress will ultimately improve your life, it's worth the discomfort, right? If being sweaty for twenty minutes while having a difficult conversation with your manager means that, actually, there's the possibility you won't have to work Sunday evenings any more, that surely has to be a good trade?

The best way to approach a difficult conversation is to:

- give the other person the benefit of the doubt;
- drop your assumptions and your expectations of how they will react;

- remember that you're not a mind reader, and therefore don't necessarily know the intentions behind whatever actions or behaviours have landed you in this conversation;
- focus on bringing solutions to the conversation, and not just a list of problems.

And, above all else, I've found that making the conscious decision to be as honest and authentic as possible not only feels good but is also the simplest way of having a productive conversation. There are quite a few books out there that promise to help you with these very conversations, so if you want to drill down into this subject even more I've listed a few in the Resources section.

This doesn't mean dropping all of your psychological defences or saying whatever reactive comes to mind. For me, having an authentic-yet-difficult conversation means that I am not caught up in *performing*. It's about finding the right balance of being honest and true to myself, while still keeping in mind what my goal from the meeting is, and the best strategy for achieving the most desirable outcome.

This doesn't mean emulating how a strong, powerful woman on TV might handle a conversation. This doesn't mean spouting off a scripted monologue that your sister helped you write the night before. It means staying calmly connected to your needs and your goal from this conversation ('I need my manager to let me hire another staff member because I'm drowning in work') and maintaining your integrity without getting too caught up in a negotiations performance.

A big lesson I learned from the book *Difficult Conversations* by Douglas Stone, Bruce Patton and Sheila Heen is the concept of considering how this conversation might be seen by someone as an attack on their identity or their image at work. If they identify as being a very good manager, and you're coming to them to say that, actually, there are ways they could improve how they manage you or ways in which you feel let down or hurt by them, this might be difficult for them to hear, or even put them on the defensive.

However, while it's useful to consider the other person's viewpoint, and to approach the conversation with empathy and a sense of curiosity about how or why the miscommunications or points of frustration between you might be occurring, you still don't know how things will go.

I'll quite often have full-blown arguments and conversations with people in my head before I actually go and meet them. So many times I've got all ramped up, thinking about what they'll say and then what I'll say, and then what they'll argue and what my reaction will be, and every time I'm wrong. Magical thinking – thinking that you're a mind reader, thinking that you absolutely know what someone else is feeling about a situation and have some sense of control over it – gets you nowhere, especially with the discomfort of honest conversations. Going into a difficult conversation anticipating a certain reaction is not helpful, and will no doubt cloud your ability to listen and communicate.

An HR specialist I spoke with suggests that, if you're struggling to connect or communicate effectively with your manager, you could try a change of scenery: 'Take your manager out to a completely new environment to have different kinds of conversations.' Sometimes people walk through the office door and their environment will make them behave in a different way, and taking a literal walk in the park with them will often produce a different outcome from the way they interact with you at work.

Have you actually asked for what you need?

Whether it's part-time working, an ergonomic chair, a regular 1:1 or more staffing support – you must use your voice, and speak up for yourself by clearly asking for what you need on a regular basis. (Sorry.)

As an example, if you need regular feedback from your manager, and you're frustrated because you're not getting it, you *must* be honest with yourself: have you explicitly asked your manager for this? Does your manager know that regular feedback is something you need in order to feel satisfied in your job? Or are you angry because your manager *should* know this, and yet doesn't, and therefore doesn't do it?

This is a trap I fall into, because I find it so difficult to ask for help. I start to think that, well, if this person were *actually* good at being a manager they would just *know* that I need this. Why should I have to ask? Just in the same way that people expect a romantic partner who truly understands them as a person to just *know* what you need.

Sadly, life isn't like that, either in or out of work. If you're not getting something you need, YOU ALWAYS HAVE TO ASK FOR IT. Because the crazy thing is, otherwise, your manager (or your life partner) might actually think they *are already satisfying you*. So much so, that they might even think they're doing it brilliantly. It's up to you to disabuse them. Here's how:

You, making the brave choice to ask for what you need – 'Tom, would you be able to give me feedback on the performance of my projects in our regular 1:1 catch-ups? I find it extremely helpful with my overall objectives to know how they're performing on a weekly basis. For example, it would be useful to know how the Giraffe Project was received by the client.'

Your completely unaware boss: 'Oh, yeah, sorry, I thought I told you how great it was in the email after you sent it through. They loved it.'

You, being even more specific about what you're after: 'Great, but a thumbs-up emoji isn't quite cutting it. I'd like constructive feedback on what worked, and what we can improve for next time.'

Your not completely aware boss who apparently thinks emojis are acceptable to use as feedback: 'Sure, yes, OK, I'll do that. I didn't realize. I'm glad you said something!'

This is obviously a bit more straightforward if you're asking for something very specific, such as regular feedback, or flexible working hours. It gets more complicated if it's for something like a new job title, a salary increase, more staff, or perhaps even a different manager, and you might need to put forward a business case or do some proper negotiating.

If you need a clearer definition of what your manager expects from you, this is also something you might need to ask for.

Give yourself permission to pause before you react

Getting an email that makes your blood pressure spike and gives you a quick shot of adrenaline can feel like an absolute attack. But a perfect antidote to this is giving yourself some time to pause before you respond. This doesn't mean ignoring your inbox to avoid feelings of stress (I wish!) – it means preventing further miscommunications and escalated conversations by being the voice of calm and reason.

Now, we all know the high you can feel when you're writing a witty, scathing response to an irritating email. It feels brilliant. It feels like finally, *finally*, you will show them who the real boss is.

However – and this applies almost 100 per cent of the time – sending an email of any sort when you're pissed off, ashamed or experiencing high levels of any emotion is not a good idea. This message is not going to come across the way you want it to. No matter how brilliant it feels to write, no matter how clearly you think you've made your point, no matter how many nine-letter words you include, no matter how eloquent the mic drop, it's not going to go down well. Assumptions will have been made on either side, and responding to a sassy email with another sassy email is playing with fire. Particularly when dealing with your manager.

The best way to approach your response is to give yourself some space to reflect and notice how you're feeling before you start furiously typing your reply. Stop and breathe. Try to notice how you're feeling. Are you anxious? Angry? Try to reflect on *why* you might be feeling this way. Is it, for example, because you feel like your boss is shaming you? Once you've taken a beat, just acknowledge how this email has made you feel and why; only *then* should you try to formulate a response with as much compassion and empathy as you can muster. Approach your response in the way you wish they had in writing their first email to you.*

---

* For more on this, check out the SBNRR method in the Resources section of this book.

It's also worth keeping in mind that an email might not be the best way to respond to what they've said. While it's definitely a bit more daunting, once you're feeling calmer and have reflected for a while, why not grab five minutes with the email writer either in person, on the phone, or even on a Zoom call (with video turned on!) so you can de-escalate the conversation face to face, or in a different forum? It's amazing how quickly some people will back down when they're speaking to you in person.

Taking a beat before you reply doesn't have to be confined to emails or chat messages, either. If you're in a 1:1 meeting or Zoom call with your manager and they say something really upsetting, or drop a bombshell like, 'You won't be getting your bonus this quarter due to a poor performance rating,' you will no doubt feel a burst of emotion or shock that puts you in prime territory to react badly, or speak in a way you might regret later.

So, instead, you have permission to stop, take a breath, and say, 'Actually, I need some time to process this before I respond and I don't think we're going to have a productive conversation at the moment. I would like to reschedule this meeting.'

This is much better than storming off and slamming the door without saying anything or, worse, spewing out all the vitriol that's just entered your head. Instead, if you feel like you are two seconds away from losing your shit, bawling your eyes out or being so overwhelmed by anger or anxiety that you can't control your response, you can simply press the pause button and resume when you're ready.

Similarly, when it feels like someone is trying to catch you out in a meeting in front of your colleagues ('What were the stats for the Q4 sales again? You have those numbers, right?'), rather than scurrying through your notes or panicking and trying to find the numbers in your email you can just stop, take a breath and say, 'I certainly do have those numbers, but not off the top of my head. I'd be happy to send them to you after.'

I wish I had given myself permission to do this more. To give myself pause, and to have chosen more often not to respond to an inflammable email with a lit match. To have taken a breath and said, 'Actually, I don't know, I'll find out.' To have given myself permission to pause and calmly leave a room and a situation where I was being intimidated, or shamed, with the grace of a dignified exit – rather than digging my nails into the skin of my arm underneath a table, choking back tears and effectively being rendered mute (which, in some instances, was the goal).

Practise mindful listening, even in stressful meetings

Mindful listening might sound a bit silly, but, like the pause before you respond, learning how to listen mindfully in conversations both in and out of work honestly has the potential to help completely transform the way you communicate in your relationships.

Listening mindfully means that when you're hearing somebody speak, their words become the only thing in your head. You're not thinking, 'OH! Yes! This reminds me of the story about that time we were in Spain and I lost my luggage,' and then interrupting to tell them this very anecdote. It also doesn't mean worrying about what your response is going to be and crafting the best, witty reply. (Which, chances are, will fall wide of the mark or seem irrelevant by the time they're done speaking anyway because you'll no doubt have missed whatever question they asked you.)

Because I've been in therapy for so long, and have read so many psychology books, the absolute worst thing I do when I'm listening to someone speak is to psychoanalyse them as they talk, and immediately try to think of a way I can help them. Often this will result in me focusing on an issue that they're battling with on a psychological level and then thinking of books or podcasts they could use to help and then deciding the best way I could suggest this to them. All of this when I should be LISTENING.

A mindful-leadership course I attended included a mindful-listening exercise that was extremely helpful. Two people take turns sitting and listening to the other person talk for two or three minutes. Then, when they're done, the one practising listening responds by saying, 'What I heard you say was . . .' and summarizes what the other person has shared. Doing this is hard, because you're trying to listen and retain information without your brain shouting REMEMBER THIS REMEMBER THIS REMEMBER THIS OH MY GOD YOU'RE GOING TO FORGET THIS!

It's a genuinely helpful exercise to practise, because in the midst of a difficult conversation 'What I heard you say was . . .' helps expose assumptions, miscommunications or potential misunderstandings in the moment. You can also explicitly follow this statement up by asking, 'Have I got that right?' This gives the other person a chance to correct you if you've misunderstood. This exercise might also help both you and your manager learn where communication breakdowns are happening in real time, and help you recognize that, *Oh wow, when my manager says something that I view as harsh, they really don't intend it to be harsh and I'm jumping to conclusions around their intent.*

Set clear boundaries (and enforce them)

If you're at your wits' end because your manager calls you at 9.30 p.m. to have a 'quick chat' about a meeting that's happening the next morning, or stands looking over your shoulder while they dictate how you should do a piece of work, then you may need to set – and, crucially, *enforce* – some boundaries with them. These could be around the times of day your manager can reach you or the style or timing of feedback they give you, or perhaps it's more of a micromanagement issue that you need to give *them* feedback on.

Sadly, defining boundaries isn't as easy as just brainstorming the things you'd like your manager to stop doing immediately. Instead, you need to find ways to address why specific behaviours or management practices prevent you from doing your best work. It's setting out what's OK and what's not OK from your manager, and then deciding how best to communicate that.

How to manage upwards effectively

Managing upwards basically means managing your manager. 'WTF I don't get paid to manage my manager!' I hear you say – and you're right; it's probably one of the many things you end up doing at work that you're not *technically* paid for. And yeah, it can sound a little daunting. But the thing is, you're probably already having to do it anyway. Double surprise: all of the above advice *is* managing upwards. Congrats! The secret to dealing with a difficult manager is to put effort into managing them. BEING AN ADULT IS GREAT.

Depending on your relationship with your manager, this can be exhausting and sometimes feel like a whole other job. Worse, the more experience we have and the longer we're in our careers, the more responsibility we have and the more complex our roles become – and this will involve more and more managing up. The higher up the chain you go, the less hand-holding you get. The harsh reality is, if your manager is the CEO of a company, or the MD or the head of a massive department, they are going to have significantly less time for you. They will expect you to be aware of your own needs, and to speak up if you need something. To ask. To give feedback. To be proactive and act without instruction. And your conversations with them will probably happen between board meetings, when you have a twenty-seven-second window of opportunity while taking a brisk walk to explain to them what you need as succinctly as possible. Which is, well, hard. And not something everyone can (or wants to) do.

Maddie Armitage, the Chief Data and Product Officer of the marketing communications company Dentsu Aegis Network, says that when it comes to managing up, understanding your manager's needs and what pressures they're facing is a must, but first you need to understand the political landscape your manager is working in:

> Building a personal relationship with your manager is always
> key. I think once you start to understand what their
> challenges are and what they're facing day-to-day, you will
> then be able to relate better to how they work, and be able to
> support and help them do that. Once you understand what
> the requirements are from above, your way to successfully

*manage upwards is to help deliver on those requirements. My
direct question to my boss has always been, 'How can I help
you, how can I support you, what are the things that I can do
to make your life easier?' So, if you have that front of mind, it
will help to build your relationship, create trust, help you
navigate the organization and think outside of your own
world, to think bigger.*

Cheryl Fergusson, VP of Talent at Heist Studios, who has
over twenty years' experience of people development, says
that how you manage upwards 'depends on the way the organization flows'. She says that if you're struggling to manage
your manager, you should keep an eye out for the members of
staff with whom they seem to work best. 'It can be useful to
find out what is it that works so well with this person, so you
can personally adapt or change the way you interact with your
manager.'

She suggests that, if appropriate, you could ask to have a
confidential chat with this person and just say, ' "Could you
give me some advice on how I could make my relationship
with my manager more effective?" Because, actually, a lot of
people at more senior levels will see that as a really great
behaviour. You're proactively helping yourself learn how to
connect differently.'

But what if my manager is actually trying to destroy me?

Here's the thing.

All of the above advice is only helpful if your manager is a
reasonable person, one who listens and one who cares enough

about their role and their responsibility to you as a manager and a leader to take your feedback on board. Not every manager is going to do this perfectly, but I think we can all recognize when someone is actually listening and trying. This person might be just a bit crap, but we can all find a way to work with a bit crap. The a-bit-crap manager is disappointing but has good intentions, unlike the doesn't-give-a-flying-fuck manager. Sometimes there's nothing you can say or do to fix a relationship with someone who fundamentally *does not give a shit* about listening to you or supporting your career the way you need.

I am all for empathy, I am all for improving communication, being honest, being authentic and doing the right thing. But there are times when 'everyone is just doing their best' simply isn't good enough, especially not when that person's version of 'their best' is fucking up your career development and mental health.

Sometimes people are threatened or incompetent or wrong. Sometimes your boss simply does not like you and does want you to leave. Sometimes people just don't know what to do with you, and that's not your fault.

The thing is, what other books and 'experts' won't admit is: YOU MIGHT TRY ALL OF THE ABOVE AND THERE'S A CHANCE IT WON'T WORK.

You might bend over backwards, do all sorts of empathetic and psychological gymnastics to try to make this job, this relationship, this management work for you – and fail.

Think of the advice in this chapter as a flow chart or a set of tick boxes.

❏ Have I had a difficult conversation with my manager where I explicitly stated my needs?
❏ Have I tried relating to them in a different manner?

- ❏ Have I tried to understand the pressures and expectations they're experiencing, and tried to help them with those requirements?
- ❏ Have I set and implemented clear boundaries around my working hours?
- ❏ Have I done all of the above several times?

If it all points to 'YES' and then 'BUT I AM STILL FUCK-ING MISERABLE', you might want to fast forward to Chapter 10 about what to look for in a new job so that this hopefully doesn't happen again.

(But just in case . . .)

One of the most important things I did when I was going through my very difficult, year-long struggle with Post-it manager was to write everything down. I took screen grabs, made notes after particularly difficult meetings, saved emails – everything. This helped me a lot, because seeing it all laid out in black and white put things into perspective for me that, no, it wasn't just me – this situation was BONKERS.

If you are being bullied or harassed or feel that you might one day need to make a formal complaint of some kind,* I strongly suggest you start screengrabbing emails, WhatsApp messages, anything that might help prove your case. Take notes after you have uncomfortable meetings. Save them on a USB stick or in your online storage area. Not only is this very useful, it will make you feel like a private detective, which is always exciting. Every cloud, right?

---

* A few suggestions for how to find the help you need are in the Resources section of this book.

The brick wall

The different tactics I've described are designed to help improve your relationship and communication with your manager while giving yourself the space and tools you need to do your job to the best of your ability, in a way that protects your integrity and your mental well-being. They are all methods that I've learned will help to deal with a difficult manager. The difference for me is that I wasn't just dealing with a difficult manager when I learned about these tools, I was dealing with someone who did not want me on her team and was doing her damnedest to manage me off her team by building a brick wall to keep me out. I know that I did everything I could to try to improve that relationship. I know that I went above and beyond and put up with more than any person should put up with.

I know that a more reasonable manager would have listened to any of the above suggestions at any given point and worked with me, even if that was to help me to find a different role within the company: 'Clearly, this isn't right for you, but let me help you find a role in another team that I think you'll thrive in.'

In the end, and despite everything I'd learned, I failed.

Eventually, it became intolerable for me to stay, so I left.

I don't regret the effort I put into trying to make it work. I learned so much about myself, and about what I actually wanted out of a job, and out of my career. If I had just said 'Fuck this!' and left, I would have missed out on gaining all of the skills I'm now armed with when it comes to managing upwards, and having difficult conversations. And I wouldn't be putting it all in this book for you now.

Leaving is a strategy, not a defeat, but it is one to be used only after all others have failed. Going through the above pointers, trying different tactics and taking the time to do your due diligence that you're not rushing to conclusions or making some bad assumptions about your manager's intentions really matters. It teaches us a big lesson about relationships, and how to have difficult conversations, voice our needs and ask for help. To give ourselves permission to say, 'I don't know', or to leave the room gracefully if we know we're being shamed or purposefully humiliated. Managers can learn from their poor behaviour[5] – but they'll never be able to change and grow if they're never pulled up on it.

2

Envy + Jealousy:
Dealing with comparison culture at work

I've struggled my entire life with feelings of envy, comparison and competitiveness with other women, particularly at work. Despite these feelings being completely natural and, actually, pretty normal, it feels rather unbecoming to acknowledge that the competitive feelings and envy I've felt towards other women in my industry have been, at times, overwhelming. I have painfully awkward memories of pre-teen dramas between myself and other girls at school that were ultimately passed off as 'just jealousy'. As an adult, however, I learned that explaining away a conflict between two women as being 'just jealousy' greatly oversimplifies the issue, and doesn't begin to acknowledge what's going on.

Early on in my career in the UK I found myself in a very precarious situation with one woman in particular – let's call her Jane – who befriended me, and then shortly afterwards proceeded to take some serious inspiration from the website I ran and launched her own very similar version of it. Jane took so much inspiration from my website that the similarities were pretty hard to just ignore. She trod the borders between 'inspiration', 'plagiarism' and 'intellectual property infringement' to the millimetre, and while there were many likenesses, it wasn't a straightforward 'copy and paste' situation that felt solid enough for me to do anything about it.

Plus, as someone who, even now, is terrified of confrontation, I didn't have either enough confidence or the psychological tools back then to be able to confront her. Instead, I proceeded to compete with her obsessively from afar for the next couple of years and never said anything to her about it. I wanted to *crush* her, but I didn't want to have to *talk* to her. I was enraged and obsessed, and it caused me much more stress and wasted energy than was ever needed.

The fact of the matter was that, irrespective of who thought of what first, this whole situation stung even more because she was ultimately more successful than me – she built up a bigger social following than I had and published a book off the back of her site. I remember seeing it in one of my favourite bookshops and feeling sick to my stomach. It didn't feel plausible that this woman could 'steal' my idea, and then execute it better than I could – but, from various standpoints, she had done just that.

This situation with Jane was difficult because so much of my persona and self-worth were embedded in my work. It felt like she was getting away with some sort of psychological fraud or impersonation. But had I been able to choose discomfort over resentment, and just spoken to her about it, and asked her about the similarities in our sites, and given her the chance to explain, the outcome could have been very different. I didn't need to be stuck in a cesspool of envy and competitiveness; I inadvertently chose to stay in one. I learned the hard way that any time spent obsessing over another person's social feeds and what they're doing is time wasted on *not* creating or doing my own thing.

Envy vs jealousy

Interestingly, jealousy and envy are actually two different things, even though they tend to travel together.[1] Envy is when we feel we lack a desired attribute enjoyed by another. ('Phoebe Waller-Bridge is so funny and talented; I want to be a multi-Emmy and BAFTA award-winning actress and screen-writer, too!') Jealousy is when something we already have is threatened by another person – a suspicion or feeling threatened. ('My girlfriend keeps sexting her yoga instructor and lying about it!') *Psychology Today* has a great explanation of the difference between jealousy and envy on its website: 'jealousy always involves a third party that's seen as a rival for affection or attention', whereas envy involves only two people, and the general feeling is 'I want what you have'.[2]

I spoke with Hilda Burke – psychotherapist, couples counsellor and author of *The Phone Addiction Workbook* – about envy, and she explained that, crucially, envy is something that is entirely natural and a feeling we actually start to experience from a very young age:

> *Envy can stir up pre-verbal feelings in us. Ultimately, it brings us back to the time when we first wanted what someone else had – our mother's attention is usually the first one – and couldn't fully express that. So when we're envying someone else's achievements, what we're experiencing is something very young within us. As such, we need to go gently on ourselves. It's good for us to admit our jealousy, if only to ourselves. So many of us think we 'shouldn't' feel jealous so we suppress these*

feelings, and like any suppressed feelings they will likely surface in other ways, maybe a bitchy comment here or there.

Feeling competitive is natural. So is feeling envious, or even jealous. But more often than not, women are told that being competitive is shameful. Research shows that men compete with others more openly, even brazenly, and women try to keep the fact that we're competitive on the down low.[3] Women do it more covertly, behind the scenes, like a silent-but-deadly fart, whereas men will loudly and proudly let rip like a foghorn, their gaseous outburst bellowing through the land – unyielding, unencumbered, unafraid. Basically, competitive men are from Gryffindor, competitive women are from Slytherin. (These are, of course, binary views of gendered behaviours that don't reflect more nuanced realities, but I hope you'll allow me the crude analysis to make my point and land a Hogwarts reference.)

Misunderstood sisterhood

So why do women find it hard to be openly competitive towards each other and why does competing with men feel different from competing with women?

Hilda Burke says she thinks there's extra pressure on women to act 'sisterly' towards each other at the moment, given the current political climate:

I see so many Instagram posts about how women support each other and pick each other up. That's all well and good, but the net impact of such generic messages is often guilt in many around experiencing quite natural feelings of envy and jealousy towards other women. Due to the gender [pay] gap, a man getting ahead, winning what looks like an easy

promotion, can be dismissed as just being down to the fact
that he's a man. Whereas with another woman, one might
feel that we could get what she has – so why haven't we?

It gets even more complicated when we feel unsupported
and let down by a female manager or leadership figure. As
Marianne, the teacher from northern California, shared with
me, one of the most disappointing and hurtful working relationships she had was while working as a teacher. The situation
with one of her female managers 'ended up being the most
non-supportive relationship. She was so toxic. I did not feel
safe in this woman's charge; I did not feel supported at all, and
I felt lied to and manipulated.'

This is something that I've heard a lot, the specific kind of
disappointment that occurs when a woman lets us down. And
it's most definitely something I've experienced. But how fair is
it to be extra harsh or extra disappointed in someone, to 'expect
different' from them, because of their gender?

My friend Viv Groskop, the author of *Lift as You Climb: Women
and the Art of Ambition*, has an interesting take on this. I asked
her why she thinks it can hurt so much more when a woman
lets another woman down. She said that, while she gets that
it's a natural response, she thinks it's actually sexist: 'Women
have as much right as a man to be incompetent, unsupportive
or unpleasant!'

She continues, 'I hope this won't sound too harsh, but I think
there is a lot of naivety around on the topic of "sisterhood". You
have to think of it as something that you offer to others, rather
than something that you expect others to give to you. Spend
time with and focus on the women who are supportive towards
you, rather than wasting your breath on the ones who aren't.'

Viv's absolutely right about sticking with the women who
are supportive, and that the concept of sisterhood is often

misunderstood. I've been excellent at misunderstanding it for most of my life. There's a very strange, primal pull I personally feel towards other women in the workplace, particularly when working in a male-dominated field. In a social setting, if someone expects me to get on with someone else simply because she's the only other woman in the room, or the only other 'other half' present, I would find this repugnant. However, in the workplace I am instantly drawn to other women and have such high expectations and excitement at the possibilities: *Will this be my new work wife? Are we going to be friends?* JOIN ME, COMRADE.

And, well, this is bonkers! And dangerous! Because so often this high expectation that this woman will be my new BFF can swiftly spiral if she doesn't meet my crazy expectations or respond to my LET'S BE BUDDIES mating call from across the office. The narrative then goes from *OMG, are we going to be best friends* to *Do I actually hate her? Does she hate me? Why doesn't she ever want to have lunch with me? She barely says hello to me. Our manager likes her better than me. I bet she thinks I'm unqualified because I didn't go to Oxford.* Which can then fully escalate to, *This bitch is now my sworn enemy.* Which is not great, and is a narrative completely based on my own, crazy-ass assumptions. But I think, unfortunately, this is something that a lot of us have experienced.

Writer and author Daisy Buchanan has more experience with the literal sisterhood than most, as she grew up with five sisters. *Five!* Her book *The Sisterhood: A Love Letter to the Women Who Have Shaped Me* explores the love and ferocity that exist between women, and I asked her about the challenges of female-centric working environments, considering the vast amount of experience she has with them in her own family. 'When we talk about women in the workforce, it's assumed that we're all on each other's side,' she says. 'We're also assumed to have the same goals, ambitions and motivations. And if we find other women at work difficult or irritating, it makes us bad, unsupportive feminists.' Daisy brings up an excellent point, because at the moment, it feels like there is zero allowance for criticism of women by women on an individual level – or perhaps of any kind.

Comedian Iliza Shlesinger has a great bit about this in her Netflix comedy special *Unveiled*. She rails against the fact that, because of the current political climate, women can't disagree with each other because we're terrified of being accused of being a 'bad feminist' or shaming other women.

She says:

Liking another woman should not be mandated, that's not feminism . . . The idea that because she showed up I'm supposed to have this abundant love [for her]. I can promise you this as a feminist: I'm excited you showed up, I'm excited you're capable, I do not hate you because you're younger than me, or prettier than me or as successful; however, you showed up and so did I, so let's get it started because life's a competition.

I tend to agree with Iliza on this, but I know the sentiment of what she's saying feels audacious, because at its heart, unabashedly competing with other women feels taboo, or unfeminist. And it's what fuels this added layer to all of our interactions with other women at work. Daisy says:

Personally, and this is not true for everyone, my interactions with female colleagues have always been much more intense than with male ones . . . I crave their approval more, I want to applaud them more loudly, and when I feel that one of us has let down the other, it feels so much more shaming and painful.

We crave a bond, a sisterhood, between the women at work, either as peers or as matriarchal leaders – and then we accidentally impose all of these high expectations on each other, assuming we all want the same thing. And when we're inevitably disappointed by each other, it's upsetting! And we become conflicted for other reasons as well, because, as much as we want to be part of the squad, what happens if we're ambitious? If we want to compete, if we want to climb and progress – that's not sisterly, is it? That's not ladylike. And when the shit starts to hit the fan, who can we trust? The women we're competing with? Don't we want to be in a sisterhood? Don't we want to show that women aren't catty and are perfectly capable of working together?

So – what do we do? If we continue to swallow our feelings of envy and competition and jealousy, and be half-hearted mentors and fair-weather friends, all in the name of progress and sisterhood and leaning in, nothing will ever change. And if nothing changes we'll still be here, years later, collectively wondering why we're bloody miserable all the time and, actually, none of these relationships are fulfilling and, *Oh god, women are so much work! This is why working with men is sooo much easier! #coolgirls #oneofthelads.*

Twenty-something workers vs forty-something bosses

In addition to the envy that can exist between female colleagues, there's this invisible, unnamed tension that can be present at work between younger and older women in the office.

If there are difficulties with communication, or the relationship between a manager and her report is a bit fraught, it's very easy to jump to the 'Ungh, she's just threatened!' narrative. It is dismissive and an oversimplification of what's going on, but the idea that a manager could be threatened by her staff member – particularly if she's younger, especially if she's ambitious – is very plausible.*

The concept of feeling threatened by the next up-and-coming youngster isn't new, or even particularly a women-only issue – men absolutely experience this. But the difference is that men are allowed to age. And if they're feeling threatened, they're expected to act out a bit, to throw their weight around. To compete overtly. They're not 'old men', they're 'silver foxes' who 'age like fine wines' and are allowed to gain weight and be human beings. Of course, there are expectations put on them too, just as there are on women, but their careers are never viewed to be over once they hit 'a certain age'. I mean, just look at my old ex-*Top Gear* chums.

Meanwhile, women 'dry up' and become culturally and socially irrelevant and invisible unless they alter their cells and defy physics and the laws of space and time. They restrict, tighten, plump and hoist themselves into younger versions of their body and faces – they fight tooth and nail to stay relevant and visible. How tiring. How disappointing. How unfair. And how perfectly natural or even expected it might be to then feel threatened or irritated when someone younger, who appears to have had a much easier ride in their professional life than you, comes waltzing in, thinking she can reach the height of your career but in just two or three years' time. And, unlike their male counterparts, women aren't meant to throw their weight around (or have any weight at all, for that matter), because if

---

* It's particularly tricky to talk about and describe this in a way that is neither sexist nor ageist nor any combination of the two – so, I'm going to do my best to not offend everyone here . . .

they do act threateningly, they're a sad stereotype. There's nothing but shame for women who get competitive with other women, regardless of their age.

This might have something to do with the narrative that girls are exposed to from childhood, particularly in fairy tales. Take, for example, the Evil Queen in *Snow White*, the Evil Stepmother in *Cinderella*, Maleficent in *Sleeping Beauty*, Ursula in *The Little Mermaid*, and even the Wicked Witch of the West in *The Wizard of Oz*. Young girls are shown that older women will become so envious of the youth and beauty of their younger counterparts that they will stop at nothing to seize control and get what they want. They'll earn your trust and then lock you up, feed you poison, steal your voice, steal your man, and then (after a dramatic-yet-oh-so-catchy musical number) they'll totally try to kill you. Older women are not to be trusted. They are the villains in your fairy tale.

So, at work, if we're already struggling with feelings of envy and competition with our peers and we're then caught in a power struggle with our older female boss who we think is probably out to destroy us, Evil Queen style – we are not going to 'lean in' to some sort of Sisterhood of the Travelling Power Suit. We're going to kick against it.

As executive coach and author Bonnie Marcus wrote for *Forbes Women*:

> We expect women to collaborate and mentor each other to be successful. But that's not necessarily what happens. The dark toxic side is triggered by the increased scrutiny that women experience. The female rivalry is fuelled by a workplace culture that does not provide a level playing field for women, equal pay, and/or equal opportunity for women to reach leadership positions. Women are set up to compete. They are

set up to compete with each other because only so many
women are tapped for the C-suite.[4]

The environment you're working in can also play a big part in either exacerbating or diffusing unhealthy levels of competition. I spoke with twenty-five-year-old Tara Jane O'Reilly, who is employed in one of the oldest working environments in the world – British politics – as a staff member for an MP. I asked her about what the general relationship between the women in Westminster is like and she told me that the majority of women are supportive, irrespective of political party, role or age. But she says that, while there are more women than there used to be, that's led to its own complications:

There is a supportive culture, but Westminster also breeds a
kind of toxic competition. I've met some women who definitely
have a vibe of 'I worked my ass off to get here and there's only
room for one woman in the room and that woman's going to be
me'. I do come across women like that – older women. And
some younger women I've met who . . . I guess they see
themselves as feminists, but they don't quite realize that
they're accidentally elbowing other women [out of the way]
when they're trying to put themselves forward.

If we internalize the narrative of 'older woman is threatened by younger woman and probably wants her dead', and we're not taught how to process feelings of envy, or come to terms with what healthy competition feels like, the 'she's just jealous' explanation probably isn't a true explanation of what's going on. It's never just one thing and not the other.

Is it correct to say that women with more experience and more seniority, who have grown up in much different circumstances from the women just entering the workforce, feel threatened, envious, competitive or territorial when it comes to their younger women counterparts? Yes, sometimes it is. But not always.

Is it also true that younger women don't realize when they're stepping on someone's toes, that their ambition may leave a few blind spots in their behaviour, and that they can accidentally be dismissive of their more senior leader's accomplishments or experience? Same answer.

Are we comfortable acknowledging and discussing both sides of this issue? Absolutely fucking not.

WTF do we do about this, then?

I've felt at numerous times in my career that I've been on the receiving end of some serious 'I'm threatened by you' vibes from various female managers – although envy might explain some of the irrational behaviour I've had from some of my male bosses, too.

But just as you can't ask a colleague, 'Hey, are you envious of me?' you definitely cannot ask your older boss, 'Hey, are you threatened by my youth and potential?' (For the love of God, don't do this!) You have to approach this particularly sticky scenario with the same principles as you would a difficult situation with your boss that we examined in the previous chapter. This is a big, hefty example of managing upwards, and it will require some serious flexing of your empathy muscles.

Although it may feel like she's 'just threatened' by you, we know it's not that simple. And it's never going to be the only thing contributing to a difficult or strained relationship with your boss. It's not the totality of your relationship, but a contributing factor. Your manager isn't a two-dimensional Disney villain consumed by her singular mission of your destruction.*

Knowing that this feeling of being threatened might be part of what's going on is useful, because it can help us be a bit more empathetic or understanding of what lies beneath the surface. It doesn't make it better, or excuse her behaviour, but awareness and empathy are always crucial when you're trying to repair a relationship – or, at the very least, make it bearable.

You can be honest with your manager and express what's at the core of your frustrations. Instead of saying, 'You're an envious bitch and I know you're holding me back because you don't want me to surpass you,' try discussing what's at the root of the problem, which, for example, could be that you feel unsupported. You could try saying something like: 'I'm not feeling very supported by you as a manager right now,' or, 'I don't feel like you're being supportive of my efforts to go for a promotion.'

And once you know *how* you're feeling, think about some solutions. What exactly do you want your manager to do? She's unlikely to turn into your biggest cheerleader overnight or morph into a different person, but what would be some concrete things she could do that would help you feel more supported? Your manager may be receptive to your feedback, and might ask: 'What would being supported by me look like for you?'

Have solutions and examples ready: 'Can we please put together a personal development plan that I can work on over the next six months? I need constructive feedback and examples of what I need to work on to get that promotion, and to

---

* Actually, I'm pretty sure I have worked for someone like this, but it's really rare . . . I think.

know you support my efforts,' and/or, 'I want you to have my back in team meetings; if someone is critical of me and my team, I really need your back-up. For example, you could say that you think my team are doing the best we can and that you trust we'll deliver the project on time,' and/or, 'If you think I'm not focusing enough or that I'm taking too long to complete, let's discuss this 1:1 so that we're on the same page before our big meetings.'

Alternatively, let's say that your manager goes on the defensive and says, 'Well, I *do* think I'm supportive of you, how exactly am I not supportive?' – this is where your documentation comes into play. While conversations shouldn't be about content – like who said what and when – if she claims she is being supportive, have examples ready: 'In the last round of reviews I asked to discuss my progression in my role, and you laughed a bit and told me I wasn't ready for that kind of promotion. But I don't know what that means, and this is the first time I've been told I'm not performing as I should,' or, 'In the team meeting last week when Michael was critical of my work and said he didn't believe I would deliver the Trash Panda Project on time, you agreed with him that it didn't look good and told me I needed to "focus" and "just get it done".'

If she goes into a 'I WAS ROOTING FOR YOU, WE WERE ALL ROOTING FOR YOU!' Tyra Banks-style tirade, or, like my old manager once said to me after I gave her some tough feedback on how I felt she didn't trust me to do my job, 'I want you to succeed more than you do,' then I'd advise ending the meeting, using the ol' 'I don't think this is going to be a productive conversation right now, let's reschedule' nugget.

Overall, the system isn't set up for our success. Yes, there are some women who simply don't want to help others, but what would happen if each of us took responsibility for our own shortcomings, if we worked through what's at the root of our own envious feelings? What would happen if we dropped the expectations and the facade of an imposed, automatic 'sisterhood' that exists between women at work, and let organic, honest connections arise instead? What would happen if our leadership figures talked about competition and displayed competitiveness in a healthy way? What if we felt able to compete, because we all felt safe enough to work through our envy?

And how can you tell if you yourself are wandering into Evil Queen territory, regardless of your age? Maddie Armitage suggests this great way of assessing your feelings:

I suppose the test is this. Say you have someone on your team that's fantastic, super smart, a rising star, at the top of their game, and everybody loves them. You constantly get positive feedback saying 'she's amazing, I wish I had her on my team'. Ask yourself how does that make you feel? Does that make you feel proud? Does that make you feel fucking awesome? Or, does that make you feel threatened? If the answer is the latter, you probably need to invest some time self-developing to conquer those fears. The most successful leaders I know look to hire great people with the goal to create a high-performing team of happy individuals. If those people turn out to be better than you, that's great – that's succession planning and that's what every good manager wants.

Is the green-eyed monster actually a monster after all?

Being on either side of jealousy or envy is equally difficult. It's a very strange dance that exists between women, whether in the workplace, in real life or on social media. At work it can manifest as an ally who backs you up in team meetings and is nice as pie to your face, while giving you a negative peer review and complaining about you to your manager behind your back. Sometimes both are willing participants – frenemies who are chummy one day and on the next withholding their likes on Instagram or not sharing key information about a project. And sometimes it's something that is purely one-sided that exists solely in your head.

Whether the feelings of envy between subjects are mutual almost doesn't matter – because envy is always more revealing about what we think of ourselves than it is about the other person.

When I spoke to therapist Kate Hogan about how to tackle envy and competition between female colleagues, and, indeed, other women in our lives, she said that awareness and identifying the feelings you're experiencing are crucial. You have to ask yourself what exactly is causing you to feel envious. She says, 'A lot of the time with envy and comparison and competitiveness it actually gives us an opportunity to think about what we want for ourselves.' Envy can be a signal that there's something about what this woman is doing that you might want for yourself. Is there a version of what she's doing that might work for you? What exactly is it that's triggering those feelings of envy?

What about if you get the impression you're on the receiving end of some jealousy or envy? Kate says that it's best not to jump to conclusions:

It depends how their behaviour is affecting you. Are you able to just think, 'OK, well that's their stuff.' But it's not always easy to think that. I think it's hard to make that assumption or express that opinion to someone, 'Hey, are you jealous?' I think it's always good to try and approach the subject in a specific moment, as it happens. So, 'Hey I noticed that you seem a bit down, what's going on with you, is everything OK?' Just don't assume they're jealous.

What Kate says echoes many of the best practices for dealing with a difficult manager given in the first chapter – not making assumptions, approaching the situation with empathy and a curiosity for the emotions and feelings that are fuelling the situation. Which sounds *exhausting* when it's so much easier simply to think, 'Well, Louise from sales is just a jealous bitch who hates me! Fuck her!' But, Kate's totally right; the self-reflection never ends.

Viv Groskop agrees that these feelings indicate insecurity and self-doubt, so it's important we address the situation. She says:

Do you need to be starting a gratitude diary or a list of your achievements in order to remind yourself that you're also pretty capable and maybe even worthy of envy? Why are you comparing yourself to someone else? The reality about people we envy is usually that if we were to know more about their life, we would discover something that is not to be envied. It's like that old saying, 'Everyone is fighting a battle you know nothing about. So be kind.'

Not knowing the full facts of what someone else is going through is a huge factor to keep in mind when you're feeling that familiar, envy-fuelled burn in your gut. Daisy Buchanan shares a similar view to Viv when it comes to processing your feeling of envy, and appreciating that you don't understand all that's going on behind the scenes of someone's glowing achievements. Daisy told me that there have been times when she's been 'emotionally wrecked' with envy not because of other people's domestic bliss – it's not babies and people buying homes that burns – but rather people killing it in their career.

She says when a friend of hers recently received some brilliant career news, she'd already seen, because they're close, the trajectory leading up to this fantastic achievement and what she calls 'the long, long concentrated amounts of effort, the highs, lows and dollops of despair before getting what she wanted'. However, she says that the way people talked about her friend's success on social media made the achievement sound 'unbeatably enormous' because the totality of her struggle and journey wasn't reflected in those social soundbites. 'It made me realize that if I hadn't been privy to the process and I just saw her as a distant peer, I would have been in an acid bath of insecurity.'

Crucially, from this Daisy says that she's also learned how to listen to what her own envy is telling her about her desires, and she's turned those pangs of discontent into successes of her own: 'I spent years sitting around fuming because no one was asking me to host a podcast before it occurred to my idiot brain that perhaps I should just make the podcast myself.' (She did. It's called 'You're Booked', and on it she's interviewed guests ranging from the novelist David Nicholls to the psychotherapist Philippa Perry.)

I'm very much into this attitude of taking responsibility for your own feelings of insecurity, listening to those feelings, and then – crucially – taking action. Notice what those feelings of envy are trying to tell you and then address them. What do you need to do to help yourself feel better so you can stop putting your precious energy into the Janes of this world! THEY ARE EVERYWHERE! So, what can you do to help yourself feel sufficiently self-aware and confident in your own abilities? Is it therapy? Is it, as Viv suggests, a gratitude practice? Weight lifting? Journalling? Is it, like Daisy, choosing to finally start your own podcast instead of seething with rage that 'The Jane Podcast' is on the most-downloaded list every week?

Whatever you choose, that confidence and that self-assuredness should kick in when some lady on Instagram triggers a feeling of wild envy in your gut, so you know to put your phone down and think, *Fuck I am so grateful for my body, but I guess I'm feeling a little static at the moment. That's great that fitness influencer is going to Pilates for the thirteenth time this week and cooking vegan lasagne tonight from scratch! Maybe I can do a little 'Yoga with Adriene' at home to help feel a bit better. And maybe eat a vegetable instead of a block of cheese tonight.*

And when someone makes you want to flip your shit at work by presenting an idea in a meeting that you had worked on together but has conveniently left your name off, this self-assuredness means that you take some deep breaths (remember those difficult-conversations principles) and just ask her about it in a calm, non-confrontational way: 'Hey, Sue! I really enjoyed your presentation today in the team meeting, and I enjoyed the work we did together on it last week. I feel like we put equal amounts of effort into this and that it was a joint process, so I'm just wondering why you didn't include my name on it or mention me?'

Uncomfortable and potentially awkward as fuck, right? Who wants to eat a vegetable and exercise rather than just sitting around screengrabbing someone on Instagram's gym selfie and sending it to your best friend with a rolling eyes emoji, instead! Who wants to actually *talk* to Sue about a potential mistake or misunderstanding she made when you could just send an ALL CAPS Slack message about it to your work wife instead! NOBODY. Nobody wants to do that! It sucks!

However – how are you going to feel after you eat a vege-table and exercise? Tired perhaps, but overall, healthier. How are you going to feel after talking with Sue? Maybe a bit sweaty palmed, but no doubt better. Relieved, even.

But, let's be real, there's also the possibility that you'll pull a muscle, or that Sue basically tells you to go fuck yourself and that you didn't work on the presentation as much as she did and that it's her work, not yours. You might walk away from that conversation even more enraged than you were before – but at least you know that you spoke with her about it, and can gauge where to take things from there.

OK so maybe we're all envious, competitive monsters and it's fine

We all find ourselves spiralling into jealousy from time to time. And it's fine. It's how we respond that matters. I used to get panicked and stressed while checking social media while I was away on holiday – in the lull of me trying to enjoy myself and not working. In any moment of inaction I was gripped by comparing myself to Jane and obsessing over what she or any of the other people I decided were my nemeses at the time were doing. It was a horrible kind of overwhelming panic that was more of a slow-burning sizzle than a rolling boil – the kind that sits on your chest, and not in the good way.

What has eased this over time for me has been a multi-pronged attack. To summarize the last ten-plus years of personal development on what I've personally done to cut back on spiralling out on envy:

- I no longer try to befriend people who make me feel like shit on the internet.
- If someone makes me feel like shit, I no longer ignore it because I'm desperate to be liked by them.
- I don't allow myself to hate-follow people and feed my inner comparison gremlin.
- If I know someone professionally or I'm sufficiently friendly with them to feel weird about unfollowing, I mute them. (I highly recommend the mute button!)
- PSYCHOTHERAPY: doing a ton of work on the areas of my life that were sore spots for envy – my career, my hobbies, how I feel about my body.
- I lean into the good stuff, the things I enjoy – reading, watching period dramas on TV, yoga.
- I work on projects and make a living doing what I actually like and feel satisfied from (easier said than done).
- I'm honest with myself when I am feeling envious.
- I talk about my envy gremlins with other women I trust.

A good approach to processing your feelings of envy at work is to start by assessing similar feelings in your world outside work: your triggering sister-in-law, that one mum from the school run, your best friend who never seems impressed by your good news, your old school friend you stalk on Instagram even though you don't follow her and actually kind of hate her. What do they all make you feel?

I am not above feeling envious or petty these days. I just have a different perspective on it now, as I channel my energy into thinking about what I desire out of life, and why certain people bring back that familiar, anxious, envious feeling in my gut. You'll feel amazingly free once you start to loosen the grip you've allowed your adversaries to keep on you. Free your-self from thinking you must have an enemy! Trust me, it's much too time consuming.

Unlike in 2009, I hardly ever think about Jane these days. And when I do, I mostly just feel regret that I never said any-thing to her. I'm no longer angry with her or feel competitive, and our lives have gone very different ways. I have no idea what battle she was fighting when she started copying my ideas all those years ago, but I'm going to guess that, whatever it was, it was pretty painful for her.

We truly never know what's in the lives of other people, which is why it's so important to remember that our envy is always ultimately about us, and not the other person.

3

Success + Sanity:

How to progress in your career without burning out

When I first had the idea to write about how to progress in your career without burning out, it was no doubt a selfish pursuit of knowledge. I wanted to write this in the hope of finding an answer for myself.

The big question – 'Can we progress in our careers without burning out over and over again?' – is at the heart of my concerns not only for my own career, but also for the wider workplace in general. Can we be happy, succeed and have a full-time job at the same time? Can we achieve in our careers without great cost to our personal lives? Can we ever properly integrate our true selves and our careers? Must we constantly be at war with the two, at the expense of our sanity and happiness?

I thought, when researching this chapter, that it would mainly feature the advice from people who have found the right combination – who have discovered the secret ingredients for a potion of magical wellness, balance and sanity that also had room for ambition, success and achievement.

To be completely honest, and with no disrespect to my interview subjects – I saw more struggle and suffering than I did balance. Many of the women I spoke with were recovering from their latest battle with work. They had learned some tough lessons and were trying new approaches to how they work. Most had a strategy to achieve a healthier balance – some were actively applying for new jobs. They, like me, have had to learn some harsh lessons, and have had to discover for themselves where the line is, where the boundaries of their own sanity truly lie. Many had spent years being very hard on themselves – for not achieving enough, fast enough; for burning out in the first place when they should have known better – without realizing that they were only doing the best they could in what were mostly fucked-up situations. My slightly ironic catchphrase when I was editor-in-chief at *The Pool* was, 'We're all just doing our best.' Some days I said this encouragingly, some days I said it in defence of our team, on other days it was an antidote for some ridiculous setback or other, and there were times that it was said through tears, when it became clear that the hopes for the business staying afloat were dwindling rapidly.

I know, of course, that while work stress affects everyone, regardless of gender, the contributing factors to the stress experienced at work will likely be different if you're from a minority group. Just as, globally, the gender wage gap gets larger when you factor in ethnicity and race, when it comes to work stress, each additional filter you include means it gets more complex, more acute. So, if you, like me (despite being mixed race), pass as or appear to be white, the way you experience work and stress will be similar to, but still different from, the kind of work stress that a trans colleague, BIPOC, lesbian or disabled colleague will. As Maura Cheeks wrote on the Lenny Letter website,[1] 'Being black and female in the workplace means constantly having to walk a tightrope, balancing your own emotions with the perceptions and intentions of others, making everyone feel comfortable, instead of nervous, in the process.'

According to the research done by the Lean In organization, which champions women's rights in the workplace, black women and women with disabilities face more barriers to advancement in the companies they work for, get less support from their managers and receive less sponsorship than other groups of women.[2] This, combined with everyday discrimination, sexism and no doubt plenty of micro-aggressions – means that the stress and impact on the mental health of these women will be worse than the average work stress of their white colleagues. This isn't to dismiss the pain or experiences of anyone, but rather to acknowledge that none of our experiences are the same, and that there are very real and concrete reasons why some women will experience different layers of work stress than others.

The one common factor I've found amongst the people I've interviewed for this book is that *so many of us* stretch ourselves beyond 'our best'; we're so far past the average person's 'best' that we lose all perspective. Like in the *Friends* episode 'The One Where Chandler Crosses the Line' and Joey says to Chandler, 'You're so far past the line you can't even see the line! The line is a dot to you!' That's how so many women are with things like 'achievement' or 'good' or 'their best'. Our internal compass for knowing what's good or enough is broken, and we speed past milestones and achievements so fast, so furiously, we sometimes miss them altogether.

The result of this tendency to overwork ourselves in pursuit of achievement is often a strange combination of emotional and physical symptoms, such as exhaustion, stress, anxiety, depression, digestive issues, skin rashes, muscular tension, eye twitches and A LOT OF CRYING.

The word that's commonly now used to describe this amalgam of feelings is 'burnout'. There have been many articles and personal essays written about different people's experiences of burnout, but I think we need to talk more about its root causes, how we can work to both prevent it and recover from it, rather than just comparing battle wounds and swapping office-based horror stories.

This chapter explores what burnout is, what its causes are and how we can start to balance our lives in a way that doesn't give burnout an environment to thrive in. It also invites you to start exploring where your own ideas of success come from, and how your opinions of what a 'proper work ethic' and 'hard work' look like were formed. And, ultimately, it hopes to answer the question of whether or not we can work, succeed and achieve without burning out over and over again. Is it possible? I sure fucking hope so.

Like our sexuality, burnout also exists on a spectrum

'Burnout' isn't a new word, but definitely one that's become more 'buzzwordy' and used quite commonly in the last few years. It's often used interchangeably (and sometimes incorrectly) with other words that usually represent its symptoms, such as *exhaustion*, *stress*, *fatigue*, *anxiety* and even *depression*. The World Health Organization included 'burnout' in its International Classification of Diseases list as an 'occupational phenomenon'[3] (but not, it should be pointed out, as a medical condition) – defining it as a syndrome of 'chronic workplace stress that has not been successfully managed', which 'includes feelings of energy depletion or exhaustion, result[ing] in increased mental distance from one's job and reduced professional efficacy'.

But, as with other mental health problems, these symptoms of burnout are not the sum of its parts, and some can exist without the others. Because of this, I like to think of it as occupying a spectrum.

'I've never fully understood exactly which part is burnout,' Tina Walsberger, the marketing director of the Edinburgh International Festival, said to me when I asked her if she'd ever experienced burnout. 'You can feel really exhausted, but then you're like, "Is this it, am I there?"' Tina says that, while she agrees that burnout exists on a spectrum, she doesn't necessarily think that she has been 'burnt out' in the way that it's usually described or written about in magazines:

> *I've never not been able to function. But I've had all sorts of exhaustion – emotional exhaustion, physical exhaustion. Sometimes you can have almost a spiritual exhaustion and feel like you don't have the meaning you intended to have in your work life or your personal life. I've definitely felt exhausted on a whole bunch of levels, but certainly not to the point where I've stopped functioning.*

This is a perfect example of how not everyone experiences burnout the same way, or feels comfortable classifying what they've experienced as such. Some people experience some symptoms but not others, and no two people's experience of what they choose to call 'burnout' will be exactly alike.

Tara Jane O'Reilly, who works for an MP, described her version of burnout to me, and while her experience was similar to

Tina's, her symptoms were different. They began in the summer of 2019, after working through a particularly 'vitriolic' period in Parliament from January to July, back when Theresa May was still prime minister and MPs were all 'working on' (i.e. fighting over) Brexit, without a proper break. As part of the overall working culture in Westminster, she explained that there was a kind of 'guilt complex' amongst MPs and their staff that, when they were given time off, they felt that they should be focused on 'fixing the country' instead of recharging. But when Parliament's summer recess finally came round, and Tara says she went from '100 per cent to zero' overnight, the sudden change proved to be the breaking point for her own mental health:

> I just couldn't handle it, I couldn't handle the change. It honest to god felt like I had been shoved off a cliff, and I basically had a breakdown. I was having panic attacks every single day, I was vomiting, my IBS was triggered again, I lost loads of weight, I gave myself gastritis. I ended up seeing a therapist for the rest of the summer, which was great, and I also went back on antidepressants for my anxiety. But, it was because I couldn't handle the sudden change from seeing people all the time, seeing MPs all the time, seeing my colleagues, seeing journalists . . . and it made me realize how intense my job had been up until that point.

Our bodies respond in different ways to different kinds of pressure, exhaustion and extreme amounts of stress. But no two people feel and process pain in exactly the same way, or have the same level of resilience.

One person might seem to be functioning quite highly at work, but is actually experiencing near-debilitating anxiety and fatigue in private, screaming on the inside, dogged by

72

stomach cramps and insomnia. Equally, just because someone is exhausted, unable to come into work and struggling to eat doesn't make them 'weak' or necessarily 'more burnt out' than the person who works every day. Nobody wins a BAFTA for Best Performance in the Weekly Team Meeting Despite Having a Panic Attack 20 Minutes Ago – we all lose. It sucks. Exhaustion or burnout is not something that one should aim for or use as a measurement for success. It's not a goal, a destination or an inevitable symptom of the truly ambitious or those with the most hustle.

Instead, I believe it's a terrible by-product of terrible work systems, an always-on culture, testing working practices, poor management and an overall lack of regard for well-being – in the physical, mental and emotional sense – and it's not something we should accept or ignore.

The cult of busy boss ladies

The fingerprints of what created burnout are all over our culture. It's the trope of starving artists, our glorification of the young, slightly mad, work-obsessed entrepreneurs. The girl-bosses hustling on Instagram. The people who brag (and it *is* a brag) that it's December and they've only just realized they've 'had no more than two days off in a row this entire year' or that they're 'taking their first week off in eight months'. The people whose standard response to 'How are you?' is 'Just soooo busy.' When I hear people trying to shock others by saying how long it's been since they've gone on holiday, I don't think it's glamorous or inspirational or aspirational to be an overworked, tired, strung-out lady boss. I don't think that's 'bossing it', I think that's *lack-of-boundaries*-ing it. I am deeply and wholly unimpressed.

A much more accurate version of the usual bollocks quotes

you see on 'inspiring business boss lady' communities online would be:

- 'Ignoring My Wellbeing 24/7.'
- 'Constant ~~Hustle~~ Anxiety Diarrhoea.'
- NO LIMITS! (OR BOUNDARIES! OR REGARD FOR MY HEALTH!)
- BE THE CEO YOUR PARENTS WANTED YOU TO MARRY . . . *or, if that's not your* THING THAT'S TOTALLY OK TOO WHATEVER YOU WANT IS FINE.
- 'You Have the Same Amount of Hours in a Day as Beyoncé – But She Has Money and Help and You Don't so Stop Comparing Yourself to the Unrealistic Standards of Celebrities.'
- LIKE A ~~BOSS~~ SUPPORTIVE MANAGER WHO RESPECTS YOUR BOUNDARIES.
- BUT FIRST, ~~COFFEE~~ PSYCHOLOGICAL SAFETY.

I mean, these probably won't be made into pretty, pastel posters with swirly fonts or overpriced daytime planners anytime soon, but at least they're accurate.

When I used to see people on Instagram on overscheduled book tours or constant work trips, bouncing between international offices or back-to-back conferences, I'd be overcome with competitive envy. *I* wanted to be shuttled from venue to venue, posting tired-but-glamorous photos in the back of an Uber wearing massive sunglasses and a giant coffee at 4.30 a.m. on the way to the airport for my next big work event. *I* wanted to be taking group selfies with my work squad of boss bitches who all 'work hard and play hard'. *I* wanted to write terribly long captions on my hot selfie in a #gifted dress on a #gifted trip to Soho Farmhouse about how I'm 'exhausted but happy and finally recharging' after a 'super manic four weeks of no sleep' working on my 'top-secret project'.

But now, when I see those photos and read those types of captions, it just makes me tired. And quite empathetic to how tired these people must secretly be, too (even if they are, also, painfully annoying). Because, for the most part, posts like this are terribly disingenuous. They're not real, or healthy, truthful, or something to admire. Even if they're like 'OMG so anxious and stressed' but posing carefully over a cocktail at Annabel's it's like *OK SURE, BABES*. #relatable

We don't all need to be hot messes, sharing our every panic attack or intrusive thought on Instagram, and we don't need to be an 'OMG I can't adult today' exaggerated caricature of a millennial with mental health problems either. What I'm trying to say is that none of that is authentic – it's performative and even reductive. Because at the heart of the troubles many of us have with 'adulting' is a real, generational issue. It's not laziness, sensitivity or a deficiency – it's a symptom of a wider cultural problem.

Our culture of burnout and over-productivity was laid bare as the coronavirus pandemic progressed. 'We're not working from home in a pandemic,' we were told by different people in various ways, 'You're at home, in a pandemic, trying to work.' Instead of hustling, the popular thing to do was to encourage others to look after themselves, to remind us all that self-care mattered more than ever, and that rest was important too. 'It's OK if all you can do is eat ketchup and cry,' we were told. 'It's cool if you can't wash your hair and only wear onesies now, lol.' All of which was absolutely correct and valid. However, as the various lockdowns were extended and our time at home progressed, the more memes and illustrations and pastel quote tiles telling us to REST popped up everywhere. It seemed on every social platform you were constantly reminded that *IT'S OK TO NOT BE PRODUCTIVE, WE ARE IN A PANDEMIC! IT'S OK TO NOT BE DOING ANYTHING! WE ARE IN A PANDEMIC! IT'S OK IF YOU ARE HAVING A LOT OF STRANGE FEEL-INGS, WE ARE IN A PANDEMIC!*

All the while we were being told that it was OK to gain weight, to struggle with your mental health, to feel lonely and to not be productive *in a pandemic*, the implication seeming to be that those things are all OK *only* in a pandemic. So, what about when we're not in a pandemic? Surely, we need to address why we feel we must always be productive, even when we're not experiencing a global health crisis? Why did we need a pandemic to serve as an excuse for . . . being a human who has feelings (and sometimes eats them) and needs rest and play as much as they do purpose and work?

Even stranger, the more quarantine-themed self-care memes and articles and photo-series, book clubs, podcasts and webi-nars that popped up eventually made some of us realize, 'Wait a second! *You* said I should be resting! But you seem to be doing an awful lot.' The Girlboss Hustle Monster didn't fade away into a cloud of self-care and self-preserving unproductivity during lockdown – she just changed her outfit. She was there, reading three books a week and sharing her poetry. She was baking cookies without eggs, flour or sugar that somehow still looked nice. She was running a half-marathon for NHS chari-ties in her back garden (she's the second cousin of Captain Sir Tom, after all) and also hosting a live meditation session on Instagram in the afternoon. She also launched a podcast/live video-series/newsletter/community because, somehow, some way, it became her job to tell you it's fine for YOU to not be doing anything, but she's, like, *different OK*? She is just ALWAYS CREATING, pandemic be damned!

And while, yes, it was wonderful still to have new things

being created in a time of grief and isolation, there is also a big difference between doing things out of true service for your community and for those in need, and just perpetuating a habit of needing to be constantly on, of creating and serving your ego, and desperately trying to keep up with the capitalistic churn of social media.

In early 2020, back in the old normal, the Advertising Standards Authority actually banned an advert from the company People Per Hour for gender stereotyping.[4] It featured a smiling woman next to the slogan 'You do the girl boss thing. We'll do the SEO thing.' They apologized, admitting it 'might come across as sexist and demeaning to women' and said it was taking steps to remove 'girl' from the advert.

The term 'girlboss' was made known to most by Nasty Gal founder Sophia Amoruso with her 2014 business memoir called #GIRLBOSS. Sheryl Sandberg's Lean In organization also helped propel this idea of 'boss women' with their 2014 'Ban Bossy' campaign[5] – the launch video of which featured Beyoncé confidently saying, 'I'm not bossy, I'm the boss.' While Sandberg and Amoruso disagreed on whether or not you should call a woman 'bossy'[6] – 'girlboss' and its many derivatives and colloquial cousins have survived long past their period of favour amongst most millennial feminists.

Most of the mid-to-late 2010s were riddled with pink-and-black stationery, water bottles, T-shirts and laptop stickers with 'empowering' 'feminist' phrases that included the word 'Boss'. While there were encouraging reports, such the 2017 study by American Express that claimed the number of women-owned businesses generating annual revenue of more than $1 million had increased by almost 50 per cent in the last eleven years[7] – it's also worth noting that a lot of girlboss culture was fuelled by *buying* and *wearing* things (hey there, capitalism!) that declared your status as a *young woman who was working on big things with big ambition* – i.e., a girl who was a boss. Hundreds of Instagram accounts and online communities for working women were launched across the globe – all of which seem to come with inspiring quotes on their Instagram accounts, sponsored events and branded notebooks. (As well as legitimate mentoring schemes, knowledge shares and workshops.) We also saw the rise of 'Gram-ready women-only working clubs, which many have argued is just corporate, privileged feminism disguised as intersectional, sustainable, empowerment[8] – while plenty of others claim that they're inspiring, useful and good for women-run businesses.

Journalist Vicky Spratt wrote an article in January 2020 for the *Refinery29* website titled 'Let 2020 be the Year We Get Rid of Girlboss Culture for Good',[9] in which she described how the phrase infantilizes women and denies their agency, saying that it 'diminishes us and denigrates our authority'. She wrote that if people weren't so collectively scared of women's power, we wouldn't need to make it more palatable by 'rolling it in glitter and pinkwashing it' – as that's exactly what girlboss culture does. It makes the idea of powerful women easier to accept (or market) by colouring it millennial pink and giving it a catchy name, thus rendering it benign, if not a bit silly. Reading this article, I was immediately reminded of the time some weeks earlier, when I took a photo of a massive advert for the 'buy now, pay later' finance service Klarna on the facade of the Koko Club in London. With the same colour scheme as Amoruso's book cover, the advert read 'I like to shop like a boss, ASOS' in big, bold letters. I posted it to my Instagram Stories with the caption 'I hate everything about this'. Buying unsustainable, fast fashion and potentially putting yourself into debt doesn't make anyone a 'boss'.[10] Coincidentally, hours after posting that photo, the advert was destroyed in a fire at the club.[11] (Thankfully no one was hurt and, no, I didn't start it.)

At the peak of 'lady bossing it' culture came a pivotal and quite exposing cultural moment that forced a dramatic shift in the conversation. In January 2019 journalist Anne Helen Peterson popularized the term 'burnout', introducing the phrase to many who had never heard it used in this way before. In an article titled 'How Millennials Became the Burnout Generation', published on *BuzzFeed*,[12] Peterson wrote about her struggles to complete mundane, seemingly simple chores like going to the post office – a sort of task-based paralysis that she felt huge amounts of shame over. She explained that this was a symptom of burning out, and that she had personally burnt out because she had 'internalized the idea that I should be working all of the time' – something, she says, that happened because everything and everyone in her life had explicitly and implicitly reinforced the idea since she was young. She pointed out that women, and especially those who have children, have a 'second shift' to do after their day job has finished, consisting of both domestic and emotional labour. She said that the millennial condition was forged in a culture that is always 'on', always working, always hustling, and that the extent of what we do, how hard we work, is often ignored or belittled. The mental loads we carry are enormous, and heavy. And, often, we pay the price with our ambition.

What will dry up first, my eggs or my ambition?

Eighteen months before the term 'burnout' gained momentum, back when I was still at Google and low-key freaking out at all times, my friend Kate sent me an article from *The Cut* by Lisa Miller called 'The Ambition Collision'.[13] The first line read: 'What is this midlife crisis among the 30-year-olds I know?' And it was the first time I had read about this *feeling* so many of my co-workers and friends my age had been experiencing. It described perfectly this plateau many of us were experiencing in our careers. We entered the workplace full of ambition and hope – we've been raised to believe we can achieve anything we set our mind to. We grew up with the Spice Girls' brand of 'girl power' and came of age to Beyoncé's brand of 'flawless' empowerment that Miller described as encouraging women to 'perform their empowerment, and never submit'. However, with many of the women around my age and older, we were about five to ten years into our career and we were suddenly . . . well, kinda done. So many of us had reached a stage where we just felt a kind of desolate numbness. A problem we couldn't quite describe. It wasn't just 'stress' or 'anxiety', it was a combination of the two, plus many other emotions, that left a lot of us feeling . . . I dunno, tired. Like, *really* tired. Like 'maybe-I-just-give-all-this-up-and-move-to-a-small-coastal-village-and-pay-my-rent-by-selling-jewellery-and-soap-made-from-waste-materials-and-adopt-five-rescue-dogs' tired.

Even though many of us don't think we've experienced 'proper burnout', we'll still recognize this feeling of just wishing you could hit pause. To escape. And while the fire in our bellies to hit the next job title, the next salary bracket, the next achievement has always been enough to fuel our bodies and minds into enduring more and more bullshit, to push ourselves higher, faster, stronger . . . suddenly, the need to lie down and just rest a bit – say for roughly eight to twelve years – feels much more attractive then emotionally killing ourselves striving for the next promotion. Our ambition hangs by a thread, and it's fucking depressing.

The articles I mentioned, although written eighteen months

apart and by American women working at New York-based publications, both captured a feeling and even a condition experienced by millennial women in many different Western countries across many different industries. And that *feeling* described by Miller and Peterson hasn't gone away since they were both published, but has rather intensified with time.

In 2015 – two years before Miller's article appeared – a survey by Bain & Company had actually found that companies drained the ambitions of their young women employees in only two years, and that their aspirations and confidence eroded in mid-career, which they found wasn't the case for their male counterparts.[14] In 2018 there was a 'review of reviews' in the US that collated forty-eight research studies focused on anxiety, and found that anxiety rates were on the rise for young women – with work being a major source.[15] A study from Montreal University found that women burnt out at a faster rate than their male counterparts, largely due to the stress and impact of being in positions with low levels of authority and decision-making powers that make little use of their skills.[16] Sound familiar?

It's this escalation that has led me to where I am today, writing this book, trying to find an answer. Because what I *don't* want is for everyone to either quit their jobs to focus on family only, or quit their jobs to do yoga on a beach in Bali for eighteen months and then decide to work for themselves, selling homemade pottery on Etsy.*

I recently read an article in a women's magazine (stereotypically while getting my hair done) about a woman who, on paper, had a career that was similar to but much more exciting

---

* No offence to crafters or people who make a living selling handmade goods on Etsy. You are much more talented than I am, hence why this seems so obscure to me

than mine. She rocketed to the heights of her industry very quickly – complete with all the anxiety, beta blockers, stress, partying and exhaustion that come with it. After 'burning out', she chose to pack it all in, go travelling and retrain as a therapist. She describes her relationship to work now using terms like 'less ambition' or 'slow ambition' or 'quiet ambition' – meaning that somehow this decelerated pace of life means she has a *different kind* of ambition than the sort that led her on a dangerous path of bad habits and poor health.

I must admit that this story triggered a lot of envy for me – that she had the money and the circumstances to make the decision to just . . . quit. She wasn't fired, she didn't lose her job, she made the choice. She made the decision to travel, and to then retrain in a new field – a process that's both expensive and lengthy. If you can afford this, good for you! How lucky, how blessed you are! I'm envious of the financial freedom that enabled her to take that path (which, as you know from Chapter 2, is *all about me*, and not her). But I disagree with this rebranding of ambition – it's not about having less or more, or whether it's gentle, soft and slow. It's not about avoiding ambition, or hiding from it on a beach.

Ambition isn't the problem. Ambition doesn't need rebranding, it's *us* who need *rewiring*.

Like burnout, we need to relearn and accept that ambition and success are unique to each of us. It's up to *us* as individuals to define what ambition is, what it feels like for us personally, and to explore what we're willing to pay for the achievements that this ambition is meant to propel us towards.

Is success actually a job title or a pay raise? Or is it figuring out the sweet spot between job satisfaction, good-enough pay and the enrichment of your personal life? At the risk of sounding mega-corny, surely it is the *quality* of the journey, rather than the destination? Harvard psychologist Dr Tal Ben-Shahar actually coined a term for having false expectations about reaching a goal: 'arrival fallacy'. He describes the term as 'the illusion that once we make it, once we attain our goal or reach our destination, we will reach lasting happiness'. Hits home, right? This is why being in tune with your own desire and the reasons why you're working towards something is so important. We'll go into this in more detail in Chapter 7, but having goals can act as a guiding light or a compass for the journey of your life, rather than just being a destination that you work blindly towards.

This reminds me of how we make vacations and holidays a lot harder than they need to be. Why must life be the equivalent of that stressful, mad rush of packing for a holiday, and then huffing and puffing in the security line and chewing your nails off waiting for the gate to be announced before *finally* you can slightly unclench on the plane, only to then reclench when you land, and then stressing out over making sure you check in at the hotel on time, and you're only able to exhale and 'finally enjoy' the holiday when you're, like, three days in and finally understand how the breakfast buffet works and know how to properly say 'please', 'thank you' and 'goodnight' in the language of the country you're visiting?

Yes, you need to pack and plan, and it can be stressful from time to time, but does that mean you need to spend SO MUCH TIME with your asshole clenched so tight you're squeezing out diamonds? Must everything be 'so busy'? WHAT IS THE FUCKING POINT?

But before we can just 'get over it' or simply unclench our superglued sphincters, we have to get to the root of *why*. Never mind the conditioning from society and the wider problems with companies and your insane manager – sure, those definitely don't help, and they have a huge responsibility in all of this, but a crucial element is that little part inside you that thinks you have to damn near murder yourself in order to 'achieve' something. What is fuelling that? Where did that come from? And what is it serving? What does your ambition actually stem from?

What's fuelling our work ethic and why do we overwork ourselves?

The reasons so many of us overwork ourselves are personal, and their origins are usually rooted in our childhood. Not to get all Freudian on you, but the way we view work and achievement, and how they're interconnected with our self-esteem and self-worth, have a lot to answer for when it comes to both our balanced and our unbalanced (and burnt-out) work practices.

Sometimes, our work ethic can be fuelled by our childhood dreams. Keira, a thirty-five-year-old woman in London, had dreamt of working as a wildlife TV producer since she was a little girl. She studied animal biology at university, and became a specialist in social media and digital videos back when both were in their infancy. When she was hired for her expertise by the BBC's natural history unit in Bristol, it should have been a dream come true. Instead, it turned into an unbearably painful working experience that ultimately led to her having a 'proper breakdown'. The job itself wasn't right for Keira for many different reasons, most of which were based in people's fear and suspicion of new technology and the change Keira represented. Plus, she was living away from home 'in this squat with like ten people' and started to feel terribly down:

I went to the doctor and they were like, 'Do you think you might be stressed?' and I burst into tears, and it was at that moment that I realized, 'Oh, perhaps I am! Oh, god, fuck!' That was before I had ever fully acknowledged the idea of having your mental health tied to work because I was always just like, Carry on, do all the things, be busy, take this opportunity it's amazing.

After a year of trying everything she could think of to make it work, Keira left her job, and essentially had to let her childhood dream – a dream that had shaped most of her life's decisions up until this point – die. She had to let it go, with all the heartbreak and grief that came with it.

Childhood dreams like Keira's are definitely at the core of why some of us work the way we do – stretching ourselves to a goal that's somehow become part of our identity, despite it belonging to another time, and another version of us. But sometimes it's the work ethic of our parents that we observe in childhood that's the biggest influence in shaping how we view our own careers.

Miranda from London, who is in her early forties and works in tech, says that her relationship to work was forged by the juxtaposition of her father's obsessive passion for his job and a dissatisfied stay-at-home mum. 'I love what I do. Passionately. And that's a problem,' she tells me:

I grew up with a dad who loved his job, and everything was about his job. For me, that's been the greatest benefit and the worst curse. If I call him now and ask him how he is, he'll tell me first of all about his work – he's sixty-five. I also grew up with a really unhappy, housewife mum. She didn't want to be at home full-time, but she didn't really have a choice. And that's coloured everything I do.

Lucy, a thirty-three-year-old from Birmingham, also has a father dedicated to his work:

My dad is a doctor, he's a surgeon, and he has this incredibly rigorous work ethic which I think I learned at a really young age. Having that kind of work ethic means that I can get a lot done in a short period of time, I can get as much output as possible – but it also means that I'm insanely conscientious, which results in me being nervous that people think I'm getting away with something or that I'm not working hard. I get worried if people think I'm not working.

But sometimes the correlation between work and our parents' work ethic isn't just as simple or straightforward as in Miranda's and Lucy's stories. These value systems are complex, deeply engrained and sometimes uncontrollable. During my research I met Virginia, a woman who was actually diagnosed with 'work addiction' by a psychiatrist and was told to join Workaholics Anonymous. Despite sounding quite fictitious, WA is, in fact, 100 per cent real. It was founded in 1983 and is based on the Alcoholics Anonymous framework, complete with its own twelve-steps programme, group meetings and recovery handbook.

Before her diagnosis, Virginia says that she had a history of taking on an extreme amount of work. She says her turbulent upbringing, marked by poverty and abuse, in a single-parent household meant she 'lost herself at school' – not because she necessarily liked it, but because she loved the work and 'loved the achieving'. Despite the chaos going on at home, Virginia says her mother was extremely hardworking, being employed as a cleaner, studying for an Open University degree and supporting her children tirelessly with everything they needed to have a better life, even when she was ill herself. Early in her life, Virginia says that there was a strong link made between work, safety and self-esteem, which resulted in a 'vicious circle', as the more she was rewarded for her work ethic, the more entrenched the link became.

By the time she was sixteen, Virginia says she was attempting 'what felt like a hundred GCSEs', playing in three orchestras, and dancing with a ballet company in London, even though she lived 300 miles away. 'I would go up to London on a sleeper train after school on the Friday. Rehearse, perform, then get the sleeper train back on Sunday night, do my homework and go straight to school. I was also Juliet in the school production of *Romeo and Juliet*. It was just insane.'

Perhaps unsurprisingly, she had 'a little breakdown' at seventeen, and it became clear that there was something critical being acted out by Virginia at this young age. This idea that 'no matter how shit things were, you just work really hard' was engrained in her from so early on that she learned to 'bury difficulties with hard work' – so the harder things were, the more she threw herself into work. She didn't know that overworking herself was both a symptom and a source of her pain. Even after a suicide attempt, she was back at work twenty-four hours later.

During her teens and early twenties, Virginia worked as, in no particular order, a cocktail waitress in Leicester Square, a barista in numerous cafés, a barmaid in various pubs, a waitress in an Italian restaurant, a sales assistant in a junk shop, an urban shepherd, a press officer at an agency selling celebrity stories to publishers, a life model ('they'd let me put my degree notes up on the wall so I could revise while I was modelling'), a teacher's assistant and a netball coach.

It was after having another breakdown at twenty-three that Virginia was first diagnosed by a psychiatrist as having bipolar disorder – a conclusion she disagreed with and so was given the alternative diagnosis of 'work addiction' and told to complete the twelve-step programme at WA. At the time, she thought it was a joke: 'In my head, a workaholic is like a 1980s CEO man, with a massive phone and briefcase, who ignores his family and works all the time – *that's* a workaholic. Someone who just does like twenty jobs in cafés and shepherding and working in a junk shop and netball coaching, that's not a workaholic.'

But despite her trepidation, Virginia went to the WA meetings, and attended regularly for eight months. She says that she found a lot of the WA programme to be 'dripping in privilege' and at times 'farcical' – and to be honest, after she read me some passages from the book of recovery about 'building an altar to your unmanageability' while wearing a prayer shawl, and writing down your 'key defects' on bits of paper, folding them into origami boats and then letting them 'float away on a river or pond' – I can see what she means. But even if the origami boats of defects weren't helpful, she found being surrounded by people thirty or more years older than her, serving as mirrors for how she didn't want her life to end up, was. The WA programme also represented the first time she had comprehensively rejected anything, 'Thinking, *Yeah, this is a pile of rubbish and I'm going to choose to leave it* is probably the first thing I've ever left.' Which, for Virginia, was a huge first step.

Virginia says that she could have made the same breakthroughs 'a lot quicker' if she just had access to a good therapist, but that ultimately, the WA meetings gave her space to talk about herself every week, allowing her to see and understand the ideas she inherited about work and self-worth. Coming from a working-class background where 'everyone's working themselves to the bone', she says she realized that she inherited her mother's work ethic, as well as that of her grandmother, an extremely well-read single parent of four children who worked several low-paying jobs until she was seventy. Virginia says she was raised and surrounded by 'women pushed to the edge of survival' who 'worked fucking hard' but 'weren't happy or fulfilled'. Both her mother and her grandmother showed her that 'you can be an agent of your own amelioration' – but only if you work as hard as you possibly can. Even if you're tired. Even if you're depressed. Even if you're ill or tried to kill yourself a few hours ago. She learned by example that life is hard and you have to push and work your way through it if you ever want to see the other side. If there even *is* another side.

And it's this work ethic, and the link she made early on between working, self-esteem and safety, that fuelled the compulsion to stretch herself as thin as possible. She says:

> If you've been brought up with conflict and loss, you'll do anything to avoid it, or run towards it. Certainly in my case, the idea of quitting a job or being sacked because you hadn't, for example, accepted all the groping – that's another fissure that I think I did everything to avoid. It's a fear. We only do dysfunctional things because we're afraid of something. I was recreating chaos. But being able to acknowledge why you're doing the things you're doing was really helpful.

I found Virginia's story so powerful for this very reason. She was able-bodied, highly intelligent and capable, which enabled her to push herself to the very limits of her own capabilities and to the breaking point – of her body, her mind, even her own life. It was her resilience and high pain threshold that actually made her so dangerous and able to do such harm to herself. Ultimately, it was the acknowledgement and understanding of what was behind this feverish need to work, to push and stretch, that led to her recovery.

These days, it's unlikely an NHS psychiatrist would recommend the WA programme. Virginia reckons if the same thing happened now, she'd simply be given antidepressants, maybe some sleep aids, be signed off work for two weeks and not be offered any form of therapy.

Virginia is an extreme example of overworking yourself. But while most of us may not be taking up life modelling, urban shepherding, or netball coaching – the sentiment of working yourself to the bone as a way of numbing yourself, or unconsciously recreating at work the chaos we lived with as young children, is something that many of us can relate to.

It's the awareness and the understanding of what motivates our work ethic, and what fuels our desire, that is the key to relieving ourselves of this crisis of ambition.

The secret sauce for avoiding burnout

Not to totally spoil this for you, but it turns out that keeping your shit together is immensely boring. Prepare thyself.

While many of the women I've spoken to have suffered immensely, they've also learned a great deal, and accumulated a huge amount of wisdom from what they wish they had done differently, and how they plan to work in the future. I've combined this with what I've also personally gathered from my experiences of extreme stress, anxiety, and – I suppose – burnout. I've learned a lot about taking care of myself over the last four years, particularly throughout 2019, and this combination of harsh lessons learned by other women and my own experiences have led to the following advice on how to work without losing your mind.

Establishing the sort of hero's journey origin story for your work ethic and your relationship to work (and particularly overwork) is most important. Doing this with the aid of a life coach, therapist, or even books borrowed from your local library (if you still have one) would be very useful. You could also start by just asking yourself a series of questions, and making notes for a few minutes on each. A good place to start might be to think about who your work role models are. What have you learned from them? What memories do you have of your parents' relationship to work? What advice have your parents given to you about work? Do you agree with it?

Once you've figured out where your work ethic comes from, the next steps towards being able to achieve and succeed in your career without continuously burning out are:

- Defining what success, achievement and ambition are for you.
- Establishing what you desire in your personal life.
- Establishing what you desire in your working life.
- Integrating these two areas so you can start thinking about your life as a whole.
- Making a damn plan and setting some boundaries along the way.

You essentially want to figure out what you want in your personal life and in your work life (which we focus on in Chapter 7), and how you can marry those two things so that you're a whole person who is neither work obsessed nor gives it all up and camps out on the beach.

A big part of managing all of this is managing your own energy.

When I spoke with Tina Walsberger about burnout, she mentioned that she's a big fan of Tony Schwartz's philosophy on energy. Schwartz is the CEO and founder of The Energy Project, an initiative that, according to its website, 'helps people manage their four key reservoirs of energy – physical, emotional, mental and spiritual – by learning to move rhythmically between spending and refuelling energy'.[17] While I hadn't heard about Schwartz or The Energy Project until Tina mentioned them to me, I found what she said about her own approach to managing the different areas of her own energy to be extremely helpful.

'I do a lot of things and I find that you have to work on it all the time, it's not a box that's ticked and then it's done.' She says that she works out a lot, and is conscious about eating healthily (although she says she's a massive sugar fiend) so, physically, she knows how to manage her energy. But she realized after moving across the world from Sydney to Edinburgh for work that human connection is an essential part of her emotional energy, and without it, she's left emotionally drained. She told me about how she struggled at work when she first moved, as she felt both culturally and personally disconnected from her co-workers. She says that, while other people are fine being disconnected from their colleagues as they've got their friends and families outside of work, this didn't work for her because she's always 'valued feeling connected to the people around me; I don't really separate those two worlds'.

Paying attention to your energy (and the different areas of your energy) is a big (and boring) part of managing your own well-being. And if frameworks like The Energy Project don't click for you, you might prefer to think of your energy as a kind of debit system – you only have so much energy and so much time, and depending on your resilience levels, some things will deplete your energy quicker and more harshly than others. Different areas have different side effects. Spreading your precious energy across several categories and areas of your life also means that you're not overcaring about one specific area or person.

A personal example of this is that in one of my previous jobs I always gave 100 per cent of my mental and physical energy to my work, but also, on top of that – I used to give waaaay too much space to Post-it manager in my mind. She used to take up so much precious space where so many other things could have been, but I let her spread out and set up camp. And not just a humble, family-holiday style camp. We're talking Harry Potter at the Quidditch World Cup-style accommodations, magically expandable tents and all. A much more public example of what I mean is Donald Trump's obsession with Hillary Clinton and her damn emails. In response to some new allegation or investigation, or maybe even a tweet from the President, in May 2019 Secretary Clinton told MSNBC host Rachel Maddow that she was 'living rent free inside of Donald Trump's brain'. Which is a helpful way of thinking about how much time, energy and space you're giving your general workload, or perhaps a difficult manager or maddening colleague in your own mind.

Who or what is living rent free in your brain?

A therapist I had when I was in my late teens marvelled at how very seriously I was taking my job at Starbucks. Not because it wasn't worthy or important enough to warrant this much stress, but rather that I was allowing it to create so much chaos in my life. One day she asked me, 'Do you think anyone would notice if you didn't give them 110 per cent every day? What would happen if you went back to 80? Or even 65?' I was dumbfounded. This question has stuck with me, and I was reminded of it during a conversation I had with a twenty-nine-year-old journalist named Aisling about how she's been dealing with her own form of burnout and how unhappy she currently is with her job. She said that she essentially applied this same philosophy in order to make her job both manageable and bearable:

> I was giving nearly 100 per cent every day, and I could feel the joy draining out of other areas of my life. I couldn't enjoy a weekend. I couldn't enjoy a holiday because I was always on, and now I'm maybe giving 70 per cent. I still work really hard, I very much have that Head Girl mentality. But now I'm giving about 70 per cent and it's comfortable. There are days – and this is the most disheartening part of my job – where I know if I just did like 10 per cent no one would even know. I really don't want to because I still care, but honestly I don't think anyone would notice except myself or maybe my immediate team.

If that feels mega-uncomfortable to you, maybe think of it this way: you're not caring *less* about your job, but caring *more* about the other areas of your life. As you can't just conjure up fresh energy out of thin air (particularly if you're nearing burnout), you'll have to redistribute it from elsewhere to achieve more balance in your life.

What is the state of your friendships? What's your relationship like with your family? Are you tending to your romantic relationship? (Did you, like me, miss your last wedding anniversary because you were busy dealing with the collapse of the business you were working for?) Are you single because you 'don't have time to date', or are you genuinely cool being without a partner at the moment? Do you have pets? Do you like where you live? What are your hobbies and when's the last time you participated in them? When's the last time you had *fun*?

Allowing yourself to care about multiple things, and to have multiple facets to your life, is really important. Some will be bigger than others, some might take up more energy than the others do at various times of your life. The balance will be different for each person, but you have to find what feels best for you.

Maintaining your baseline energy and wellness

Keeping your sort of baseline energy, your baseline mental health and well-being happy is a HUGE part of all of this. As Tina said, it's not just a box that's ticked once and then done, it's a daily upkeep. And *oh my god* it sucks.

I heard my absolute favourite description of this daily upkeep during a How To Academy talk with Elizabeth Gilbert.* When asked how she describes her job, Elizabeth said that her main job, and what she spends most of the hours in her day doing, is 'managing my own mental health'. And that on any given day for most of her life, her first conscious thought when she wakes up in the morning is, 'Oh fuck. FUCK!' She says she's spent hours, months and years of her life working on settling the 'exclamation point of panic that I wake up with' as best she can, 'That's my actual job. Everything [else] I do is just a hobby.'

Another useful piece of advice I heard about managing your mental health and energy on a daily basis was actually from actor and director (and husband to Kristen Bell) Dax Shepherd on his 'Armchair Expert' podcast, which he co-hosts with actress Monica Padman. On the podcast, he speaks regularly about his own mental health, his now more than fifteen years of sobriety and his own various childhood traumas. In numerous

---

* You can listen to a podcast of this talk from the How To Academy on all good podcast providers; it's also listed in the back of this book.

episodes he's mentioned that he actually has a list of the things he knows he has to do every single day in order to manage his mental health. For example, he knows he has to work out every day. He also knows that if he starts to feel bad, he needs to address his list and see what he's been doing and perhaps neglecting.

If you ignore all other advice in this book, I think this is one of the most crucial – and most simple and obvious – things to do for yourself if you're struggling (and even if you're not). I wrote my own list in February 2019 when I had just lost my job at *The Pool*. It includes groundbreaking remedies such as:

- taking a shower,
- washing my face,
- yoga and meditation,
- eating a balanced breakfast,
- actually cooking a meal,
- listening to a podcast,
- using a foam roller,
- drinking water,
- going for a walk.

I also made a note to make sure I take stock of the following:

- time spent on social media,
- overall screen time,
- TV/sofa time,
- sugar/caffeine/carbs/cheese,
- refreshing my emails.

If keeping a list of 'how to feel better' sounds mundane, boring and basic as fuck – that's because it is. It is all of these things. It's also necessary for a lot of us.

No matter what those bitches on Instagram tell you, managing your mental health is less *wellness* in Lululemon, ponytails, hard-to-pronounce exercise classes at boutique gyms and pomegranate-seed salads photographed in soft lighting, and more *basic health* in days-unwashed yet very comfortable leggings, dry-shampooed messy 'buns', nearly-cried-on-the-way-there gym sessions and being amazed at how much you wee in a day when you drink the amount of water you're actually meant to.

I feel as though the collective reaction to the pandemic may have normalized mundane, daily self-care as a point of necessity – but only time will tell if this is truly the case. Even if the masses haven't totally caught on, looking after yourself is part of the bigger picture of managing your energy and keeping the balance in your life. This is tending to your garden. These annoying, mundane tasks are all part of the bigger task of NOT LOSING YOUR FUCKING MIND. So, I'd like to invite you to put down this book (or pause the audiobook) and take some time to think about what your own checklist would look like. Start to write down ideas of the things you personally need on a daily basis to keep yourself balanced. (If you're struggling to know where to start, feel free to use some of the things from my list, or find inspiration with the No Bad Days checklist notepad.)[18]

Please don't disappear into the woods for ever

All of this – the energy maintenance, the boring lists of mundane tasks to keep you sane, the discovery of what we want and how to make it happen – is to try to keep us all from running away to beach huts and small wooden cabins and living out our days in our own self-employed ecosystems, away from the workplace and corporate companies that are increasingly having huge impacts on our governments and lives.

Sometimes we need a break, even if we know we are lucky and should be grateful for having a paying job. Sometimes our work stress is so overwhelming and has impacted so many aspects of our lives that we really do need to fuck off to Bali or, go freelance and work from home for a year and write a book. (One of these things is supremely more relaxing than the other, mind.) There is plenty of space for many of us to be self-employed. But the answer is not for us *all* to go off piste. It's not more feminist or more impressive or better or ethical or more badass to work for yourself. Sorry to burst your hustling-queen-bitch-boss-lady bubble, but you can be just as badass working a 9–5 as you can running your own business. You don't need to run your own business or constantly be juggling ten different projects in order to achieve your dreams, because the key here is, it's about *YOUR* DREAMS. What *you* want. And I don't believe that all of us are going to be content running a glamping site in the New Forest.

If we all just accept the fucked-up systematic cycle of achieving and burning out, and embrace this singular vision of what ambition and success look like, and respond by saying 'fuck this' on a permanent basis . . . then who is in the board room? Who is in the room where the decisions are being made?

Now, you could argue that we're not in those spaces anyway, so who fucking cares if we're not the ones in there when we could be spending our mornings walking our five dogs on the beach instead of commuting and sitting in meetings with a bunch of fuckwits who don't care about your ambitions . . . But the difference is, if we're trying, if we're fighting, if we're exemplifying the change we want to see, the tide will start to turn. I sincerely believe this. And there are many ways of doing this; a plethora of activists and campaigners are fighting for change everywhere you look. In the past I've taken the stance that a woman working in a big corporation or traditionally male workspace, hiring younger women, mentoring them and giving them the tools they need (and that I perhaps wasn't given myself) is performing a feminist act. The problem for me was, I didn't have my own armour when I was doing it. I didn't put my oxygen mask on first before helping others with theirs.

So, we need to reach the point where some of us fuck off for a bit, but we come back so that others can do the same. We can't let our cycles get out of sync; someone always has to be on shift. But the biggest part of this deal is that we need to start exploring and speaking up, letting our bosses know what we need to stay in the game. We need to look after ourselves and promote our cause in new ways. (Or at all, because I don't think, honestly, we're all standing up for ourselves as much as we know we should be.)

A while ago I went for breakfast with Viv Groskop and I told her how I had turned down a few job offers and that I wasn't interested in going into a 9–5 role and just wanted to write my book. She looked at me and said, 'Well, you can hide yourself writing books, but we also could really do with you out here in the workforce. We need leaders.' I laughed, but what she said stuck with me, and I have just decided to take a new role in an office. It's still freelance, but I'll be working three or four days a week with a publisher on a commercial project for a global cosmetics company. And, well, I'm nervous. Not because of the actual job but, in all honesty, because I am now terrified of burnout. The idea of becoming stressed out in my professional life fills me with anxiety. I am terrified of the prospect. I am afraid of falling back into old patterns, of believing that I will only achieve great things if I work myself into the ground. Will my newfound armour hold?

It's now up to me to go forth and succeed without burning out and TAKE MY OWN FUCKING ADVICE.

Drink some water.

Eat a banana.

Go for a walk.

Balance it out.

And, not to sound like one of the Instagram clichés that I knock so freely, but I really do believe that I've got this.

And that you can get it, too.

Boundaries + Egos:

'It's called a *job* for a reason . . .'

What does the word 'professional' even mean these days?

Sometimes complex subjects like this are easier to define in opposition. Personally, I've witnessed all kinds of 'unprofessional' behaviour in my career. Some of it was of the benign 'are you *serious*?' variety that comes with working with 'eccentric' people in tech – such as men walking around barefoot in the office canteen or using fruit scissors to cut their fingernails in the kitchen. Other unprofessional behaviour I've seen sits more in the 'bullying' category, like when the most senior person in the office arrives late to their own meeting and then berates their assistant for 'typing too loudly' . . . after asking them to take notes.

To me, 'being professional' consists of very basic rules of engagement when working for a business. Whether you're a dog walker, a lawyer, working in a super-fun start-up or a bank, there are some basics of how to be. How to behave. How to treat those around you, whether they're a colleague, client, or contact.

A large part of being professional is about reading the room. It's about knowing what is socially acceptable and abiding by the rules that apply to whatever organization you're dealing with or working in. Beyond the specifics of each workplace, professionalism is about being appropriate, inclusive and respectful, while operating from a place of kindness without being overfamiliar. It's also about setting boundaries – teaching your managers and colleagues how to work with you, and how to treat you and your time – and respecting the boundaries of others.

This chapter will show you how to set boundaries so that work is *work* – not your identity, not your 'fam', not the epicentre of your social life, but a job that you get paid for. It will also give you practical ways to keep things professional – even if nobody else around you is. Much like the 'Am I the Asshole?' subreddit,[1] for lack of a daintier phrase, this chapter is meant to help prevent you from being the asshole at work by setting boundaries, keeping your ego in check and not getting fooled into thinking the people at work are your family, no matter how lovely they might be.

While trends, buzzwords and office styles shift like the tide – particularly in 2020 – basic manners, common sense and good intentions do not, and by keeping those two things in mind, almost any sticky situation is manageable.

Why 'we're like a family' is a big fat lie

So often I've heard companies, departments and (especially) start-ups refer to themselves as 'family'. 'We're like a big family here!' or 'Welcome to the family!' It's meant to be inclusive, welcoming, and to make you feel at home. But it makes me shudder.

Families are complicated, complex systems, with many different interpersonal relationships and the expectations and needs of many different people to balance – so, yes, in that way, companies *are* like families. And, also like families, work is difficult and, at times, an absolute fucking nightmare. You can't choose your family – you are born into it and there are varying levels of responsibility, dependency and obligation attached to that. Basically . . . you put up with your family's shit because they're your family and you (probably) love them.

Your job, on the other hand, literally pays you for a service to better the company's output in its effort to make as much money as it possibly can. That's not a family, that's a business. And, for the most part, your family isn't going to fire you. Your family isn't going to downsize and make your position as second-born daughter, auntie or god-mum redundant. On the flip side, unlike your actual family, you *can* choose your job. Don't put up with shitty behaviour at work because your employer sells you some BS excuse of 'needing to pull together because we're a family'. It's not a family, and it's weird if people are trying to pass it off that way.

While some companies don't straight-up say, 'We're a family,' their general lack of boundaries and work/life balance has the same effect. Jessica, a twenty-seven-year-old writer from London, worked at a big-but-still-thinks-it's-a-start-up media company a few years ago, where a lot of her colleagues were quite young. For many, it was their first job out of university, which made the atmosphere at work feel like it was 'basically an extension of uni'. Jessica said that, while she thinks it's natural to make friends at work, she noticed the boundaries between work and home just didn't exist for a lot of her colleagues, as many of them not only lived together, but were also dating. Despite finding all that to be 'fucking weird', she says that, overall, it was a fun place to work, 'It was the first time I would wake up in the morning and genuinely think, "I am so excited to go to work."'

But after being at the company for just over a year, Jessica says she started to see 'the dark side of everything': how the company would take impressionable young people and 'use swag and free food and the cool name of a company' that these young people could leverage in social situations as 'cultural capital' to make them feel proud of where they worked. She noticed they were, over time, given increasing quantities of company-branded accessories and clothing as gifts – a jumper, a hat, a rucksack – and then 'before you know it, you're drinking with a branded cup, and writing with a branded pen, and you've got a branded blanket on your bed, and you're just like, I am *owned* by this place'. She believes this is all part of a wider tactic of keeping young people in jobs, even if they are unhappy, and to ultimately 'stop them from complaining about injustices in the workplace'.

'I think it is one of the smartest tactics used to fuck over a generation of entry-level people who are so eager to get into the industry, and so eager to keep their jobs,' she said. 'Really, it's so clever.'

Jessica also explained how this becomes even more complicated if people are, like her, from an underrepresented background, 'When you are a minority in that kind of environment, you already feel like you owe that place. Because nobody else really looks like you there, you know it's not the norm that you should be there.' She says that she felt 'just lucky to be chosen' to work at this (mostly white) company, which made things complicated when the shine started to wear off: 'When you start to feel unhappy, you're like, "*Fuck!* I feel really bad because I still feel like I owe so much of myself and my career to this place." ' But she soon learned how these 'cool' and 'fun' environments that claim to be family can quickly turn 'personal and aggressive'.

Office shag-nanigans

I've worked in a very similar situation to the one described by Jessica, and have seen how easy it is for this to happen, especially at start-ups and small companies where a lot of people are of a similar age. If you're working in a big city that you're not originally from, chances are, you don't have many social contacts. Your uni friends are elsewhere, your family far away, but your colleagues are near enough your age and are in the same situation and environment as you. It starts slowly – people chatting on Slack all day, popping out for lunch together, then drinks at the pub in the evening. And then the evening drinks become all too regular, and then 'What are you doing this weekend? Want to go for a roast?'

When someone's flatmate moves out and they need a new one, a colleague might move in. Or perhaps all of those Slack conversations and nights at the pub lead to hook-ups (are people still calling it that these days?) or even committed relationships.

This all, inevitably, then leads to drama that spills over from the virtual safety of Slack and the happy-hour-turned-karaoke-excursion from the night before, into the office. There are tears in the loos, high-tension meetings where management is no doubt oblivious to what's going on, and sudden requests to move desks or teams without a real explanation for why start rolling in.

This is stressful, tedious, upsetting and/or awkward for everyone involved.

Even if people aren't *courting* or shagging or having torrid love affairs in the office, things can still get awkward and dramatic AF if everyone is in each other's pockets all the time. And things can snowball and escalate very quickly.

If a management team sets up an environment that emphasizes fun or feels like university, or even a playground, to the point where it no longer resembles a professional working environment, it signals to the young and green, and the fresh out of uni that being fun and casual is the norm, and what really matters. *Here's a casual breakout room with beanbags and bottles of beer, let's order a pizza in and brainstorm!*

If your manager is gossiping, it makes it OK for you to gossip. If your manager is tribalistic, has their favourites and treats different people differently, this gives the office the green light to behave this way as well.

If your manager is high strung, staying late, coming in early and generally a bit of a stressed-out mess, this sets the tone for how people should behave and work. It diminishes time and stress management and everyone's personal well-being and mental health, and signals that success and seniority in the company look like *this*.

Overall, if everyone is wandering around boundaryless, behaving like they're not at work, talking like they're not at work, walking barefoot in the office canteen because that's 'their true authentic self',* this is not only pure chaos, it makes it nigh-on impossible to, ya know, get any fucking work done.

---

* I've seen this happen and it's so upsetting.

How to go from 'totes like a family' to proper colleagues

A big part of being able to work without losing your mind is cutting out the unnecessary drama, and putting the wild beast that is work back into its cage. If you want more order in your life, you must put up some boundaries. So, if you've landed yourself in a bit of a mess at work, or if you're keen to set new boundaries in your new job – this *can* be done. It's just going to take a bit of time to unpick the mess you've got into, or to get yourself used to having these fresh, new boundaries in places where before there was just wild, borderless landscape as far as the eye could see.

So, what does setting up new boundaries look like?

Jessica, our friend with the boundary-less uni-office, eventually left that company and now adopts a very different approach to her interactions with work colleagues. She says it was an adjustment when she started at a new company, 'At first I was, like, "Why does nobody want to be friends?" But now, I prefer it. I don't like it when a company says you should be a family. At my new job, I like the idea that we're a team, not a family, and that we're only as good as our shittest person. I like that.'

There are new boundaries and limits she's working with too – for example, she doesn't often add people on Instagram. 'I don't particularly want you messaging me at one in the morning, telling me about how you snogged one of the guys from work, like, no thanks. I've put that boundary in now. I don't think you should be stone-cold awful, but a boundary-less working environment in a boundary-less, open-plan office? No thanks.' She also makes it clear that once it's 5.30, she's out the door, and not contactable (unless it's a genuine emergency).

I love what Jessica has decided to do in her new role, and if you need help with where to start on this, here are a few things to keep in mind or try out for yourself if you're struggling to set boundaries with your colleagues:

- Once you start gossiping, it's very hard to stop. Avoid joining bitchy, private Slack rooms or WhatsApp groups, or anything else like that. Not only can your employer request to see chats on devices,[2] or accounts they've provided to you (*oof!*), it's terrifyingly easy to get caught somehow. You don't need that.
- If you must gossip, confide in someone out of work. And if it *has* to be with someone from work, limit it to one person that you've known for a while. Honestly. Trust me on this.
- If your social media profiles are relevant to work, it's probably not a problem if colleagues follow you because *of course* you're totally keeping in mind that anyone and everyone (clients, your bosses, etc.) can see what you post, *right*? However, if you have private social accounts, you don't need to add people. If anyone asks, you can just say, 'Ah, sorry but I don't add anyone from work, it's just a rule I have.' If they're offended or offensive, don't worry, they'll swiftly move on.
- You only have to talk about what you want to talk about. You don't have to write articles about all of your pain and trauma, even if your editor asks you to. You don't have to tell everyone all of your sad mental health stories at the pub, even if everyone else is sharing their misery. You don't have to tell anyone what you actually did at the weekend, or what your marital status is, if you don't want to. Think of

yourself as a politician and simply avoid answering the question: 'What did I do this weekend? I love weekends off, don't you? I remember, one of my favourite weekends was spent rock climbing in Wales. Tell me, have you ever been to Snowdonia?'

- You can be friendly and polite to everyone, but you don't have to like everyone. And they don't have to like you. This can be painful, especially if it means you don't get invited to the gossipy Slack groups so you don't know all the in-jokes, or if the group decides they're all going to lunch and you don't get the memo. It's hard. But you have to remember *why* you're at work. You're earning money, and you're hopefully getting some satisfaction by doing work you enjoy, and that gives you wider satisfaction in your overall life.

The tricky balance of putting boundaries on your time

I often tell people how important it is to get to work on time, to take your full lunch entitlement and to leave on time. Easy! But despite being simple in concept, in execution accurate timekeeping can get quite tricky. I often hear people say, 'But there's just no time, I have too much on!' I know people who feel they don't have time to go to the loo, or even to buy a meal deal (never mind actually eating it) because they don't have space in their day. They have back-to-back meetings and a manager who's riding their ass. They have demanding clients, and in order to prove their worth to the company, they have to just manage it all. *There is no time to wee when Betsy from The*

Meerkat Agency needs that statement of work emailed to her by 2 p.m. I know how this feels, because I have been there.

If you're starting a new job, make laying down time boundaries your number one priority. Start as you mean to go on. Have your new team and manager know that you get to work on time, that you take your lunch break and that you leave on time. It's so much easier to start fresh. Block out unbookable times in your diary – for going to the gym, for going to lunch, or for actually working and not sitting in meetings. If your new company uses G-Suite or Google Calendar, you can set your working hours, and even make a rule whereby if someone tries to book a meeting when you already have something booked, it will automatically decline the invite. Be strict with this from the beginning and things will be much easier for you. The minute you start taking meetings out of hours, or if your client's executive assistant discovers that you once cancelled dinner plans so you could attend a review with the New York office, they will always think your time is theirs. 'Oh, that meeting will overlap with something else on Cate's calendar, but I know she'll move it. Book it in.'

If you're currently drowning in the mess of your schedule at your current job, resetting the way you work and defining those boundaries is more complicated, but not impossible. It's necessary, so here's what to do:

Firstly, you need to talk with your manager and be crystal clear that you're struggling and you need their support in finding a more manageable workload because the current way of work is negatively impacting your mental health. You can say, 'It's not that I can't do the actual task, or that the job is too challenging, it's the scheduling that is not working for me. I don't have time to eat lunch or even go to the loo, and it's negatively impacting my well-being.'

You can then bring some solutions to the table and offer new ways of working that will help you, such as booking out your lunch in your diary, having their support when you need to decline certain meetings, or pushing back on being given various extra tasks. You can also ask for your boss's help on taking some things off your plate, and they might also have some feedback on how things can be improved.

Of course, your manager might just say, 'This is the nature of the job,' or, 'The work still needs doing,' or, 'If you're not up to the task, I'll find someone else who is.' Well, if the nature of a job is that nobody can pee, I'm sure your HR representative will feel otherwise. That's the *nature of how they're choosing to run their team*, not part of a job description or 'Just how this industry is'. People *choose* to work like that. You don't have to.

As far as the 'but work still needs to get done' argument, I firmly believe that work will be done more efficiently if people have time to rest their brains. More can get done in a ninety-minute block with zero interruptions after a proper lunch break than in an entire day that includes back-to-back meetings and non-stop email replies. If your boss threatens to fire you because you're struggling to eat, urinate and sleep at night, then you probably need to quit anyway. It's unreasonable, cruel and unhealthy to expect anyone to work that way, or to offer someone zero support when they explain how they're struggling.

After you have this conversation, you MUST put these things into practice:

- Book out your time, and be strict about it. Lunches are important, even if you can only take a half-hour some days. Physically leave the building or eat your reheated leftovers on another floor. People need to see your desk is vacant. If they see you sitting there, even if you're eating, demanding colleagues will just talk to you anyway. 'Hey, sorry to interrupt but . . .' This used to drive me mad, but it was my own fault for eating at my desk.

- If you're having a busy afternoon and you need a toilet break, you are entitled to quietly excuse yourself from a meeting. You don't have to announce where you're going, just say, 'Please excuse me, I'll be right back.' DON'T ASK PERMISSION. YOU'RE NOT AT SCHOOL.
- Get to work on time, leave on time. You can put in extra hours when it's absolutely necessary, but make sure you're either paid for it or get time off in lieu. Maybe you can arrange to come in late the next morning, or leave early that Friday.
- Use the word 'urgent' sparingly. Be mindful about treating things as stressful when they're not, and raising red flags only when actually necessary. If you're tearing your hair out and are always either staying late or coming in at the crack of dawn, how is your manager to know when you're going 'above and beyond'? How will they know that you need urgent help with a genuine emergency if you treat every project like it's a house on fire?

These boundaries are crucial for your well-being, and your actual output at work. They'll allow you to manage your professional reputation, your work and your sanity well. You're teaching people how to treat you at work, and hopefully setting a positive example for other people in the office at the same time.

Setting boundaries when you don't work in an office

For those of us who were able to work at home during the global pandemic, working remotely brought with it a whole new host of problems. Suddenly a huge part of the world's workforce were communicating via video calls, huddled in messy kitchens while their toddlers wailed in another room, or hid from their partner's loud conference call while stuffed in whatever corner of their home wasn't piled with laundry.

However, toiling remotely under extraordinary circumstances is not how working from home can or should be. It is also not reflective of how being self-employed and working from home on your own schedule is, either. In fact, it's important to remember that there is a big difference between working for yourself from home and working from home as a 'remote' employee. One of the key differences is that if you're working for yourself, you make your own schedule – aside from the occasional client call and the deadlines you have to adhere to, nobody is going to be watching the clock to make sure you're at your desk at 10 a.m.

However, if you're an employee working remotely then, sorry pal, you should very much be signed into Slack or whatever communication software you use so your team and manager see that you're online and available. Whether you're doing that from the loo or not is, of course, up to you. But no matter your exact situation, it's the clear communication around your working schedule and the boundaries within it that are such an important thing, perhaps *the* most important thing. At first, setting a firm 'home' and 'life' boundary when you're working from home can feel nearly impossible – but, fret not, it is doable. It just takes discipline and a few adjustments here and there.

For the most part, even when you're working from home, you still need to cover the basics that we went over earlier: take loo breaks, start and finish at reasonable times, block out time when you need to focus and reach 'flow'. Don't get in the habit of 'just quickly sending one last email' at 9 p.m. when your partner is wanting to spend time with you. You know, that sort of stuff. Here's what that looks like in action:

Make it clear *when* people can reach you. Are you a 'call me anytime, 24/7' person? If not, your customers, clients or colleagues need to know that you're available from 8 a.m. to 4 p.m. Monday to Friday, and if they contact you outside those hours they'll have to wait until the next possible business day to hear from you. You would think common sense would prevent people from phoning you at 10 p.m. for something minor, but unfortunately this is not always the case (particularly when international time zones are involved).

Make it clear *how* people can reach you. Do you want people to call your mobile? Is email best for you? Explicitly tell people which platforms you use to communicate for work and business, and stick to them. (Keep the other platforms and channels – such as social media and WhatsApp – for personal use only if that's your preference.)

Be consistent and abide by your own communication rules. If you tell people you're only available until 4 p.m., don't then call them at 7 p.m. using Facebook Video Chat. That's sending mixed messages and rolling out the welcome mat for them to do the same. Be consistent and lead by example.

You decide what an emergency or urgent situation actually is. Keep in mind that clients and managers will usually have different definitions of 'urgent' and 'emergency' from you. Have your own interpretation of what's really urgent, for example, what is a good enough reason for someone to call you at 7 a.m. on a Saturday? Let your team know what a true emergency comprises so everyone is on the same page. Granted, those higher up the food chain than you may have very different ideas on this, especially where money is involved. If your client gets you out of bed on a Saturday morning because they want to share a fun idea with you – that is not an emergency and you need to set better boundaries with them! Your manager doing the same because the business has lost millions of pounds overnight, or because Harry Styles was photographed wearing a shirt you designed, would definitely feel a bit more 'urgent'.

Give yourself the set-up or circumstances necessary to reach 'deep work', 'flow' or whatever you call high productivity. Working at the kitchen table without a monitor or keyboard for your laptop might not be the most conducive to creating your best work. If you're working from home permanently or most of the time, invest in your work space and environment. If you're trying to be productive and work from home and feel good about your life and work balance – doing it in bed in your pyjamas ain't great. (Just because Phoebe Waller-Bridge does it doesn't mean you should.)[3] For us mere mortals, showering, brushing our teeth and putting on some proper clothing – even if it's just unlaundered loungewear – will help you feel 'ready' for work (bras, makeup and shaving are, as always, optional). This helps to create a clear distinction between 'home' and 'work', even though both happen under the same roof: your bed is for sleeping and shagging – not for working on a mind-numbing presentation in Google Slides (unless, of course, this is your kink; no judgement here!)

Even if you don't have a spare room to turn into an office, there are still economical (and ergonomic) things you can do to be more productive and more comfortable. Facebook

Marketplace and eBay are excellent for cheap, second-hand office equipment. Freecycle is cheaper still! If you need to invest in noise-cancelling headphones or better lighting, these are all things to take into consideration, budget depending.

Establish your most creative and productive hours or times of day – if you're a remote worker, you might struggle to make your personal peak hours of productivity match your overall working schedule, but give it a shot. If you're freelance or work for yourself, you have freer rein and can set your own working hours. If you don't need to be confined to 9–5, and you work better as a 12–4 one day and a 5–7 the next, then do that. Your daily work also doesn't need to equal eight hours a day if you're not doing shift work or being paid by the hour, though you might want to set a rough target for your working week, just to keep yourself honest.

Communicate your boundaries with the people you work with

Don't just set your Slack to 'do not disturb' for half the day or ignore all emails or suddenly stop answering your phone during core work hours unless the people you work with know to expect this. *Boundaries are only boundaries if you actually enforce and communicate them*, otherwise they're just bullshit commandments you wrote for yourself that have zero impact or value.

You must tell your manager – or whoever needs to know – what your plans, needs and boundaries are. An example of communicating your working times and availabilities could look something like this: say you're working on a big project and you know that you work best from 10 a.m. to around lunchtime, so you need to avoid interruptions during this time and won't be attending any team meetings or responding to Slack messages or emails during this period. You could send your manager and your colleagues the following message:

Hi team! You might notice in my diary tomorrow that I'm unavailable for meetings from 10 a.m. – 1:30 p.m. as I've blocked out time to work on the Rainbow Capybara presentation. I'll have notifications turned off on Slack and WhatsApp and I won't really be checking emails at that time, but if there's an emergency – like the presentation has been called off or there's been a major shift of brief that I need to know about – please call me on my mobile. I'll be joining our 9:30 a.m. start-of-day meeting as usual to check in before I get going.

Making it clear when you will and won't be available, the reasons why, and how people can reach you if they really need to will put even the most uptight of micromanagers at ease.

How to communicate professionally at work

Whether everyone is together in an office or has several members of staff working remotely, the culture of a workplace is best reflected and encapsulated by the manner in which people communicate – be it in platform, medium or style. Some places may be very email heavy, and speak to each other in more formal tones. Some may keep the emails short and casual, and usually opt for 'jumping on a quick video call'. Other places may keep the day-to-day discussions to Slack, and then swap to email for bigger conversations that end up in seventy-message, company-wide threads, jostling for the praise and attention of the CEO (*gag*).

It's important to note that this style, these preferences and this crucial element of a workplace's culture, stem from the leadership teams. Heist Studios' Cheryl Fergusson says that when it comes to the style of communication used in an office, management have to set the tone, and they also need to be clear on how they themselves want to be spoken to, 'You might have an entrepreneur who is really relaxed, and then they get an email from a young person that's casual and not at all professional, and then the entrepreneur is shocked – but they are the ones who have created a relaxed culture.' She says that if you're a time-poor senior leader and you just want people to give you the information you need as succinctly and as quickly as possible, then you have to make that known.

Communicating appropriately and well is a huge factor in saving yourself stress and future grief. How many times have you agreed to do something, perhaps against your better judgement, and then a week later been cursing the ground everyone involved in the project walks on, hissing to yourself, *'If I had only asked X or if only I had clarified Y I never would have agreed to do this!'* Sometimes we put our foot in it and we don't even realize it until there's a surprising consequence to our actions weeks later. Sometimes we can think we're losing our mind because it feels like we're literally trying to communicate in a different language.

It could be that whoever you're dealing with is just particularly difficult, but if you're finding that your exchanges with several of your clients or contacts are especially tough, you might need to stop and examine why.

Perhaps their responses are totally fine, but you're feeling defensive or angry for other reasons, so you're projecting your feelings onto their responses. Or it might be that they actually are being short and shitty with you, in which case it's always worth having a look at your responses and communications with them – have you yourself accidentally been short and shitty yourself? Sometimes we can fall into the trap of adopting an attitude that we think is professional and powerful, one that displays our seniority and shows that we're a strong bad-ass bitch lady boss or whatever, but which actually just makes us look like an asshole. So, yeah, I'm telling you that, actually, you might be the asshole here. Sorry about that, but it's a good thing to know.

To help prevent that from happening again, here are a few pieces of situational advice that aren't necessarily specific to particular jobs or industries, or even if you're in full-time employment or freelance. They're tips for how to communicate with people in a professional environment, in a professional way, that doesn't leave you looking shitty or stupid (which should be a goal for us all, basically).

Please don't ask anyone if you can 'pick their brains'

If you're wanting to meet someone new at work, or get to know better someone you have met only once or twice, be up front about what you want. Say something like: 'Hi, Adaego! It was lovely running into you at the Wombats for Climate Change conference last week, I really enjoyed your keynote speech. I wanted to ask if I could meet you for a coffee sometime as I was hoping to ask you a few questions with regard to progressing within the company?' Be upfront about what you want, show that you know who they are, remind them that you've met in the past and be polite.

If you're emailing someone you don't know but who you're hoping could give you advice or offer a bit of insight, don't make them feel like you're asking for free consultancy or sneakily trying to get expertise out of them. Or, if the person you're asking for help is very senior or has a big following on social media, don't come across like you just want an excuse to meet them and then put it on your Instagram Stories.

Be open about what you're asking for. As author Leil Lowndes advises in her fantastic book *How to Talk to Anyone*, you should never bury the WIIFM (what's in it for me) or the WIIFY (what's in it for you) when you reach out to meet someone, or even to ask them a favour.

Here's a good example of what *not* to email someone you're hoping to meet and ask advice from for the first time:

DON'T DO THIS:

> Hi Sara
> I'm Brit, I follow you on Instagram. You don't actually follow me back, but you've probably heard about my styling business as it's been featured in Red magazine recently, and [name of Sara's biggest competitor] loves us. Maybe you saw the post on their Twitter?
>
> Anyway, I'm a big fan, and your podcast is one of my faves – I really want to launch my own. I think I'd be really good at it and a few of my followers keep asking me to do it.
>
> I'd love to pick your brains about how your podcast got so popular and how you got to make so much money from it. We should definitely meet to discuss. I am only in the city 2x a month and can only really meet in Soho in the early afternoons as I'm v busy with my client meetings, but I'm sure we can figure something out. See you soon!!!
>
> Bxx

Cringeworthy, right? Here's what this person should have said:

DO THIS INSTEAD:

> Hi Sara
> My name is Brit, and I'm the founder of The Styling App (link to website).

I'm a regular listener to and huge fan of your podcast; your latest interview with Olivia Colman about killer whales and crocheting was truly insightful. The production quality of 'The Sara Podcast' is so impressive, and I'm a huge admirer of your interviewing style.

I'm actually looking to launch a podcast for my business in the next six months, and I was wondering if you might consider meeting for a coffee so I that I might ask you a few specific questions with regard to the equipment you've decided to use, and whether you have any advice on how to approach monetization.

I appreciate that your time is extremely valuable, and I would be more than happy to work around your schedule. If a call or email would be easier for you, please do let me know.

In the meantime, please find attached a complimentary registration code for the Styling App, which I hope you will find useful.

Thank you very much
Brit

When you approach someone out of the blue like this, don't expect a response. If you do, wonderful. If not, then a gentle nudge a couple of weeks later might work:

Hi again, Sara
I was wondering whether you'd had the chance to read the email I sent you the other week (below). I do realize you must receive many such requests, so I'll understand entirely if you don't have time to reply.

I do hope you're finding the Styling App useful.
Many thanks
Brit

If they still don't get back to you, just swallow it. Don't stalk them on Twitter, or spam them every fortnight for the next six months. Also, don't slag them off to everyone you know for 'not helping women'. Sometimes people get busy and awkward; it's not personal.

Choose discomfort over ghosting people

You are never too high and mighty to stop being ghosted. Like in the third season of *The Crown*, when President Johnson simply never replied to the Queen's invitation to Balmoral* – it doesn't matter who you are, sometimes we just get ignored. The further along in your career you get, the less frequently it happens, but when it does, it's even more annoying. Like, who doesn't get back to the QUEEN? We, however, can be better than that, and choose to not ghost people. We can turn back the ghosting tide!

It's simple, really. If you're not interested in something, just politely say so – don't let silence speak on your behalf. Save everyone the mental energy of filling in the blanks. Be kind, be gracious, and write your email so that if for some reason it was ever screengrabbed and tweeted, you'd have no problem with it being out in the world. (Never mind how rude it would be of anyone to actually do that.)

Don't mimic how your boss writes emails, unless they're actually coherent

I don't know what it is, but once senior managers hit a certain level of seniority, their emails lose all form. They become alphabet soup – short, rude haikus without capitalization, punctuation or grammar. It's infuriating.

---

* This didn't actually happen, it was a pure fiction devised for TV, but it's still a good example, right?

For example, I'm sure we've all seen emails like this, from on high:

Need asap tmrw make sure Calum there

or

No just the org pres for Mon thx

or my favourite, the one-worded, cold reply:

Yes

What is more chilling than a *one word email* without any emoji to soften the blow? So often these emails don't make sense, and you can only ask for clarification so many times before you know that another request will make you seem thick as a board.

I combat this with a stubborn insistence to reply to these emails as I would if I were in charge:

Email from boss:

Paris tomorrow, C to do present, talk deets tmrw

My response:

Hi Eiko
That's great news about Paris. I'll make sure Tom knows to bring Caroline's laptop with him to the station so she can do the presentation – looking forward to hearing more about it then.
 Best
 Cate

Try to bring your boss solutions, not problems

One of the best pieces of advice I was given for how to write emails to your manager was to focus on giving them solutions, not problems. Don't complain for two paragraphs that your colleague let everyone down and so the presentation isn't done. Just tell them that the presentation will be done by 2 p.m. tomorrow and apologize for the late delivery. Your boss doesn't want to know about all the reasons why it's not done, they need to be able to tell *their* boss when it will be on their desk. If they're curious as to what happened, they will ask.

If it's that important for you to tell your boss it wasn't done on time because Tom went out on a boozy three-and-a-half-hour client lunch, tell her that in person, separately.

Acting overly entitled isn't exactly inclusive behaviour

Unless you are the actual Queen (in which case, thank you for buying the book, Ma'am), you don't get to treat people as though your time is so much more valuable than theirs, or that they're just lucky to be in the same room as you. And, even then, we know that the Queen *specifically and purposefully* does not treat people like that.

Somewhere along the lines, whether it was through ~empowering~ Instagram quotes about hustling or everyone telling each other what a queen or girlboss they are, we, as a way of combating imposter syndrome or low confidence, have developed a habit of acting a bit . . . entitled.

It's the strong-badass-bitch-lady-boss tone I mentioned before. I know it, because I have definitely, 100 per cent done this before. I also know that it was born out of insecurity and an inferiority complex, and also mimicking how some of the people around me behaved. I know that I've acted like I was VERY BUSY AND IMPORTANT and was dismissive to people who perhaps didn't deserve it, and I know that I've been unnecessarily harsh on people who were easier to be shitty to than the ones I *actually* wanted to be shitty to, but was too scared of.

Instead of doing this, especially if you're feeling shit, I encourage you to act in the spirit of Brené Brown and communicate from a place of kindness and gratitude and empathy.

Even if you don't feel like having coffee with the graduate you promised you'd see four months ago and only just remembered, even if you don't necessarily have the energy to take a video call with someone from the Vancouver office – treat them with kindness and respect.

I've been in so many meetings where people clearly didn't know or care who I was, or couldn't remember what we were meeting about or why they had ever agreed to meet with me in the first place. And as a result of all of that, I felt unhappy, dismissed, small and angry. Not great.

If someone is making you feel crap while you're in a meeting, remember that. File it away. You don't need to tweet your disgust or tell everyone you know or curse them dead. Just remember the way they made you feel, and try never to make other people feel that way in your meetings. (And then, three years later, when they desperately need something from you, keep that in mind. Not that I recommend holding grudges, but sometimes . . .)

I'd also like to point out that, in my experience, the people who are *actually* famous/important/busy are the ones who treat you the kindest. The ones who need everyone to know how busy they are, how lucky you are to be meeting them, and spend half the meeting checking their phone or looking at their watch, clearly have some sort of complex at play. It could be that they're trying to impress you, that they want you to appreciate how important and grand they are. It could be that they're stressed and they don't usually behave this way. Whatever the reason, know that it's not about you, it has everything to do with them.

Meetings made simple

Make it easy for people to say yes

Make it easy for busy people to say yes to you and to help you. Temporarily redefine boundaries if necessary and anticipate possible points of contention. Give people all the information they need to say 'yes' as succinctly as possible, without overwhelming them with details.

Nothing is worse than a huge back-and-forth email thread when all you're trying to do is meet someone, or come to a simple conclusion.

This means thinking ahead and doing a bit of organization. It might include:

- Proposing times, dates and locations for a meeting.
- Booking a meeting room.
- Providing them with options so they can just pick one, and you do the rest.
- Including vital information: Is this a video call or a phone call? Will you be calling on their mobile, or on an office landline? Is the meeting in person? What about parking and other transport?

If you're meeting a colleague within the same organization as you, you might have access to their own diary via Google

Calendar or a similar tool – if so, check for a free slot in their diary before blindly sending a calendar invite that clearly works for you. People don't like to hit 'decline' – they want to say yes to you, so don't make them have to keep telling you 'I don't work Thursdays' or 'I have a meeting at that time' if you have clear and easy access to their diary already. Be respectful of people's schedules and diaries. It's up to them to prioritize their time, not you.

As I mentioned before, being up front and honest about WIIFM and WIIFY makes it easier for them to say yes – and if the favour you're asking means a lot to you, be open about that. If it sounds like a throwaway request that you've already asked twenty other people they may not take it as seriously. But if you say that you're only asking a couple of trusted friends and you value their opinion highly and would appreciate any effort they might be able to make to help you with whatever it is you're asking them, that might make all the difference.

Avoid cancelling at the last minute

I've learned the hard way that scheduling back-to-back meetings only works if everyone attending is on time, and their agendas are such that they end on time. Otherwise, prepare to spend your day feeling very stressed out, bursting into meetings after they've already started while sweating profusely and apologizing to everyone in hushed tones until you go home.

If you have to cancel something, don't do it less than an hour before it's meant to be happening. Give at least two hours, preferably more – twenty-four hours' notice is ideal. If you're meeting someone for breakfast, do not email them at 6.45 a.m. and expect that to suffice; either show up, call them, or cancel at least the night before. Nothing is worse than dragging yourself out of bed for an early meeting, only to be told when you're nearly there that it's been called off.

'Are we still meeting?'

If you email someone to ask, 'Are we still on?' it gives them the perfect opportunity to reply, 'Oh, actually . . .' You're giving them an easy out, so you need to be a bit more clever.

The best way I've ever had someone double check that we're still meeting was an email the day before simply saying: 'I'm really looking forward to seeing you tomorrow, here's my mobile number just in case.' *Perfect.*

It's a lovely way of saying that, yes, they remember you're meeting, and that they'll enjoy your company, and it's a gentle reminder to you that the event is scheduled. It also doesn't give you an opening to cancel – because if you do cancel, you're letting them down! *They were looking forward to seeing you FFS!* Plus, once again, it's making life easy for you – providing a contact number just in case you can't find each other at the venue or whatever. I send a similar message before all my meetings now.

The complicated etiquette of virtual meetings and video calls

Whether it's Zoom or Google Meetup, Skype or Microsoft Teams – taking part in a video call or 'virtual meeting' is more complicated than you might expect. If you work at a tech company or an international firm with remote workers, you were probably already very familiar with video meetings before coronavirus happened. However, the pandemic saw more of us using these apps for virtual meetings than ever before, and it became quite clear that the etiquette of how they should run was as fuzzy as the resolution of your colleagues' webcams.

To clear a few things up, here are some best practices:

Have a dedicated moderator

For meetings with more than two people, whoever is owning the meeting needs to set up the call, and everyone on it. They need to send the calendar invites, perhaps followed up with an email of the agenda, and make it clear that the call is in fact a Zoom or Teams call, with the log-in details made super clear.

Have a clear agenda

The moderator of the meeting needs to chair it properly. They should open it by making all necessary introductions, giving a summary of what the meeting is about, and run through the agenda (which would have ideally been sent out ahead of time and should allow time to ask questions). That way, everyone knows what will be discussed, and in which order. You can even go so far as to include timings, such as 'Why Episode 10 of *Normal People* is a masterpiece – Elizabeth, ten minutes'. It's up to the moderator to let everyone know when it's their turn to speak. The moderator should also keep in mind that it's hard to speak up on a video call. Interruptions are actually very stressful – in person, you can pick up on verbal cues, you can hear someone sharply inhale in preparation to interject but on a call, there's none of that.[4] The moderator can help with giving guidance at the beginning, for example they could say something like: 'If there's an important point you feel like you need to make, please do just jump in. It's hard on video calls to tell, so please don't feel like you're being rude.' Or, if you'd rather people hold their questions and comments until the very end, make that clear, too. This might feel a bit formal, but giving video calls a bit of structure will help cut down on the aspects of 'Zoom fatigue'.

Do the necessary prep work

Virtual meetings via video are not the time or place to go over anything in granular detail. Unless you're all in a board room with snacks, nobody can properly pay attention to line-by-line detail on video call, even if someone is sharing their screen. I firmly believe that all the finer detail should be forwarded at least thirty-six hours in advance of the meeting, so participants can review it in their own time, at their own pace, and then the video call can be used for questions, concerns, pass-agg comments, full-on arguments, silent tears, etc.

Keep it to thirty minutes, max

As well as prep work, keep your video calls to no longer than thirty minutes. I'm not a fan of hour-long meetings anyway, but on video it's especially hard to concentrate. There's plenty of research into this – it's also why TED insist their talks last no longer than eighteen minutes,[5] but beyond the science, who the heck wants to sit on a video call for more than a half hour? It's exhausting! Our brains have to work harder during video calls as our communication is impaired. We can't see people's body language or their hand gestures, and their facial expressions can be much harder to read on video – so pretty much all of our non-verbal cues are gone. We're also trying to look from one face to another on multi-person calls, which in itself is tiring, because you literally cannot 'read the room'. There's also the problem of being distracted by your own face instead of paying attention to what's being discussed.[6] And if you have any neurological differences, such as being on the autism spectrum, video calls can be even more challenging.[7]

'Sorry, I was on mute!'

This is a big one, the importance of which seems to elude so many. If you're on a call with one other person, it's not such a big deal, but when there are several people on a call and you are not speaking, please, for the love of god, mute yourself. Nobody needs to hear your deep breathing, your coffee slurping, your nail biting (or, in my case, your dog snoring loudly in the background). Equally, try to remember to unmute before you start talking. 'Sorry, I was on mute!' became the slogan of working from home in 2020 (along with 'Can you see me?' and all of us screaming into the lockdown void).

In addition to muting when necessary, using headphones is also far preferable to relying on your computer's speakers. Not only do they block out background noise, but also, if you're presenting or note-taking or have to send a quick email during the meeting while your sound has to be on, they mean we don't have to listen to the clickety-clack of your keys and that horrible scraping noise of a hand touching the microphone.

'Are we doing video?'

Despite its name, it's not always clear if a video call actually means 'a call with cameras turned on'. Whoever is running the meeting needs to make it clear whether everyone should turn on their cameras. Having cameras on makes a big difference, especially for important meetings or when sensitive topics are being discussed. If you make that clear from the outset, there's no awkward 'Er, what are we doing?' when one person has their camera on and nobody else does. Equally, being on camera for several calls a day can be exhausting, so if it's just a quick catch-up that can be done with audio-only (what used to be known as a phone call), make that clear, too.

'Can you see my screen?'

If you're sharing your laptop screen for a presentation or to give a visual example to a client or a colleague, *please lord* turn off notifications. Make sure you don't have Slack or Google Hangout pop-up notifications or, even worse, texts or WhatsApp messages coming through. It's also a good idea to close all open tabs on your web browser, and to give a second glance over what you have saved in your bookmarks bar! Another element of screen sharing to keep in mind, is to *remember you're sharing your screen*. If you're zoned out while a colleague drones on about something, don't get so distracted that you flick over to Slack – particularly if it's to message your pal at work about how boring the person talking is. (I've seen this happen – it's so painful!)

Basically, this is how to work without being a dick

Ultimately, setting boundaries to keep work predominantly about work is crucial, as is treating all of those connected to your professional world with respect and kindness. Be transparent and honest with others, just as you'd want people to be with you.

I've found that consciously treating people the way I would want to be treated at work can absolutely reduce my own stress levels, and has made my working life easier. As ever, it means that I'm super uncomfortable and sweaty sometimes, but asking questions and doing due diligence can pay off in spades in the long run and can help build your own reputation in ways that you might not even be aware of.

Leadership+
Responsibility:

How to be the best manager you never had

There's an odd belief in the world of work that being a manager is somehow the holy grail of seniority – this idea that once you manage a team, you've hit a milestone of success. Management is big business. There are countless books on management, management consultants and experts, and lots of different frameworks and tactics and theories and methods on how to manage people – much of which is just management snake oil, or the business equivalent of Goop's vaginal jade eggs.

Even if you're not currently a manager, and even if you don't necessarily think that's on the cards for you, it's still worth giving this chapter a read to prepare yourself. Essentially, the qualities that make a 'good' manager are also qualities that can make you a positive role model and leadership figure. It might also help you work out why you're struggling with a difficult manager. Frankly, I don't think that being a 'good' manager is all that complicated – it's actually quite simple – but just because something is simple, doesn't mean that it's easy.

Good managers are a little uncomfortable a lot of the time, and the rest of the time are very uncomfortable indeed, to the point of thinking, 'Why the hell am I doing this?' Which is why people opt for the easier route of people-pleasing or taking out their own personal insecurities on their teams rather than addressing them head-on.

Being a 'good manager' is about choosing to be responsible and professional over fun and popular. It's about making hard decisions and following through. It's about giving tough but necessary feedback and facing awkward situations head-on when you'd rather drown yourself in tequila to escape. It's generally unglamorous and occasionally highly uncomfortable, but, as I said, it's also quite simple. This chapter is all about breaking down what a good manager is, and how to work through these points of discomfort – plus some helpful examples of what to do and what not to do to become one.

But first, I think it's important to take a look at *why* I think there are so many bad managers out there, running wild and playing fast and loose with our careers.

The system is not set up for you to succeed as a 'good manager'

As I've already mentioned, poor management is absolutely everywhere. It's an issue that runs across international borders, oceans, industry and sector. I believe the main reasons for this are:

- a complete absence of alternative career trajectories that don't include people management as a marker for success or progression;
- lack of acceptance that being an expert in an area does not give someone the same skill set needed to people manage;
- lack of succession planning within organizational structures;
- lack of training and continued learning and support for managers, old and new;
- lack of understanding of the importance of emotional intelligence and psychological awareness needed for those in management roles.

Looking at the first point, I think it's important to highlight that using management as a reward for doing well at your job *simply doesn't make any fucking sense*, and yet this sort of progression is the absolute norm. Doing your job well and leading a team are two very different things that require very different skill sets. If you display a proclivity and, crucially, an actual interest in a leadership position – wonderful, let's get you trained up! If not, and you're just great at your job, why would anyone just hand you a team of people to deal with as some sort of treat? 'You smashed your H2 goals, Rani! We're so impressed with you and your work – so instead of a bonus, how about dealing with four other people's bullshit day in and day out? Congrats!' Now, to be fair, dealing with other people's BS isn't exactly a kind description of people management, but if you've managed people before, you know that it's also not that wide of the mark.

Managing people involves dealing with them on their very best days and their very worst. It involves managing, on a daily basis, your team members' expectations and sometimes the nitty-gritty details of their work. Managing well doesn't mean just meeting someone once a month and letting them get on with it – only your highest performers require the lightest of touches, and even some of those need constant feedback and checking in. It's time consuming AF. And so, sometimes, managing can very much feel like dealing with multiple people's bullshit day in and day out – like parenting! But, ultimately, it is incredibly rewarding . . . which is why you actually have to be interested in managing a team, not only to be good at it but also to enjoy the moments of positivity and celebration.

When you've worked for a crappy manager, your surface-level distaste or distrust of that person can easily lead you to believe that this person as a whole is rubbish, or perhaps a complete idiot for not being better at managing you. However, it might not be their fault entirely. Kimberlie Walker, a HR specialist from Dorset, says she often sees examples of it being down to the company rather than the individuals if their management style is lacking, because it's the company that ultimately decides who is promoted. She says that, no matter the location, industry, or business size, she'll quite regularly have a conversation with a client that goes like this:

COMPANY: Good news, we promoted Rhoda and she's now a manager with five direct reports!
KW: OK brilliant. What training or development have you given her? Does she know what she's doing?
COMPANY: Yes, she did appraisals last month.
KW: OK, sure, and who supported her with that?
COMPANY: No one, we just gave her the form to fill out and told her to get on with it.

KW: Right . . . so, tell me, why exactly did you promote Rhoda?

COMPANY: Well, she's an expert in her field with over twenty years of experience; she knows absolutely everything in her area . . .

KW: OK, why does that qualify her to be a people manager, though?

COMPANY: Er . . . well . . . ah . . . [*slowly backs out of the room*]

In all honesty, this sounds like the type of management training I've been given in the last ten years . . . as in, there has hardly been any. It's like, 'Congrats! Here's your team and it's review time! Here's a ridiculous form to fill out, now go have some awkward conversations about why they're not getting the pay rise they wanted! Good luck!'

Note to the wise: If you're being offered a promotion or the reward of management status for doing well in your own role, Walker advises you to ask immediately what support you'll be given in this new role, and to judge whether or not you accept it, based on what they say.

Cheryl Fergusson from Heist Studios also agrees that the training for new managers is dreadful. When I ask her what kind of training most companies should be providing for their new managers, she makes the excellent point that there's not exactly a one-size-fits-all two-day management-training course that you can pop your new managers along to and expect them to flourish. She says that an organization has to provide 'constant support and knowledge' for managers, especially for those who aren't 'naturals'. Even if you're not a natural manager, it doesn't mean that you can't still be a good people manager. She says, 'It's about looking at what their strengths are, and how they could be used to manage more effectively.'

Even if you're quite proactive and have asked for training or development, it doesn't always mean that you'll get it. A twenty-nine-year-old woman I spoke to inherited a team of two when she started a new role, and she quickly became aware of her own limitations when it came to managing them. She was very self-aware and proactively did the research to find out which courses she should attend, and presented those to the Learning and Development department at her company. She was later informed via email that the department she works in doesn't actually have access to the budget for training and development, so she couldn't go on the courses. They didn't provide any alternatives, either.

Money is often the main reason management training and development isn't offered or prioritized, as it can actually be quite hard to make a business case for it. The HR specialists I spoke to about this all agreed that it's hard to convince board members and those in charge of budgets to fork out the cash for training courses, because it's not easily tied back to a bottom line or its efficacy proved with direct data. And if a board of directors have a choice between putting £10k into a marketing budget to get new customers – an obvious 'cause-and-effect' figure that is easily tracked – or putting that money into training and developing a group of people they already have working as managers, it's a tough choice. Most companies will go with the marketing option, as they can then see results directly and quickly, while the benefits of training and long-term development are less quantifiable. Prioritizing marketing is good for a company's budgets and pleases its board members, but detrimental to its management team, and all who work for them. It's a vicious, stupid cycle.

What a 'good manager' looks like

I asked almost everyone I interviewed for this book what they think makes a good manager *good*. While I found some distinct commonalities between the answers, I noted that everyone had different wants and expectations of a manager, depending on their experience level, where they were at in their career, and their overall personal preferences. This is an important point. One person's nightmare boss is another person's ideal manager. After reflecting on all my managers in recent years, I realized that there are some who, in hindsight and in comparison to the real monsters I worked for, really weren't all that bad. At the time, all I could do was complain and get frustrated about how crap they were, but actually, they just weren't what I needed at that point in my career. Now, years later, I'd be happier working for them (*in theory . . . I think?*).

Saying that, most of these 'good manager' common characteristics need to be present in order for them to manage well, but the level, volume or frequency at which each of those characteristics is necessary will vary, both from person to person and at various points in an individual's career.

Based on my experience and the feedback from the women I spoke with, here are the top characteristics that good managers seem to have in common (pop back to 'How bad managers behave' on page 20 to compare to the characteristics of a bad manager; it's interesting to compare and contrast). A good manager:

- leads by example,
- 'practises what they preach',

- follows through on plans,
- is open to feedback,
- takes feedback on board and implements it,
- can admit when they're wrong or have made a mistake,
- treats everyone with respect,
- has high emotional intelligence,
- is observant, able to pick up on non-verbal communication, subtext, reading between the lines,
- has a lot of empathy for those they work with,
- is a good listener,
- adjusts management style for each person they're managing,
- has good personal boundaries,
- is simultaneously friendly and professional,
- treats staff members as equals without being overfamiliar/inappropriate,
- knows when to just 'be a human',
- encourages others to also have personal boundaries,
- has an interest in people; is a 'people person',
- is happy to talk with people in the office,
- tries to relate to others,
- remembers important details (for example, asks about staff member's dog, or their family in Yorkshire, etc.),
- is transparent about
  - their own work load,
  - issues that are going on in the company,
  - how decisions are made (reviews, pay rises, etc.),
- is supportive,
- challenges/coaches you to be better, to stretch yourself,
- helps with career development,
- empowers you to have autonomy and be confident in your role,
- 'has your back'.

One of the best pieces of advice I was given when I was newly promoted to managing editor at *BuzzFeed* was from our Australian editor at the time, Simon Crerar. He told me about one of the best managing editors he ever worked for, and the thing he said about her that struck me as key was, 'She always, always had our back.' As someone who is keen to be dutiful, responsible, and always 'do the right thing', this immediately clicked with me, and helped shape my own management style. I firmly believe in protecting my team, fighting for my team, and, when it came to *The Pool*, going down with my team. (A captain should go down with her ship, right? Be there to provide comfort, information and some sense of stewardship – not jump into a fancy, executive lifeboat.)

Sarah Drinkwater, a director at the Omidyar Network investment company, has a similar philosophy when it comes to backing up her team. She says, 'Something I hope to offer my team, is that if they make a mistake, we're going to have words about it and make sure it doesn't happen again, but in a group setting, I will *always* back them. Part of your job as a manager is to provide cover for your staff.'

Providing cover, and also an awareness of when things are a bit 'off', is also a big positive. Another woman I spoke with, Helen MacBain, said that her current manager is one of the best she's ever worked for, even though (or perhaps because?) he's based in the States while she's in the UK. She says that she appreciates how open and honest he is, and that he doesn't try to cover up or defend the company when something is not quite right in a meeting: 'He'll ping me afterwards and say, "Hey, we should we catch up after that; that was a weird call." ' Ultimately, what she thinks makes him a good manager is that she's 'made to feel like an equal, and respected as an intelligent human being who has valuable skills'.

Being treated as an equal by their manager is important to

a lot of people – and particularly important to those who are quite senior or have many years of experience. It makes them feel seen, and their experience acknowledged – a nod to the fact that sometimes you might be older than or have just as much experience as your manager but, for whatever reason, they're on a management track and you're not. For me, I think it's more important to treat everyone with equal respect while still adjusting your management style for each person that you manage.

When I was nineteen and promoted to 'shift supervisor' at Starbucks, it was my first time ever being 'in charge'. I was working with many different types of people, of varying ages and backgrounds, and one of the most useful pieces of feedback I got from one of my managers was this: 'You can't talk to everybody the same way.' And, well, I had been. And they were so right to point this out, because the way I'd give instructions to a new seventeen-year-old recruit was not necessarily the way I should ask a forty-seven-year-old with ten years' experience to do something. It was valuable advice, and also made me cringe to think about how I'd been speaking to certain people.

I'd also like to note that not being a 'people person' isn't necessarily a make-or-break character flaw because, well, it can be faked. I'm introverted and am generally not by any means a 'people person' – and by people, I mean 'the general public, specifically when they're on public transport or anywhere near an airport' (any queue at an airport is my personal hell). But I care about individuals, and I know the right things to say and the right noises to make, even when I don't particularly *like* someone, so although I would never describe myself as a people *person*, I think I'm a damn good people *manager*. Sometimes being professional is about acting, and that's totally OK. It's not even a case of 'fake it 'til you make it'; more 'fake it 'cause you have to'. I'm never going to fake my way into being a person who 'just loves people' and that's just fine!

Psychological safety: the real key to team building

In order to be a supportive, transparent, empathetic manager, you need to create a supportive, transparent, empathetic working environment. A key component of this is 'psychological safety' – which sounds complicated and deep but is actually very straightforward. It's also the key to, if not the foundation for, building a team whose members all feel supported and able to do their best work.

The concept of psychological safety in work teams was first identified by Amy Edmondson, a professor at Harvard Business School, back in 1999. She defines it as 'a belief that one will not be punished or humiliated for speaking up with ideas, questions, concerns or mistakes'.[1] Through her research with physicians and nurses, where she examined which types of teams generated more medical errors, Edmondson found that the 'best' teams reported a higher rate of errors – not because she believed they were actually making more mistakes than the other teams, but that these teams had a *culture of openness* that made them more willing to admit to errors and talk about their mistakes.

I had never heard of psychological safety before joining Google, which makes sense, as it was Google that actually helped popularize the phrase when their HR teams published a study in November 2015.[2] The study found that psychological safety was one of the top characteristics of high-performing teams – along with qualities such as dependability, structure and clarity. It's ironic to me that I learned about it from a team that had none, but this just goes to show that a big company's overall culture and values can't penetrate the walls of a poorly managed team.*

A key part to all of this is building an environment in which your team feels encouraged and empowered to use their voice and speak up when necessary. In her TEDx talk on the subject, Edmondson says that, as managers and leaders, you can create this psychologically safe environment for your teams firstly by framing work or projects as a learning problem, not an execution problem, and making it explicitly clear that there is interdependency needed, and that there will be a level of uncertainty when solving this problem. Then, she says, acknowledge your own fallibility and that you, too, are capable of making mistakes. You can do this by simply saying something like, 'I might miss something, so please let me know if I do.' She also advises that you model curiosity by asking a lot of questions, which immediately means your team has to voice their replies.

Basically, you can't be a kick-ass manager if your team is terrified of talking to you (and each other), and you can't do creative or innovative work if everyone is too terrified to voice their wild ideas. Psychological safety is basically the secret ingredient to productive, happy teams.

---

* If you're a leader in your organization or a manager, give Amy Edmondson's TEDx talk on psychological safety in the Resources section a watch; she gives pointers on how you can make sure your team has it.

Beware of 'boss baby' behaviour

I'm of the opinion that once people hit a certain level of seniority, usually that of an executive director, or make it into the hallowed C-suite, they become a bit unhinged. It's as if they just accept that, in order to deal with all the levels of bullshit and pressure they're going to need to endure if they're going to get that sweet salary, bonus, private healthcare and share options package, they're just going to give up their ability to emote appropriately, display empathy, and keep their shit together. And as a result, they often turn into a 'boss baby', much like Alec Baldwin's character from the animated film *The Boss Baby*.

In almost every organization I've worked in, the senior managers and those in very senior leadership positions just seem to blatantly ignore their own schedule. Never mind it being a generational or technical issue where they 'don't really get Google Calendar', they behave like they've never seen a clock or a desk diary before. Spare me your 'Oh, I don't wear a watch' bullshit. These managers completely over-rely on their executive assistants to remind them of their schedules, and their EAs are then forced into treating them like stroppy children dragging their feet on the school run, scooter in tow: 'Sofia! Your next meeting is in thirteen minutes on the other side of the building, you need to drink that turmeric latté and walk at the same time. Where's your bag? Is your laptop in it? What do you mean you don't know where it is, it's in there! I checked! Let's go. Let's *go*. LET'S GO!'

I've seen so many embarrassed assistants walking their fussy toddler bosses across offices, shepherding them from one meeting to the next, because they, for some reason, can't figure out where anything is, *ever*. They must be reminded to eat lunch, to drink water, even of the names of people on their own team, and their poor assistants get blamed for over- or under-scheduling them, or for not reminding them the in-house restaurant stops serving lunch at 2.30. It's *insane*. Like, you are not so busy and important that you get to treat someone else as though they're your personal servant or lady-in-waiting. This isn't the seventeenth century and you're not a fucking queen, mate. Get it together.

In one place I worked, I had a manager whom no one on our entire team could ever find. He would just disappear. 'Where's Nigel?' became the sentence I dreaded, because somehow people always expected *me* to know where he was. And, spoiler alert, *I had no fucking clue*. We all turned into detectives ('Is his coat still here?' 'No, that's the jumper he always leaves on his chair . . .') and would comb through his Google Calendar to try to figure out where he might be. Sometimes he'd gone for a haircut. Sometimes he was on a call. Sometimes he was in the pub. On one occasion he was in a disciplinary HR meeting with someone and forgot to set the event as 'private'. The height of unprofessionalism.

All of this is to say – behave like an adult; *be the grown up in the room*. Take responsibility for your own schedule and the logistics of being the boss. It's fine to need support, to have an assistant (if you work at a company that has enough budget to provide you with one, that is). But when people start to behave as though they're so important that they actually become incompetent and unable to function as a normal human being, it's embarrassing for everyone involved. You're not Mariah Carey. Or eleven months old, for that matter.

Please don't shout at people, but also don't let people shout at you

As a manager, I think it's important to make people feel at ease with your presence, not afraid. It's to be expected that, as someone in charge, people might be a little intimidated, a little nervous around you – you're the big boss! But you don't want people so afraid they're shitting their pants and unable to form sentences when you ask them a question. When you enter a room, you want to own it. Think Michelle Obama not Alan Sugar – you want people to be inspired and impressed. You don't want to enter a room and for the temperature to suddenly drop and for the lights to dim, like you're actually a Dementor squeezed into a nice dress from & Other Stories: 'Everyone, Elise has flown over from Azkaban for our two o'clock team meeting! Now, just a quick housekeeping reminder to not make direct eye contact or any sudden movements around Elise. If you do start to feel your life force slowly slipping away while in her presence, please feel free to use one of our HR-approved hand signals, but let's hold off using that Patronas charm until she's at least set out this quarter's KPIs. OK? Great!'

If you notice people getting uneasy and uncomfortable in your presence, you might need to spend some time exploring why this is – even if this means asking for feedback from some of your team members. This comes back to being observant: it can't *always* be everybody else. If you think that 'everyone just is really jealous and intimidated by me' or that 'everyone around me is just totally incompetent' these are both huge warning signs that there's something bigger going on, and that some self-reflection and 360° feedback is in order.

I've worked for people who are unpredictable, loose cannons who will literally shout at their staff or will happily say something shockingly rude and insulting to a member of their team, right in the middle of a meeting, in front of other people. These people are very rare, but they exist. Please, I beg you, never adopt this style of management. Don't shout at people – just like I described in Chapter 1, if you're angry or feel like you're going to freak out from either anxiety or irritation – it's OK to end a meeting and get out of the situation until you're able to compose yourself and think straight.

I dealt with a crappy situation not so long ago when someone on my team got angry with me and started raising their voice. Their tone was one of disgust and contempt, and *hoo boy* did I feel it. This was a new experience for me, as I'd never had a member of my own team talk to me like this at work. Shocked as I was, I tried to handle the situation as best I could. In that moment, it didn't feel like this person had much respect for me, or my position as their editor, and it felt like I didn't hold the power in the room. I could have quickly regained it by swiftly ending the meeting, but I didn't. Instead, I slogged my way through, letting her rage against me, her distaste of how I was doing my job now very well known, both of us red-faced – she with anger, I with shame. Afterwards, I rage-cried in the bathroom, having the conversation I wished I'd been able to have with her playing over and over again in my head.

What I should have said was: 'You clearly are very upset about this, but it's not OK to talk to me or anyone else on this team like this. We can revisit this conversation after you've calmed down, but for now this meeting is over, and I need you to leave the office and take a walk to cool off. I will check back in with you later today.'

I beat myself up over it, and it was one of those things that kept popping into my head as I tried to fall asleep that night. The next day I let her know that how she spoke to me was not on, and she apologized. Clearly, she was under a lot of stress and was taking that out on me. Sure, as a manager you have to be a sounding board, but you're not a punch bag. People don't get to shout and curse at you simply because they disagree with something, or even if they're upset. That's not OK. My relationship with this person was damaged by the incident, but we managed to be civil throughout the remainder of our working relationship. Sometimes, that's all you can hope for. Civility.

Which brings me to this:

Not everyone is always going to like you (I'm really sorry)

You're a boss of people. You set their tasks and assess their performance. You have to be the grown-up in the room, and often this sucks.

At various times you'll find that your team will kick off, push back and question your decisions – it's all part of their growth and development. In the world of work, you are the parent. You do what you think is best for them, even if they don't appreciate it at the time. You have to listen when they're upset, and gently (and sometimes not-so-gently) guide them when they're a bit lost. (Again, this is not code for 'stand there and take it if they scream at you', there have to be boundaries.)

The biggest part of the equation that makes it work is their trust in you. They need to know that, even if you're making a decision that they don't necessarily like, they can trust that you're doing the right thing. You build this trust by consistently displaying the characteristics mentioned earlier in this chapter, and when it comes to getting your team to trust you to make big decisions, the following points are key:

- Be transparent.
- Listen to concerns and feedback.
- Take questions and answer them as honestly as is appropriate/possible.
- Don't bullshit people or use 'corporate speak' to explain or excuse things away.
- Admit when you're wrong, and when a decision didn't have the outcome you'd planned on.

Even when you're transparent and honest and have trust, there are times when it will feel like you have a bunch of overgrown teenagers and the occasional toddler under you. And it can become overwhelming when it feels like they all hate your guts, but this is part of the deal.

They might not always understand you, but ultimately, I think people can tell when you care about their careers, their development and their goals. That is more important than whether or not they kiss your ass or follow you on Instagram or like the decisions you make. They might not tell you 'OMG you're the best boss ever', but they'll certainly appreciate it when you help develop their skills in a way that means they're promoted, or are able to reach goals they had struggled with before. Even if your staff don't always realize that you do so, I think it's more important to have their back in ways that they might not even be aware of. To defend them in rooms they're not in, and to be the umbrella that shields your wider team from shit. Even when it's painful, like, 'wow we might all lose our jobs if we don't hit our target next quarter' kind of shit.

You must put your responsibility and your duty to your team above your own ego.

Management is basically *super* fun, guys.

You're going to get management FOMO, but you'll live

Earlier in my career, I used to get my snowflake millennial feelings hurt when my team members didn't invite me out to lunch. I mean, I was their boss. Who invites their boss out to lunch? If they had invited me I would have said no, anyway. But it's the *otherness* of being in management that can be difficult.

It's particularly so if you've recently been promoted from within – especially when you're now managing people you were on good terms with, or even friends with. This can raise many problems (all of which can be solved by setting clear boundaries and being honest about what's OK and what's not OK to chat about at work – yay boundaries!) but learning to get used to management FOMO is hard.

You suddenly exist in this weird land where you have far fewer peers, and if you're a younger manager, you might not necessarily get on with the other folk on your level owing to your age and/or experience. Confidentiality also restricts the connections you can make at work. You don't have as many people to talk to about what's going on with your day-to-day. For example, if you don't have someone to bitch about doing annual reviews with, or a friend to turn to when you have to fire someone and you're feeling nervous about it, it really, really sucks.

This is another excellent reason not to think that management is some exciting reward or sign of importance: it's isolating!

And hard work! And you can't even get drunk and complain about it like you used to because your whole team goes to the nearest pub to the office most nights and you don't want to see them!

Other than 'toughen up, buttercup' when it comes to this peculiar type of FOMO, I can tell you that finding at least one person on your level, even on another team, can really help. This means you have someone to grab lunch with occasionally, and swap horror stories and advice with. Ye olde social media is good for this too – there are lots of groups out there where you might be able to connect with other people on your level, outside of your organization.* Within your organization, if you need proper, concrete advice that's specific to your team, you can always try reaching out to the other managers on your level, or even your own manager. Alternatively, do some research into what's available to you with regard to employee resource groups. Often there will be some sort of 'inspirational business ladies' group that, despite their cringe-worthy names and logos, can be absolute lifesavers at work.

Be respectful of everyone's time

This lies in 'don't be a boss baby' territory. In addition to not over-relying on an assistant (if you have one), don't be so unorganized and 'busy' that you miss meetings, or cancel appointments five minutes after they were scheduled to start. You have no idea how much time someone has spent preparing or psyching themselves up for a meeting with you, and

---

* It should go without saying that you should never post anything that could breach the confidentiality of your organization, or anyone in it, but I'll say it anyway.

how much of a let down it can be when something they've prepared for gets cancelled at the last minute.

Try your very best to not be late for anything. Don't keep rescheduling or cancelling, especially 1:1s with your direct reports – this is unbearably irritating and frustrating for your staff, and can give them the impression that you're avoiding them, particularly if it's to discuss something awkward. Make room for them, and treat their time and their schedules as if they're just as valuable as yours.

Also try to be mindful of others' anxieties and insecurities. For example, if you reschedule your 1:1 for 5 p.m. on a Friday, most people (myself included) will assume this is the most convenient time for you either to fire them or give them some bad news. If you know your report is anxious, maybe just send a note along with the calendar invite saying, 'Apologies for this meeting late in the day, it was the only time I had available.'

All of the above is even more important if you're managing someone who works remotely, or in a different office or even country than you. Scheduling meetings in their time zone or at a time of day that works best for them – not just your schedule – is important. Try to include them in as many team activities as you can – heck, even make some team events virtual so it all feels equal for those who are in the office, or based elsewhere. Managing someone who you don't see every day can be difficult – you lose all of the non-verbal cues, all of the impromptu chats that can happen in an office. However, you can still show up for them the same way you do with your other reports.

This might mean you have more regular catch-ups with them than you do with your 'in person' staff. Ask them about their ways of working, and what works best for them. Asking questions is key; it gives them space to tell you about themselves and how they work, rather than you dictating to them how it is you think they should be working remotely.

Discipline and giving difficult feedback

Nothing causes anxiety-fuelled diarrhoea quite like having to take disciplinary action against one of your staff members, or giving difficult feedback.

Many, many books have been published on this, and the various methods that are commonly put forward on long training days usually look like complicated grid systems or charts or are presented as sandwiches or something equally anodyne. While a lot of these frameworks are useful for training situations or new managers, I personally find them rather overwhelming and believe that most tend to overcomplicate things. I spend too much time trying to remember what the next step is, or what I'm supposed to do if they say X or Y. Role playing can be helpful, but it's usually embarrassing and never represents what actually happens.

It's difficult, then, for me to give specific advice on how to handle most of these situations because they really are, well, situational, particularly if you're having to take disciplinary action. So I'll just provide a few guidelines and key points to keep in mind when they arise.

First, if you're a new manager, speak with your line manager or another member of your senior leadership team and get some coaching on how best to handle the conversation. Ask if they might be able to support you in the room if you need it.

Most importantly, if it's discipline related, your HR manager should be advising you how to handle the situation in order to ensure that whatever you do or say is legal, conforms with company policy and is generally by the book. They should also be able to give you clear pointers on what to say, what not to say and which areas to avoid. In most cases, they should absolutely be in the room with you.

All of the 'having difficult conversations' advice given at various points of this book are applicable to when you have to give a team member difficult feedback, but you should also try both to keep things balanced and to display empathy and kindness.

To keep it balanced, try not to focus only on their areas of opportunity, but throw in what their strengths are, too, as it can soften the blow and not make them feel like they're completely crap at their job (unless, well, that's the problem).

Showing empathy and kindness doesn't mean sugar-coating things or lying – but you can be clear and direct without being an asshole. You can speak plainly but remain empathetic; for example: 'Chris, as we discussed before, you didn't hit your sales target for this year – the final numbers have come in and you're about 40 per cent lower than was expected, which means you're quite far off your agreed target. Because of this, your performance rating for this half of the year is a 2.5, and is categorized as "needs improvement". I know it is probably tough to hear, but let me walk you through what that means for you now, and how we can work together to help get you up to an "exceeds expectations" standard by our next round of reviews, OK?'

Compare this with: 'So, Chris, your performance rating is a 2.5, as in "needs improvement". You actually came in the lowest out of all our team in sales, and I have to say, the whole team is surprised and disappointed by your performance this quarter. I'm not quite sure how you can come back from this, but we need you to get your act together for Q1, OK?'

The thing about 'bad' reviews, is that they should never be

a surprise. You or your staff shouldn't ever be blindsided by a poor rating or negative feedback from your manager (or your peers). I've been hit by a genuinely shitty performance review only once in my career, and it came as a shock – Post-it Woman strikes again! I knew my manager didn't exactly like me or love my work, but ultimately I wasn't aware of anything that might affect the overall judgement of my performance and output. So when I was then given this poor rating, and a lengthy (awful, cringeworthy, shame-inducing) document detailing all the negative feedback that my manager and some of my colleagues apparently had given with regard to me and my performance, I was both shocked and enraged.

Of course, this situation was very complex, had been going on for over a year, and I was ultimately being managed out, but you should *always* know, and be made aware on a weekly basis, how you're performing. Any issues, and odd bits of feedback, you should know about all of it. And, above it all, your manager should have your back. They should listen to you, advise you and support you in overcoming any challenge that might arise. You shouldn't be left on your own to just figure it out and hope your next rating is better. You should also never feel that, if someone goes to your manager with some gossipy tittle-tattle, they will take it as gospel and put you in a position of having to defend yourself.

Managing in a crisis

As the coronavirus pandemic gathered pace, the businesses and companies impacted were sent very quickly into full-blown crisis mode across every aspect of their business. From ill members of staff to remote working to IT issues with everyone working remotely to furloughing or laying off staff and closing entire departments or completely shutting down – managers and those in leadership positions were very quickly forced to deal with issues and situations that most had never had to tackle before – and certainly not all at once, during something as intense and as threatening as a global pandemic and threatened economic collapse.

But no matter the exact circumstances or situation, managing in a crisis will put anyone's management skills to the test. While there wasn't a 'How to Manage in a Global Pandemic' rule book to consult (although I'm sure several will have now been published), there are certain things to keep in mind during a crisis of any kind.

Be transparent. Even if you don't have all the answers, share the ones you're able to. Say that you're stressed. Say that you're confused and concerned, too. But also be aware of how your salary, job security and overall situation differ from those of the employees you might be laying off, or asking more and more of during turbulent times. For example, if you're the COO of a company and you're having to explain that you're laying off 300 people and you tell everyone that you're 'super sad and you've not slept in, like, *a whole month*' because of this – perhaps be aware that you're announcing the layoffs via the Zoom app on your secondary iPad, from the comfort of your giant Kensington apartment, while wearing a £250 hoodie and AirPods.

Over communicate. If you don't communicate properly during a crisis, people will fill in the blanks for you. Rumours will get ever bigger and more dramatic. Things will spiral more than they need to. Therefore, in addition to being transparent, you'll need to over communicate. Even if you're just telling people you don't have any news, the fact that you're openly telling them that is important. Even if you hear murmurs that people are pissed off that you called a meeting to tell them *nothing*, I firmly believe it's better for them to be mad at the lack of new information – which isn't necessarily your fault – than being mad that you've apparently dropped off the face of the earth or are hiding from your staff because you can't bear to have uncomfortable conversations – which is 100 per cent your fault.

Be a human being. Show some empathy. When there are layoffs, people being furloughed, rumours of financial ruin or a personnel scandal brewing, people tend to freak out a bit. Feelings run rampant. People find it super difficult to keep their shit together, so be respectful of that. Speak normally to people, don't spew corporate sound bites or government party slogans ('STAY ALERT!') at them. Be honest – even if you can't tell them everything you know at this point, say that you are telling them all you can. Exercise displaying empathy. Practise mindful listening. Just letting people know they're being heard can make a big difference. During the global pandemic, my manager at the time (shout-out to Samm!) did a wonderful job of having check-ins with her team at the beginning and end of each week, just to see how everyone was doing. We didn't have to talk shop, we could reminisce about Polly Pockets or cry laughing at the Connell's Chain Instagram account. These calls acknowledged that there was something bigger than client briefs happening in our lives, and that our colleagues could be a source of distraction and support in a time of uncertainty and chaos. It made a big difference.

Don't freak out in public. Especially when rumours are flying around social media, it might feel really tempting to 'set the record straight' in a long Twitter thread or a series of seething Instagram Stories that you think won't matter because they'll disappear in twenty-four hours . . . in short, *don't*. But if it looks worse to stay silent than to acknowledge a workplace situation, particularly if you're a senior manager or leadership figure that's known in the industry, then don't stay silent either. It's not a binary choice. There are ways to make dignified but honest statements online, even if sometimes they need to be made via your PR team or your peers. It's always best to stay level-headed and to try to take the highest road possible. If you're in the middle of a crisis, you don't need social media drama to make things even worse for you.

Find solace in your peers, not your direct reports. As much as you want to drown your drama with shots of tequila with your team – it's best to just set up a tab for them and let them all get on with it without you. When things are tough, it's best they have the space to talk with each other and commiserate, and even if they all love you, your presence can create a weird dynamic. Even when being honest and transparent, you still need to remember your role in everything. They don't need their leadership figure falling apart in the pub. You can fall apart with the folks on your same level, in a different pub from the ones your team goes to.

Telling someone they no longer have a job is, well, terrible

Most managers, certainly those with higher levels of emotional intelligence and empathy, never want to have to make anyone redundant or unemployed. Firing someone is nearly always an absolute last resort. Unfortunately, sometimes it's the only option available if a person's behaviour is completely unacceptable. Even redundancies are invariably tricky (unless they're voluntary), because they, too, are forced by business reasons, such as budget and structure, and are usually at the instruction of those at the top of the company pyramid. It all sucks, basically.

I've had to make several people redundant, and even fire some in my time as a manager. Without exception, they were long, stressful, admin-filled, uncomfortable processes that nobody emerged from feeling good.

Once, as part of a new role, almost my first task was to restructure the existing team. Let me tell you – if you're new to a business and you have to introduce yourself by making long-serving staff members redundant . . . it's not fun. It doesn't exactly make for a settled team, either, but sometimes big changes are necessary for future growth.

This process was made more difficult than was probably necessary by the intense, visceral reaction to the news of one of the victims. They were appalled, furious, if not completely disgusted that I would have the audacity to render their position redundant. Which, you know, I get. I didn't expect them to love it, or even necessarily understand it, but their vitriolic reaction blew me away. Despite having only been at the company a very short time, I was accused of some pretty dreadful stuff by this person, and had to read through seething, threatening letters to me drawn up by their lawyer. I knew it was the right decision to be making for the business, and for the team going forward, but the way this person looked and spoke to me during the meetings throughout their consultation period was unlike anything I had ever known. Throughout the process, I had to bite my tongue and be as professional as possible – even when, during the particularly tough meeting in which we broke the bad news, I looked over to see that the HR representative who was there to help me with the process was obliviously drinking tea from a mug that read, 'SORRY NOT SORRY' in an obnoxiously twee font. Thankfully, this went unnoticed by anyone else, but I was mortified.

Going through the redundancy process as a manager is definitely rough, but once you get through it, you'll then know what it's like. You'll have the experience, and you'll be better prepared for it the next time it happens. I once worked with a new manager who was issuing redundancy notifications for the first time in his career. He was really unsettled, completely freaked out by it. Before and after his first such meeting, he kept saying things like: 'Oh god, I can't believe I'm doing this. What are they going to do next! What if they have a family? I feel horrible!' But the problem with his reaction was that what he was saying was rooted not in kindness and empathy for this person but in his own guilt and discomfort. And, honestly, if you can't get past your own feelings to make the right but uncomfortable decisions for the business – you're going to struggle higher up along the chain of command. I actually found his incessant 'Oh god I feel so awful!' chatter extremely unhelpful.

Of course it sucks – it sucks for everyone involved for different reasons – but it's undoubtedly harder for the person losing their job than it is for the person telling them. Someone being made redundant in a lawful, empathetic, fair way will always receive some sort of severance package, and often support in finding another role. Letting them go in the kindest, most humane way possible is the best you can do. You can't run a business, or be in a position of great power and authority (and salary) if you're paralysed by the idea of putting someone – or even several people – out of work. I'm sorry if that sounds harsh, but it's the way the world operates. You're only a ruthless prick if you don't do it legally, or if you do it for the wrong reasons, or tell people in the shittiest way possible. Or if, for instance, you suddenly stop paying your entire staff and your suppliers without any notice, and then, for instance, instead of taking responsibility for lying to everyone about how much debt the company was actually in and trying to make it right, you choose to hide behind lawyers and scurry off into the night like some sort of rat . . . *for instance*. (Yes, this happened to me.) But if you're making the right decision for your business and giving people paid notice, and you're being kind and humane, then you're doing the best you can for both your staff and your business. Them's the breaks.

Actions speak louder than company-wide emails

It's all well and good to set up 'unconscious bias' training sessions for your team, or to sit on a Diversity & Inclusion panel and make earnest declarations about how *important* it is to you and your organization. You can even create a 'Head of D&I' position and send emails about what you stand for, or tweet about the gender pay gap, and 'celebrate' International Women's Day in the office – but it's your *actions* that matter. It's the things you say, and the way you say them, when nobody other than your team is around to hear you.

Do you say you care about Black Lives Matter and diversity but consistently hire cis, white, straight people while claiming, 'It's just really hard to attract diversity in this industry'? Do you place a symbolic rainbow somewhere in the office or suggest sponsoring a Pride float in your local parade, but forget to use the correct pronouns for the non-binary person on your team, or don't change the toilets to gender neutral as has been requested several times? Do you claim to be an intersectional feminist, or even run a 'feminist business',* but can't move past your own internalized misogyny and envy issues

---

* These don't exist, FYI. Feminist leaders and values can exist in a company, but companies are capitalist entities, not feminist ones.

and therefore can't treat certain women on your team with the same respect with which you treat the others? Do you say you're an ally to those with neurological differences, but don't try to accommodate their needs in the office? If so, YOU ARE NOT GENUINE ABOUT BEING INCLUSIVE. It is ALL of these actions, these throwaway comments, your hiring choices, your priorities and the culture of your team that will speak on your behalf.

If you're a manager, it is your responsibility to take all issues of diversity, inclusion, respect and equality seriously. To be curious about the things you don't understand, and to be vulnerable in your efforts in finding out more. Even though I had a difficult time in the specific team I was working in, I must say that the diversity and inclusion workshops and training sessions made available to me at Google were excellent. I was struck by a senior staff member who shared his own journey to understanding his trans and BIPOC colleagues, and how it took him a long time to overcome his military background's rigid way of interacting with the people he had worked with, and accept that he had to ask questions and make himself vulnerable (and therefore be brave) in order to finally achieve a more open mindset.

Even if these opportunities aren't immediately available to you within your own organization – seek them out. There are many resources online – books like *Why I'm No Longer Talking to White People About Race*, podcasts like 'Nancy' and 'Getting Curious with Jonathan Van Ness' AND YouTube channels like Franchesca Ramsey's* – that can provide insight into the lives of so many different kinds of people.

The big thing to realize here is that your team and your colleagues will remember how you handle hiring, and how

---

* See the Resources section for details of all these.

you treat members of staff who come from a different background from them. Being a 'good manager', and I'd even venture to say a 'decent person', means putting your money and your values where your mouth is. Do what you say you're going to do. If you care about something, don't just harp on about it, make it happen in your organization. Be the change you wish to see in the workplace.

Basically, be kind

Treat people with respect and kindness. Be a human being, with boundaries and rules. Remember that this is a job, and you're not everyone's parent, even though it might feel that way sometimes. Be transparent. Even when it's embarrassing, even when it's tough. Even when you have to tell a room full of people their jobs are disappearing, you have to show up for them. You have to be the grown-up in the room. Be honest. When things are tough, you can cry with them. You can be a person.

When people eventually go on to do other jobs, they won't always remember the targets, the OKRs* or the endless 1:1 meetings you had together. But they will always, always remember the way that you made them feel, and what they learned from you. It doesn't have to be perfect, but just do your best to make sure it's good.

---

* Objectives and key results.

Authenticity + Mental Health:

The myth of bringing your 'whole self' to work

On my first day at Google as a new recruit, I'll never forget sitting in the big orientation meeting amongst a mixture of new contract workers and full-time employees, and hearing a very senior woman in the company stand up on stage and talk about how lucky she feels to work for a company that encourages all employees to bring their whole selves to work.

Bring your whole self to work.

At the time, I thought this was wonderful. *How nice that they accept that we're human beings with feelings and brains and eccentricities*, I thought. *Gosh, I can't wait to be accepted for being the real me!*

Now, after a few years of reflection, this is my wish for you: any time you hear someone say 'bring your whole self to work'

I want it to trigger an automatic response in your brain that sounds like Admiral Ackbar from *Star Wars* yelling 'IT'S A TRAP!' Because, my friend, *it is a trap*.

I don't think Google or any other company saying they want you to bring your whole self to work is *lying*, as such. On the contrary, I think *they* think they genuinely mean it, as does everyone who uses the phrase (which is also the subject of both a TED talk and a book). The problem is, that they don't understand what bringing your whole self to work actually means. Part of the problem lies in defining just what your whole self is.

The benevolent and benign message at its core is that an employee should bring their values with them to work – the things they care about. Their personality. Their vulnerabilities and their strengths. It means that they don't want their employees to hide the different parts of themselves that make them unique and special. In more progressive companies, this phrase is also used as a signal to employees that they're cognizant of issues such as mental health, diversity and inclusion. They don't expect you to be homogeneous, corporate robots devoid of personal lives, personal style and actual feelings. Which, I think, is a very good thing. I love the idea of 'wholehearted' living, epitomized by Brené Brown in her audiobook *The Power of Vulnerability*. I have absolutely no qualms about companies acknowledging that their staff members are actual humans, and that their opinions and colour and essence make workplaces richer, better, brighter.

But . . . (and it's a *big* but) when a company says, *Bring your whole self to work!* they are leaving so many things unsaid, because what they *actually* mean is, *We're OK if you bring the lite, legal, politically correct, palatable version of your personal life to work in moments where it's appropriate. But, actually, we don't want or know how to handle anything too weird, or too deep, too complex or too scary because we actually have no fucking clue how to deal with that. Let's keep it cute.*

Encouraging employees to bring their *whole* selves to work suggests that everyone's 'whole self' is clean 'n' tidy and office-ready when, really, most of our whole selves involve some pretty dark shit. For every charming, sunny quirk there's a messy, neurotic compulsion lurking on the other side. We are all complex, contradictory beings, with light and dark, ups and downs.

Asking someone to show their true, authentic, whole self at work is like inviting a vampire into your house – you have absolutely no clue what's going to go down. (Are things going to be sexy or scary? Will you die? Who knows!) Quite frankly, it's naive. It's as if they think the wildest that people's 'whole selves' get is being gay, or needing to leave early to go to therapy on Thursday afternoons, or revealing that they were once on antidepressants but found meditation in Bali in the summer of 2011 and haven't needed them since. That all your struggles and messes have happened already – that they're not current, or still to occur, or something they'll ever have to deal with or support you with.

They are not expecting, for example, someone to admit they're part of a right-wing extremist activist group and go big-game hunting on their holidays. Or that they have schizophrenia and once spent twelve months in a mental health facility. Or that they tried to take their own life at the weekend. They're not expecting to hear about the side-effects of your chronic illness, the fact that you're also the primary caregiver for your disabled sibling, or that you're in the middle of a custody battle for your children. That you've just found God and would love to talk to them about your Lord and Saviour Jesus Christ.

Our 'whole selves' are a wide and deep spectrum of issues,

conditions, beliefs, practices and characteristics. And there's only a slim slice of our true selves that businesses are (barely) equipped to deal with, or that's (kinda) fit for a professional working environment. Plus, our whole self is a *vulnerable* one. Like that creepy, foetal Voldemort in the last *Harry Potter* film, our whole selves include the naked, unarmoured, underdeveloped bits of ourselves that aren't exactly ready for public consumption. We only show this part to those we trust, those who are deserving of our intimacy and who, in turn, will treat it with kind and gentle respect. You don't need to bring this part of you to the office. Your manager, and the people who you work with, don't need to see this. Leave that little dude shivering under a bench in the King's Cross of your mind, tucked away safe. He doesn't need to be chilling with you at work, splayed out on your desk like a buffet of vulnerability: 'Oh, hey guys! This is my soul-crushing fear that I'm totally inadequate and that no matter what I do and what I achieve, I'll never be enough – which, like, probably stems from my belief that *I'm* the real reason my mom left me and my brother when I was four! But, enough about me, how was your weekend?'

Not only does anyone at your work 100 per cent not need to know that, they don't *deserve* to be privy to such intimacies. Because what are they going to do with it? They can't hold space for you the way a loved one, a trusted friend or a trained therapist can. They can't help you. They can't fix it. And work is a competitive place, it's a complex ecosystem that more often than not tends to get a bit toxic. And, as therapist Kate Hogan told me, if you're in a hostile environment, it's not *safe* to be vulnerable. (Remember this. Write it down. *If you're in a hostile working environment, you don't have to be vulnerable.* It's not *safe!*) Who knows what could be done with that information? And also, can you imagine if someone brought it up when you just asked how their weekend was? Your brain would no doubt scream, *Oh my god this is too awkward, TMI, get me the fuck out of here!* because, really, that *is* awkward and has no place at work.

Companies, and the managers within them, are simply not set up for or capable of dealing with our whole selves. I have hope that they will be in the future, and that as mental health awareness and training become better and more integrated into the makeup of companies then this will change. I hope that the insight that many people gained into mental health during the coronavirus pandemic – that we're all human beings with complex feelings – has stuck. But, for now, they're simply not equipped – so, don't fall for it or get fooled into thinking they mean it. They don't. They can't. And, even if they did, it's a bad idea.

I think you should only ever bring about 60–75 per cent of your 'whole self' to work, but I fully agree with the *concept* at the heart of 'bring your whole self to work': authenticity. Authenticity, I think, is a vital part of your work life. And the hardest one to get right. It's a balance of being your authentic self while keeping your emotions and your more 'sensitive material' contained. It's tricky, but doable. You just have to be willing to get a bit uncomfortable (which might as well be the subtitle of this book, tbh).

And what *this* chapter aims to do is to help you look after your own mental health, feelings and emotions at work in a resilient, contained and intentional way – one that's authentic to you. So that you're not risking overexposure, or the mess that can come with bringing your 'whole self' to the office.

I firmly believe that you have to be the chief protector of your own mental health at work. Nobody else can, will, or should do this for you. So, let's get uncomfortable, shall we?

The uncomfortable reality of dealing with mental health issues at work

We are not robots. And although I don't think we need to bring 100 per cent of ourselves to work, you can't exactly leave your brain, psychology and emotions at home either. And nor should you. Unless you have a serious dissociative disorder like Elliot Alderson in *Mr Robot*, this is also pretty much impossible.

Your mental health is part of who you are, we all have it. Mental *illness* is different from poor mental health, and people don't always get the language around this right. There's a difference between the two. Journalist Natasha Hinde wrote an excellent article about this for the *Huffington Post*,[1] explaining the differences between the various terms that are used – and incorrectly used interchangeably – when discussing mental health.

Mental health can also be described as 'emotional health' or 'well-being'.

A mental health *issue* (or problem) is when someone is showing signs that something else is going on for them – this could be, for example, tearfulness, anger or anxiety. Panic or anxiety attacks or depressive symptoms are also signals of mental health issues or problems. The good news is that the Mental Health Foundation say that most people who experience mental health issues learn to live with them or recover from them. The speed or manner in which people bounce back from these issues depends on their individual mental resilience or mental strength, and this differs from person to person. It also depends on individual genetic and personal circumstances.

A mental illness is when mental health problems affect a

person's ability to function in their everyday lives and it impacts their work, relationships and social lives. The organization Mental Health at Work uses the term 'mental illness' as an umbrella term for 'conditions that affect how a person thinks and feels'.

Mental illnesses can range from eating disorders and depression, to obsessive compulsive disorder, bipolar disorder and schizophrenia. It's important to understand the differences between the phrases and terms, because when you conflate issues or confuse what these sensitive descriptions mean, it makes it so much harder to talk about them or for people to gain an understanding of how to deal with them, especially at work.

I spoke with Maggy Van Eijk, author of *Remember This When You're Sad*, about dealing with one's mental health at work. She told me about the analogy that the company she works for in the Netherlands uses to describe its philosophy around mental health at work: 'If you're on a football team and you break your leg,' she says, 'they're not going to kick you off the team; you're just going to sit on the bench for a bit.' And so, if you're experiencing mental health problems or illness at work, it's OK, you're not off the team, you just need to rest up, and you'll be back in the game once you're feeling better.

I thought a lot about this analogy, and, while I think it does help normalize (and simplify) the way we regard mental health problems, Maggy and I both agreed that it doesn't adequately address the other parts of the equation. Like, well, why did it get to the point where you broke your leg? Was your coach pushing you too hard? Did you get taken out by a member of the opposing team? Were you resting enough, and do you have a physio to help you recover?

Companies aren't great at dealing with mental health issues at work. While new foundations like Mental Health at Work have been formed, and many companies are training mental health first responders, I think this is more a case of addressing symptoms and putting fires out (and not getting sued). Some places are very good at rallying in a crisis – they can have someone help you when you're having a panic attack – but they're not addressing the chaotic, panic-inducing culture their leadership teams feed and foster on a daily basis. And, even then, I would venture to say that most places aren't going to know what to do for someone who is suffering from mental heath problems or illnesses.

One woman I interviewed for this book had to fight for her company to provide her with trauma counselling after the images and videos she had to review as a requirement of her job made her unwell (a fact that the company hadn't necessarily anticipated or planned for). A journalist I know bravely wrote a beautiful personal essay about her own depression and suicidal thoughts for the publication she worked for – and while her editor's initial response was to tell her the piece was 'brave', they then showed astounding insensitivity by suggesting that she illustrate the article *by returning to the scene* where her near-suicide took place, and having a photo taken. (I mean, fucking hell!)

While some of us are being told to bring our whole selves to work by big tech companies, it turns out that being disciplined or punished for mental health problems or illnesses is something of a trend, not only amongst the women I interviewed for this book but also amongst the wider working population. The Mental Health at Work 2018 summary report 'Seizing the Momentum', compiled by Business in the Community, found that 11 per cent of employees who disclosed a mental health issue faced 'disciplinary action, demotion or dismissal';[2] even more worrying, this figure has actually increased since 2016, when the figure was only at 9 per cent.[3]

Marianne, the former teacher we met in Chapters 1 and 2,

told me that in the last year of her teaching career she was involved in a serious car accident that left her suffering from symptoms of PTSD as well as a brain injury. Her temporal lobe was damaged, which resulted in both behavioural and cognitive symptoms that she had zero control over. These included unintentionally aggressive behaviour. Despite her managers being made fully aware of her symptoms and their cause, she was provided with no support – instead, she was disciplined for her 'aggressive' behaviour and passed up for a promotion.

Another woman I spoke with, Greta, told me about an upsetting situation at a company she used to work for, where her behaviour and performance at work deteriorated as a result of having an undiagnosed mental illness (and essentially having a breakdown), which led to a disciplinary hearing. Greta says that before she was given an official diagnosis, she reached the point where she just wouldn't show up for work in the morning, later calling in to say she'd had food poisoning or with another elaborate excuse. Even when she found the courage to admit to her manager that she missed work due to being in A&E for self-harm injuries, she would play down the seriousness of the situation by making 'weird jokes' about what was going on. She says she would even respond to work emails in the A&E waiting room. Her manager knew her behaviour was erratic and was aware that self-harming was involved, but neither Greta's manager nor the company she worked for at the time knew the full extent of what was going on. They saw only her poor behaviour, the *effects* of her mental illness, rather than the cause. Greta told me:

> What I should have done, is come in and said, 'It's really not going right for me, I need to take a leave of absence,' and just have had a couple weeks off, got some proper help, and then come back. But I was in this weird no-man's land where I kept

up pretence that I was fine. I think my manager assumed that I was fine, and that me trying to make light of everything wasn't an attempt to try and hide how shit everything was, but that I was genuinely taking liberties. I can understand that, from a work point of view, it just seemed like I was taking the piss.

When she found out that there would be a disciplinary hearing about her behaviour, Greta found her HR manager to be of little help, and was even shown an email written by her manager suggesting they just fire her. Because of this lack of support, she says she found it difficult to attend the pre-hearing meetings without crying, and that she had to get help from an external trade union as she was struggling to advocate for herself. As she put it: 'I just couldn't deal with it.'

Greta's hearing was eventually escalated and senior management backed down when the union got involved. Her manager at the time was new to management, and was most certainly out of her depth when it came to the kind of crisis that Greta was experiencing. I personally know how difficult it can be as the manager in a situation like this, and how challenging it is from a business perspective to have key members of staff off sick or behaving erratically due to mental health issues that you may not have full information about. Overall, neither the company Greta worked for, nor her manager, nor her manager's manager was in possession of the full facts concerning her mental health. As a result, Greta says that the most important lesson she has taken from the situation has been understanding that she overused humour to disguise the true situation. 'It's not just my manager's fault,' she says. 'I'm largely to blame.'

While it's certainly very self-aware and diplomatic of Greta to take responsibility for what happened, and to acknowledge her own partial culpability, and while I know how challenging it can be on the management side of a situation like this, I'm still stunned by the general lack of empathy shown by the senior figures in Greta's company, and the fact that there was very little effort made to get to the heart of what was causing her behavioural issues.

While she is now in a much better, healthier state and working at a different, more supportive company, Greta says that the trauma of the disciplinary hearing, and the way she was treated at work during this fragile, devastating period of her life still haunt her: 'I think about it daily.'

Keeping your shit together, authentically

Greta's and Marianne's stories aren't meant to scare you into keeping your mental health problems to yourself. If anything, they make sentimental and naive statements like 'bring your whole self to work' look even *more* ridiculous. It even makes me a bit angry. Like, oh, you want our whole selves, well HERE YOU GO, MOTHER FUCKERS. WHAT ARE YOU GOING TO DO WITH ALL THIS, HUH? Like Destiny's Child sexily cooing they don't think we're ready for this jelly, I don't think companies are ready for the *tidal wave of dark reality* that actually comes with welcoming people's whole selves. In some cases, I don't think it's safe. This doesn't mean you're not allowed to be a human, or show feelings or emotion, or to talk to your manager or colleagues about your mental health. I think you just need to be *selective* about the details. What is it that they need to know and why? Be direct and clear in what you need from them: self-advocating, while walking a fine line.

If you find it necessary to tell them you have a condition or illness, share that with them. If there are specific working conditions (certain equipment, flexibility with working from home) you need, let your manager know. For example, one woman I spoke to shared the story of a man on her team who has ADD, and when her company decided their open-plan office would switch to hot-desking (where nobody has assigned desks and you just sit where there's a space), the man explained that his condition meant that he needed his dedicated working environment containing his working materials as part of his daily structure. If he had to start each day searching for a calm space to work, setting up all his stuff, it would send his brain into overdrive.

Even if most companies don't know how to deal with or even understand mental health problems, properly, it's important that, at the very least, you understand *yourself*. Before you can ever establish what you should share or need to ask for at work with regard to your mental health, you first must gain an understanding of your own psychology, what your mental health needs are and how your mental health impacts your work.

Your psychological patterns and how they impact your interactions at work

Understanding your own psychological patterns is a huge part of looking after your mental health at work. This means understanding what you're bringing to the table every day. What kind of slightly unhinged emotional and psychological baggage are you dragging around with you from meeting to meeting in addition to your laptop and KeepCup? What filters or lenses are you viewing your work interactions through? Never mind rose-coloured glasses, are you wearing 'Everyone is Out to Get Me!' glasses in every meeting? Are you reading every email through a 'My Boss Hates Me No Matter What I Do!' lens? Is every conversation being heard through a 'My Colleagues Think I'm Unqualified!' filter? Do you spend more time piecing together evidence to prove your 'Samantha is Out to Get My Job' theory, than you do trying to actually understand why you have so many run-ins with her?

There is *so much happening* at work that is out of your control and so much relational and hierarchical bullshit flying around it's amazing any of us survives the working week. But the thing to keep in mind is, what do your difficult manager and OTT colleague have in common, other than a (possible) desire to see you crash and burn? What's the one element present in every single work situation you've ever been in?

You.

This isn't to say you've been *causing* the problem, or that you *are* the problem. Rather, it means that you have to keep in mind that the *way* you experience some of this stuff will be down to you – how you interpret it, how you react and what elements of it you choose to carry around.

'Are you my mummy?'

Here is a perfect example of what I mean about bringing your own psychological baggage with you to work.

In one of my earlier roles, my therapist helped me work out that I had, in my mind, somehow turned my new, female boss into a matriarchal figure in my psyche. So, when this woman 'rejected' me – when she didn't hold me to be one of her favourites, when she didn't praise my work or support what I was doing or say that she was impressed with me – it felt like a maternal rejection.

At first, when my therapist suggested I was projecting some sort of familial fantasy onto my managers at work, I was like, 'Oh here we go with the Freudian "Waaaah my childhood, aaaah my subconscious" bullshit.' But the more we talked about it, the more I was like, 'Um, OK, yes, I have totally turned my manager into some sort of mum in my mind.' Once I learned how to see my own shit clearly, it made all the shit that *wasn't* mine much clearer too. I was able to go, 'Oh, this is me, and that's you, and in this bigger situation, there is a whooooole lotta you. It's YOU poisoning the well, not me.' And I learned to sit in the mess, to exist in the discomfort, knowing what was in my control (my shit), and then what was out of my control (their shit). I was then able to contain my feelings better, to put up some proper boundaries, and then come up with some solutions for what my next steps would be.

It turns out that acting out unresolved familial trauma or dysfunction in the workplace is a real thing, and not just something particularly crazy my own brain decided to do. Completely different from (but I suppose not completely removed from) what happens when businesses refer to themselves as being 'like a family' – *Psychology Today* says that psychologists use the term 'transference' to explain what's happening when we're 're-enacting a psychodrama from the past', which they describe as being a kind of 'flashback in our adult life to the emotions and perceptions from our early life'.[4]

My therapist once described the concept of acting out in the present feelings that belong in the past as a form of time travel, which, I guess, basically makes me some kind of boring, psychodramatic Time Lord. (*Psychodramatic Time Lord* will also 100 per cent appear in the title of my memoir.) This behaviour at work can reveal itself in many different ways, and can include turning your boss or senior leaders into one (or both) of your parents, treating performance reviews like you might a report card in school, or even treating your co-workers like your siblings or classmates.

If you've had traumatic relationships or situations with any of the above, well, that's going to create some level of dysfunction at work, too. For example, the way you learned how to manage conflict in your family can then serve as a sort of template for how you deal with conflicts at work.[5] If you start to get angry at work or fall into a trap of thinking work is your family, you could find yourself slipping into dealing with your colleagues the way you work through things with your family. So if you come from an, er, expressive or explosive family that's used to shouting the doors down any time you have a disagreement, and that's 'just how you sort through stuff', the situation might get rather feisty.

These early relationships are also going to inform our own personal levels of resilience. Therapist Kate Hogan says that we all have different levels of resilience, and it's the level of difficulty we had to deal with in our childhood that's going to 'deeply affect our baseline of resilience'. And so, if we come from a dysfunctional family system that is somehow replicated at work, it's going to trigger some deep-rooted feelings.

Having had previous experiences of this, when things started to get impossible with the Post-it note writer at work, I was able to say, 'Ooooh, THIS AGAIN.' I knew that I had a habit of psychologically turning my manager into my mum, so I was able to see and assess why, perhaps, some of our interactions were more fraught than they needed to be, and why her rejection of my ideas and even my entire role felt so personal (because I made it personal in my head). Even if it *was* personal and she really didn't like me, that wasn't my stuff to worry about. All I could do was work on not turning what was happening into a familial, out-of-place psychodrama, and control the things that were actually within my control: how I reacted to her, how I responded, and then more concrete things like looking for a new job, and eventually leaving.

Keeping your mental health issues contained

In addition to understanding your own triggers or being aware of what psychodrama you're re-enacting at work – it's important that we learn to *contain* our mental health problems at work, too.

When I talk about the idea of 'containment' what I mean are elements of self-awareness, self-moderation and keeping boundaries. While 'containment' sounds a lot like 'compartmentalizing', the two are actually different. I don't mean that you should lock away your feelings in some mental Tupperware and pretend it doesn't exist. Containment is about having the resilience and capacity to manage internally and ring-fence any extreme emotions, thoughts or anxieties that arise due to stress at work.[6] Again, this isn't about denying your overall feelings or mental health issues or pretending they don't exist. It's about acknowledging them, tending to them when you need to, but, crucially, putting a fence around them when necessary: a border that those issues and feelings can't cross when you're at work or in social situations. It doesn't have to be an aggressive border – think of it as a lovely floral hedgerow rather than being kettled by riot police.

If you've ever worked in an office where everyone's feelings, traumas, conditions, neuroses and anxieties are just flying around, melted all over the place, running amok like Gremlins on speed – you'll know that it's incredibly messy, unruly and, ultimately, quite toxic. A culture of unconfined mental health issues and illnesses isn't progressive, feminist or liberal – it's feral, unhealthy and quite painful to exist in.

I am not a mental health professional or therapist, but from my own experience, I believe that if everyone made their best efforts to be aware of and keep their anxieties, neuroses and other mental health issues well contained within the lush green hedgerows of their mind (and also be honest with themselves when they know they can't), this would make a fantastic foundation for a working environment that was authentic, empathetic and responsible. The culture would be a kind one while remaining professional and business effective. Now, I need to make clear that I completely understand that, when you have a mental illness (especially, like Greta, when it's undiagnosed), containment isn't always possible. I understand that there are chemical and neurological conditions that no amount of resilience can alter. When I'm talking about working on containing your mental health problems at work, those are not the sorts of situations or conditions I mean.

Here's a personal example: on top of the more straightforward actions I take to look after my mental health, such as regular psychotherapy and my (boring) self-care checklist I shared in Chapter 3, I also have to contain my own mental health problems at work *on a daily basis* – whether that's sitting in an office or working from home.

This containment isn't always easy, but this is what it looks like for me. When I'm stressed – from work or because of something going on in my personal life – my anxiety will spike, which means I'll feel more sensitive. Through the work I've done with my therapist, I now both understand better what triggers my anxiety and, crucially, I also know the stories I start to tell myself when I'm feeling anxious about work – which is uplifting shit like: 'I'm unqualified and everyone thinks I'm a pushy, bossy bitch,' or, 'They think I'm dramatic and controlling and too difficult to work with; they're going to fire me!' I know that when I start to feel like this, and this narrative worms its way into my head, it puts me on the defensive and I begin to experience and view every interaction I'm having through the filter of my anxiety stories. If left untended and uncontained, I might start responding to my colleagues in a harsh way, because I'm acting from that place of anxiety and defensiveness. This could also culminate in me feeling quite angry and lashing out, which certainly doesn't bode well at work. (Or even just imagining that I'm being super harsh, when I'm actually not, and then feeling guilty that I've 'been a bitch' to my colleagues for the rest of the day. It's exhausting!)

How I contain these feelings is, firstly, to acknowledge how I'm feeling, which is kind of like the 'noting' concept used in meditation.[7] (*Ah, I feel anxious. OK.*) Acknowledging it is actually very powerful, because then I start to realize that, because I'm feeling this way, I'm looking for evidence to support my anxious narrative, which then helps me view interactions and even the way I read emails and Slack messages differently. Once I acknowledge it, I start to become more objective. This means I'm more aware of pausing to breathe and calm myself before I fire off reactive emails, and knowing when I need to go for a walk or take myself for a coffee to get a bit of headspace.

If I didn't contain my own anxiety and anger at work on a daily basis, in both my current and previous jobs, then my performance, my relationships with my colleagues and, I think, my overall professional reputation would be completely different. I have an anxiety Hulk constantly lurking inside me, whom I've learned how to both accept and contain. Some days I do great at this. Other days, not so much. It's a balance, and what Americans like to call 'a journey'.

Sometimes big things happen

As much as I am a control freak, and an advocate for being your own advocate, taking responsibility for your behaviour, and doing as much as you can to make a painful situation better, sometimes big things happen that are out of your control. Your mental health is one of them. Your physical health is another. Maybe you're chronically ill. Maybe you get cancer. Maybe there's a global pandemic. Maybe you've had a miscarriage. There are other big things that can happen, too. Maybe somebody close to you dies. Major life events such as divorce and bereavement provoke residual feelings that we carry with us for years afterwards, including when we go into work. We can't just 'check it at the door', as one manager early on in my career told me to do with any 'personal problems' I might have. And, specifically when it comes to a bereavement, you cannot just leave your grief tucked in bed at home, or sealed in an envelope at the bottom of your handbag.

Bereavement and grief at work

Dealing with bereavement and grief in general is difficult, traumatic and individual to each person who experiences it. It's a pain that you can only truly understand if you've felt it. And although grief can make it appear that time has stood still, it hasn't, so to make a bad situation worse, most people have to return to work (or even keep working) throughout what is probably the most painful period of their lives.

I spoke with journalist Kat Lister about her return to work

after the death of her husband, music journalist and author Pat Long, who died in August 2018. Kat and I worked together at *The Pool* and we met for the first time only days after Pat's death. Recently I sat down with Kat and asked her what her relationship with work was like, both during Pat's years-long battle with a glioblastoma brain tumour and after he died. Kat explained that in 2017 she was offered a full-time position at *The Pool*, covering another editor's sabbatical. At this point Pat was very ill, but there was no way Kat was going to turn down the role. 'It was a philosophy that defined my attitude as we hurtled from trauma to trauma – I did not want to be pitied, and I would not give up,' she says. 'It's only with hindsight that I realize that this had a significant impact on my health – both mental and physical.'

Kat told me how she continued to work until six weeks before Pat's death, and that she'll never forget how she accepted a day's work the week that he died as a way of preserving normality. 'Coming into work, I felt like I was fighting for us both. That perhaps if I could impose this normality onto our situation, I might save him – he might live.' Afterwards, she said that she felt a lot of guilt and grief about losing a day with him during the week he died, but for many people, work can provide a safe haven from dealing with the illnesses or trauma currently engulfing their personal lives. Work can be a place to escape. Kat says that *The Pool* office became her space, and that she was adamant that every morning she walked into the office, she wanted to leave her personal life at the door. It was a space in which she could be truly herself. She wanted things to be about work, 'I did not want to see that cock of the head and hear a "But how are you *really*?" '

It can also be a very tricky experience to crave the normality of work, and to be so emotionally and physically changed by the trauma of death and grief. Of her return to *The Pool* a couple of months after Pat died, Kat says:

To be completely honest, I remember very little other than the feeling that I was drifting underwater. In a lot of ways I was going through the motions of my old life without any idea as to where I was or what I was doing. But I do remember feeling safe and loved in that space. In that respect, I was fortunate – I was working with a close-knit group of women who had gone above and beyond to support me during the most traumatic period of my life.

But, as she mentioned before, while the emotional toll of grief is more expected, there's also a physical factor to contend with, which Kat says that people aren't aware of: 'We talk a lot about the psychology of grief, but we are only just beginning to explore the ways that loss can affect a mourner physically. I would regularly go into the toilets and throw up.' She also says that she still struggles to concentrate, even though it's been over a year since Pat died. 'I struggled to read, I couldn't follow conversations. Sounds hurt my ears. Restaurants and bars were no-go areas. The background noise almost felt violent to me.'

She says that, ultimately, when it comes to returning to work after a bereavement, each person has to do what feels right for them at the time, and that she herself adopted a trial-and-error approach to figuring out life after Pat, including how and when she worked. Crucially, she says that when a person is experiencing acute grief, there has to be a system in place to support that person as an individual, 'Grief isn't a one-size-fits-all experience. It requires a nuanced approach.'

Grief is a varied and personal beast and, as Kat says, it won't look the same for everyone, which is why I think reading and listening to other people's experiences of it is a powerful way of helping to process it. Author Nora McInerny has become a go-to resource for those dealing with grief, as her own story of dealing with a miscarriage and the loss of both her husband

and her father – all within months of each other – has touched and helped so many people. She's written about her experiences with grief online, as well as in her memoir *It's OK to Laugh (Crying is Cool, Too)* and her podcast 'Terrible, Thanks for Asking'. If you're feeling pressured to grieve correctly and neatly, I highly recommend giving her a follow. As she said in an interview with MPRW News, 'Grief is chaos, and it is not five neat steps. It is this weird hamster wheel you will be running on for the rest of your life. I don't believe in closure. I don't use the phrase "moving on" at all. I think these are things that stay with you and become a part of you.'[8]

Another fantastic resource that I've found comforting when dealing with any kind of grief is the 'Griefcast' podcast by Cariad Lloyd, which features brilliant and touching interviews with 'funny people talking about death and grief'.[9] Being able to laugh about how awful death is is soothing for a lot of people, and helps to normalize the intense feelings they're grappling with. There's also 'Fresh to Death',[10] a podcast on BBC Sounds from Saima Thompson and Maleena Pone, which explores the British Asian experience of death, grief and loss.

If you're struggling with grief at work, there's a brilliant organization called Back to Work After,[11] which was created by Nicky Palamarczuk. Palamarczuk is the head of social and influence at advertising agency VCCP, and she has gone 'back to work' twice – the first time was when she returned to work after maternity leave, the second after she was diagnosed with and received treatment for breast cancer only five months later. Back to Work After hosts events and shares stories in support of people who are struggling, and focuses on how others have coped, adapted and successfully returned to work after illness, maternity leave, addiction, bereavement or any other major life event that might require you to take a leave of absence from your job.

Coming out as your true self at work

Another difficult part about the challenge of bringing your whole self to work, is when who you are, and how you feel about yourself – and particularly your gender – changes.

Coming out to your colleagues about many different things can be highly challenging, whether it's about mental health issues, sexual preference, fertility issues, or that you've been diagnosed with a serious illness – it's all very, very painful. Coming out as transgender, or explaining to your colleagues that you're transitioning and that you, for example, would like to be referred to by a different name and pronoun, is particularly hard because it's completely uncharted territory for most people, and there's a distinct lack of company support for employees around it. It's especially difficult in this current political climate, where accepting that gender is a social construct, that it can be fluid, and that neither gender nor biological sex is necessarily the binary concept most people have always understood it to be, is somehow beyond both the comprehension and the respect of many (notably on Twitter, where some famous authors and comedians with bad opinions and 'gender critical feminists' like to hang out). It's upsetting, disgusting and wrong to not accept members of the trans community with the same open arms so many people have learned to give the wider LGBT+ community, and I hope by the time this book has been published attitudes will have changed, and at the bare minimum will have moved just a bit in the positive direction.

Transitioning in an open-plan office can be challenging. And even if you are transitioning at a quite progressive, modern company – there can be astounding technological hiccups that prevent people's names and pronouns from being changed in HR systems (something, for example, I was told several trans Googlers have experienced).

I spoke with my former *Pool* colleague Vic Parsons, a non-binary trans person who works as a gender and identity reporter for the LGBT+ online publication *PinkNews*, about their experience coming out as non-binary at work. Vic says they had been working full-time as a freelance sub-editor at *The Pool* for about five months, but as they didn't have a job contract they were worried about jeopardizing their income source. 'I was worried that me coming out as non-binary might be "difficult" and could lead to someone higher up deciding not to keep me on.'

Vic told me that they started going by 'Vic' in their early twenties, so their colleagues had only ever known them by that name, 'I had been in a process of coming out, to myself and others, since forever, but I'd done it very unobtrusively and gently, too gently, the other times. I had also changed my name to Vic in my early twenties, but without fully explaining to people why, which meant I was not able to correct them when they used my old name.'

After 'years of being quite unhappy', when Vic's mental health started to reach 'a real low point', they knew that coming out and asking for a change in how people treated them was 'becoming quite urgent'. Vic made the decision to come out to both their colleagues, friends, parents, and social media followers all at the same time, like ripping off the most painful plaster imaginable: 'So, this makes me cringe to think about now, but I sent a three-page letter – complete with FAQ section – to everyone on the *Pool* team email, one Friday afternoon when I wasn't in the office. The letter *really* didn't need to be that long, or that detailed,' Vic told me, 'but I think I was so nervous that I wanted to cover everything in the hopes that people would understand how I felt.'

Vic says that emailing everyone gave them the space and time to process everything, and that working in an office of mostly women, whom they describe as 'all big feminists, all LGBT+ allies', helped them feel safe to come out. Vic also says that while they got many kind and supportive messages back, when they went into work the following Monday they were still 'really anxious' and 'terrified', as coming out to so many people at once 'felt very public, very revealing, and I felt very exposed'. But, once they got to the office, all was totally fine: 'It was fairly anticlimactic, to be honest – no one made a big fuss, some people were gently, quietly supportive, but mostly it was just another Monday morning at work.'

I asked if working in an 'explicitly trans-inclusive' working environment at *PinkNews* made them view their coming out experience at a company where they were the only trans person differently. 'At *PinkNews* I feel like most people see me as a non-binary person called Vic, and treat me as such. This means I can mostly focus on the thing I'm at work to do: my job. There's a lot more to treating someone who was assigned female at birth as 'not a woman' than just using the right pronouns – using someone's pronouns is like, the first step, and honestly just basic respect for another human being. It's like pronouncing someone's name correctly. Working here has definitely made me realize how much energy I spent at *The Pool* managing "gender stuff".' But, they also note that if the company hadn't gone bust, 'it's quite possible that that would have changed over time'.

I also asked Vic what little things management and colleagues need to be aware of (and perhaps regularly fuck up on) that they may not realize, and Vic emphasized the importance of referring to people the right way, even when they're not in the room. This means not using binary terms for groups with non-binary people in it, like referring to a group as 'ladies' or 'guys', as well as consistently using the right name and pronouns. 'I hear you when you use the wrong pronoun or name for me or for any other trans person, even if I don't appear to have heard you or don't correct you, and even if you're on the other side of the room. I have special antennae. We get them from the Trans Lobby when we come out.'

So far as coming out to your colleagues is concerned, Vic's advice to non-binary people perfectly echoes that of therapist Kate Hogan about not being vulnerable in a toxic working environment. Vic says, 'You don't have to come out at work. Only do it if you want to, if you feel ready, and most importantly if it feels safe.'

Vic has been lucky to work with groups of feminists and trans LGBT+ allies where they felt safe enough to be their authentic self at work. It's harrowing to think that so many people have to choose between more suffering and negative impacts on their mental health if they don't come out, and risking their relationships with their friends and family, as well as their job safety, and unfortunately sometimes their own physical safety, if they do.

Vic and my trans colleagues at Google have been so helpful in teaching me how to be a better ally (and, really, a better, more empathetic human because that's what being an 'ally' is). And I'm forever grateful to them for their patience, their vulnerability and their resilience. If you're looking for ways to help support either yourself or your trans colleagues, I've listed a few in the Resources section.

Be yourself, or as much of it as you want to be

Our whole selves are complex creatures. We grieve, we transition, we go through illnesses both mental and physical, we have a multitude of emotions and stresses to balance at any given time. We're all vulnerable, and while vulnerabilities and emotion can contribute to the workplace, it's important they do so in a balanced, moderate way. We are imperfect beings who control neither time nor space, but we try our best anyway.

Be your authentic self, but contained.

Feel your feelings, and do your job anyway.

And when the worst happens, if you experience a death, or your health takes a turn for the worse – put yourself first. Look after you. Look after your health. Nobody can or will do it better.

If you have to make the difficult decision to come out as gay, trans or anything else at work – only do so if you want to, and if you feel safe.

From remembering to take your meds at the same time every day, or trying different methods to improve your sleep, you can absolutely pinpoint the areas that help you stay on track – even if they seem super boring, they're still mega important. This is about you, taking care of business and doing whatever it is that you need to do to be able to do your job, and do it well. Everyone's mental health is unique to them, and what works for one person won't necessarily work for the next. But we all have a duty to each other at work to commit to looking after ourselves, so that we can build a better, kinder and safer working environment.

7

Desire + Planning:
What do you actually want to do?

At some point in popular culture the question 'Where do you see yourself in five years?' became a trope in both job interviews and first dates. Somehow it became the done thing to roll your eyes and say: 'Five years? I don't know where I'm going to be in the next five minutes!' and to whimsically skip off into the Millennial Pink sunset. 'I'm simply too busy living my best life to worry about such things. Too blessed to be stressed!'

We've learned to roll our eyes because we're afraid of the answer. We dismiss it because it's too uncomfortable to say, 'Well, actually, I want to win an Oscar for Best Original Screenplay, to live in Paris with my future husband with at least two cats and be able to afford those Le Creuset ceramic pans.' So we say something sardonic and dismissively self-deprecating instead.

Much like finding the right balance for being authentic (but with boundaries!) at work, being in tune with your own desires is vital to finding satisfaction in your career and life. Knowing what you want, and accepting that 'what you want' can change and evolve over time, and being able to adapt to your changing desires, is incredibly powerful. Accepting that desires change isn't an excuse for you or anyone else to be super flaky, flitting all over the place because you changed your mind and don't want the same thing you wanted last week, or an hour ago. I don't think true desires fluctuate that much. (Your appetite might, but not the core of what you want out of life.)

There will come a time when you realize that the thing you thought you wanted for yourself for so long, no longer fits. Or when, like me, you realize that for years, you've been working extremely hard but without purpose, chasing approval from bad bosses, an identity in a job title and self-worth in a salary package. Or that, like Virginia in Chapter 3, you've been working hard for the sake of hard work, ignoring all of the warning signs that it was too much, because that was what you grew up with. *And you're no quitter.*

We can learn to harness and maintain our energy between the personal and the professional, but doing so is pointless without understanding what that energy is for, and what it's fuelling.

For some of us, what we truly want can be a cause of shame or embarrassment. It makes us vulnerable. If people know what we want, and they actively see us working towards that end, what happens if we make a mistake? Or if we don't get there? Saying what you want and working full-throttle towards it might seem brazen and audacious (which it is), but it also feels jarring, especially in a culture that still suggests that women should be seen and not heard.

However, first and foremost, making it clear to *ourselves*

what we want to achieve is intrinsic to success in our careers and in our overall happiness. Knowing what you want and not being afraid of it, means that you can actually start planning and working towards that goal ASAP. To be clear, the answer to the question 'What do I want?' isn't 'What my parents hope for' or 'What my partner expects' or 'What my mentor tells me'. No, in this instance, fuck what they want. What do YOU want?

Why a five-year plan isn't just self-help bullshit

As I mentioned in the Introduction, in the summer of 2017 I spent months going in and out of one employer's wellness centre, visiting the nurse, doctor and physical therapist. My ailments ranged from a six-week eye twitch to mysterious muscular twinges that felt like electrical pulses triggering in my neck, throat and back. It was painful and scary. After my blood work came back fine (bar a slightly raised 'bad cholesterol', no doubt due to the plethora of free croissants and pizza in our office) they concluded that the chronic eye twitch and various other physical symptoms I was experiencing were due to stress.

'Do you need to see a counsellor? We have one in the building,' the in-house nurse would ask gently, wrinkling her eyes in sympathy. 'I've been in psychotherapy for over three years, I don't think I need another therapist,' I said, feeling very defensive of my current therapist and annoyed at the notion that I was now so nuts that I needed two of them, and that I couldn't do my job without seeing one at work.

Eventually, I went to a physiotherapist, who took one look

at me and said, 'You're not breathing properly.' He then walked me through the ways you should *actually breathe* (into your diaphragm, into your lungs, full belly breaths – not short, pan-icked, up in your throat and shoulders kind of breaths), and explained how our body responds to stress. I had what he called 'universal pain', and the irony was, I was in the best physical shape I had ever been in.

Despite all the yoga I was doing, and the cycling, the duath-lon I completed, the 10ks I was running, the Krav Maga and Muay Thai kickboxing courses, the meditations on my Head-space app, I still wasn't feeling right in my body – the stress spoke louder than my physical fitness could.

And this is how I found myself in a three-day course called 'Search Inside Yourself' at the recommendation of a colleague who had found it extremely helpful. 'Search Inside Yourself' was (ironically) developed at Google, and the organization behind it now works with individuals and companies round the world. They describe themselves as a global community 'making mindfulness and emotional intelligence practical and accessible'.[1] It sounded perfect, like something I very much needed. I thought this course would finally see the end of The Great Eye Twitch of 2017.

The course included a lot of group meditation, mindful lis-tening and enforced eye contact with a complete stranger for prolonged periods of time – which made us both cry, despite only having known each other for approximately ninety seconds.

Honestly, I spent the first full day at the course constantly annoyed and often full-on angry, as captioned in my notebook from an exercise at the end of day one, asking what irritations and challenges are in our life. I wrote: *This class and its prompts; people's voices and sneezing and the loud door,* quickly followed by *THIS EYE TWITCH* in block capitals. It's fair to say I was experiencing a lot of anger, anger that my job and, specifically, my managers at the time triggered.

Another section of my notebook from that day contains the following, which is, in itself, very telling:

After this course (not because of it) I am trying to identify and sort through the feelings I'm experiencing at work. And outside of it. I'm afraid there's nothing I like, and only things I hate.

That every boss is an idiot. That every adult is incompetent.

I was angry, I was lost – and all the yoga and meditating and mysterious green protein powders in the world couldn't change that.

On the second day of the course, one of the instructors introduced an exercise on 'alignment, envisioning, and resilience' and she began by telling us the story of a woman named Roz Savage. Roz lived in the States, where she had a big, fancy, corporate job with all the trappings. By all accounts, Roz led a pretty good life. However, she started to deeply question her own existence. In a blog post, Roz decided to write two obituaries for herself: one that represented the existence she wanted – a life of fearlessness and adventure – and the one she was headed for if things carried on as they were.[2] She desperately wanted the former and, as a result, quit her job and dramatically changed her life. So much so that she is now the first (and so far only) woman to row solo across the world's 'Big Three' oceans: Atlantic, Pacific and Indian. She also holds four Guinness World Records. And this all stemmed from not liking how her obituary would read if she'd died that day.

Now that we were all fully intimidated and having personal existential crises, the instructor asked us to think about what our *own* obituaries would look like if written today, and to then write in our journals what we wanted our lives to look like in five years' time. In my case that meant writing down what I wanted Cate at thirty-seven's life to look like. We were meant to put down the first things that popped into our minds, unedited, and to write continuously for three minutes.

What I wrote changed the course of my life.

The first thing was '2 kids, 2 dogs, 2 cats'. As a woman who had often said that she wanted approximately zero children and currently had zero pets, this was an interesting revelation.

Apparently I also wanted a house in the country, and to work in the media again. To do more public-facing writing; to work with women in the media, art and culture on stories across film, TV and radio; to set up a creative agency or consultancy or production house of some kind; to be motivated and fulfilled and for my balance and fulfilment to come from both personal and professional endeavours. I wanted happiness and balance with my husband and to be in a financial position where we could pay for help with both life admin and childcare.

This is all that I wrote down, and it all felt like news to me. I was pretty stunned. And also annoyed that this morbid exercise had actually worked.

I was even more stunned when people around the room started sharing what they had discovered. One guy had the sheer audacity to take everything a step further by saying, 'The thing I realized is that if I want all of these things in five years, I need to get started now. Like, right now.'

That's what made my blood run cold. Now? I was suffering from an eye twitch and stressful confusion at work – what could I possibly be doing to produce two children and a country home when I'm an *absolute fucking mess*? How am I supposed to *write* when my days are full of stressful video calls, managing my micromanaging manager, and dealing with an extreme amount of tedious work that leaves me so drained that I can barely find the creativity to construct a tweet?

I didn't have the answers right then and there, but the question had been posed, and my subconscious had answered. It was then up to me to figure out how I was going to make that all happen.

To return to the title of this section, I can personally confirm that having a five-year plan isn't pointless, because the minute I had the reality-check question of 'What do I want in five years' time?' and the answer was a goal in my future with a timer strapped to it, I (slowly) started to get my shit together. Giving myself space to think about what I wanted for my life, without the noise of someone else's desires or judgement, ultimately changed and informed the decisions I started to make from then on. It became a subtle, guiding light in my life. I realized, *Wow, OK. So I want A, B and C? Then why am I pursuing X, Y and Z? What the hell am I doing?*

Two months after the course my husband and I brought home a puppy. Over the next couple of years I made a series of decisions that have led me to where I am now on the journey – back in the media, writing publicly and doing freelance consultancy work. I've made steps towards creating what I desired. Even when fate threw a spanner in the works, like the demise of *The Pool*, I still rose to the occasion and made decisions that would keep me in line with my overall aims.

Without that obituary-journalling exercise, I might still feel completely lost and angry, not to mention having a permanent eye twitch. Sure, I probably would have got to this point with the help of my therapist and podcasts at some point anyway, but I am so thankful that I had the question asked at that specific point in my life.

I'll be honest with you, before I attended that course I had been under the impression that having a five-year plan was only something that uptight people with unrealistic expectations of the world who have been keeping wedding ideas in a scrapbook since they were nine did. What I discovered, however, is that 'What do I want?' is the single most powerful, revealing question you can ask yourself when assessing both your career path and your life in general. It's not for a particular 'type' of person with a certain kind of job or career trajectory. There is nothing corny or embarrassing about knowing yourself. I realize that not everyone necessarily has the financial means to put their plans into action right away and start out on a completely different life path, if that's what their journalling exercise reveals. That's not what I'm suggesting. You can start to plan what your life could be in five years, and look at the small, realistic things you can do right now to make a change. Your five-year plan might actually take ten years to complete, and that's OK too.

So, how do I make a five-year plan?

When I ask myself what I want these days, the answer is usually take-out pizza. But this isn't about your *immediate* needs – it's about your overall desires. What motivates and drives you? And if you haven't asked yourself what today's you desires for the you in five years' time, you probably don't have a very defined existence or path at the moment (harsh, but true.)

Here's what you need to do:

1. Get out a pen and paper.
2. Write down [YOUR NAME] at [five years + your current age] (and try not to freak out about the age).
3. Set a timer for three minutes on your phone (or an egg-timer if you have one in your kitchen).
4. For the next three minutes, write down what you want your life to look like in five years' time – your job, where you're living, if you have kids or pets, if

you're married or divorced, if you're running marathons, writing poetry, setting up a business, going freelance or spending more time with your family. Don't edit yourself, don't think about if your best friend would approve, or if your partner would like it. Write the things that come into your head, and don't stop writing until those three minutes are up.

Once you've read back what you wrote – take some time; think about it. What you've written may surprise you and you might feel like you're not even close. Or you might be one of the rare people who do this and go: 'Wow I am totally content, I have all the things I want in five years, well done me.' Either way, know that you don't have to do anything rash or sudden. Please don't quit your job the next day. Instead, think about what major things you're going to need to change to get from point A to point B. Will you need to move? Start saving money? Take on another part-time job? Will you need to start physical training or research? Maybe there's some emotional work you have to put in before you can make any of those decisions. Whatever, the key to moving forward is MOVING.

A great way to get more specific in your wider five-year goal, and to help formulate your plan, is to use the SMART Goals framework. SMART stands for:

Specific (What do you want to accomplish?)
Measurable (How will you know when you've achieved those goals?)
Achievable (How do you achieve the goal?)
Relevant (How does it measure up against your overall objectives?)
Timely (How long will this take? What are your deadlines?)

You can use SMART goals for the key milestones on the way to your bigger goal. Other simple-but-helpful questions to ask yourself are:

- If time and money weren't factors, what would I be doing?
- What do I want my lasting legacy to be?
- What do I want to achieve in the next six weeks? The next year? The next five years?

The best thing to keep in mind when you're doing exercises and constructing frameworks like this is that they're only suggestions and are meant to help you. They are not fixed systems that you have to abide by rigidly. They're meant to help you maintain sight of your overall goal, and keep you on track to achieve it, not to make your life miserable because it took you six months to achieve an important milestone rather than the six weeks you had originally hoped for.

Are you doing the work?

Once you've identified what you desire, and what your goals are, the absolute worst thing you can do in most instances is nothing. Once you know the thing you most want is to do creative work and write a screenplay for a film, you don't just get to stay on your sofa, hate-scrolling through Instagram and wondering why no film producer has called to ask if you want to write a script for a new project they're working on. What signals are you sending out into the world? *Are you doing the work?*

Just because you *want* to start writing screenplays doesn't mean that you're *entitled* to. The universe doesn't owe you a miracle out of thin air. A genie ain't gonna appear and offer you three wishes. Liking or being interested in something, or being a consumer of something, doesn't mean that people will suddenly start paying you to make that very same thing simply because that's what you personally want. You have to put the work in. Pay your dues.

Dealing with disappointment

As with anything new – a new skill, a new job, a new project – if you're trying something for the first time you will no doubt make a mistake or experience disappointment along the way. There will be an element of your overall goal that doesn't quite work out. It's important to remember that, even when you put in the work, even when you show up and you feel like you're meeting the universe halfway, there is actually only so much that we are in control of. We actually control very few things in our overall lives, and we have to accept that chance and luck play a big part in our achievements. As Daniel Radcliffe told Lauren Laverne in his appearance on *Desert Island Discs*, 'You can be the most hard-working and the most talented, and you still need a huge amount of luck.'[3]

There will be times when we go for something we want and do not get it. If you're new to this whole listening-to-your-own-desire thing, the first few times you miss out on something you truly craved, it will be a blow. It will be painful. It will be disappointing. Personally, I've learned that the *fear* of being disappointed by not getting something I truly want is more painful than the disappointment itself. But this is a huge part of building resilience. You can't build resilience without discomfort and a bit of pain, and you can't get what you want without a bit (and sometimes a lot) of disappointment along the way.

Keep checking in

Taking personal responsibility for your plans is huge. Know that you will have to make some compromises. Your overall goal may shapeshift as time goes on, too. Five years is a long time. People can change, as can circumstances (sometimes unexpectedly and catastrophically, as we all now appreciate).

If you're currently undergoing talk therapy – psychotherapy or CBT, for example – you'll be familiar with doing emotional work on a weekly basis since someone will probably be asking how everything that's happened to you in the last seven days 'made you feel'. If you're not currently in therapy, finding a way of having regular emotional and practical check-ins with yourself will be very useful, particularly when you're working towards an overall goal.

And whether you're in therapy or not, whenever the universe does try to help out by politely setting off an emotional bomb in the middle of your life, those are great times to do the obituary exercise and to reassess your SMART goals. Even when you think you're nailing it, never be above asking (or too afraid to ask) questions like:

- What motivates me?
- What am I passionate about?
- What have I done today, in the last week, or in the last month to help achieve my five-year goal?
- Am I putting the work in?

Now that I'm over three years into my five-year plan I can – hand on heart – tell you that all the exercises I've put in this chapter have truly helped change my life and my career, and the way that I think about work, and my life overall. I can tell you that I've regularly assessed these goals, especially when I've been face-down in the mud in that arena. In her Netflix special *The Call to Courage* Brené Brown talks about how, in life, what matters most is that you show up for yourself and you get in the arena. Even if you're losing, the point is, you're there. You're trying. So, even when I have to make tweaks here and there to my overall plan, I know that the important thing is that I've learned how to show up for myself. I've learned how to compete.

Ultimately, I'm pleading with you not to bullshit or short-change yourself. It's your life, it's your work. Don't waste it. Put down your phone, get off Instagram and book that course you've been thinking about for the last six months. Go on that run so you can clear your head and get started on the dusty business plan you began to write three years ago. Get comfortable with the discomfort of asking yourself what you want, using setbacks as an opportunity to build resilience, and formulating that five-year goal and subsequent plan. Because – as those horrible motivational posters tell us – that discomfort is, after all, where the magic happens.

Parenthood +
Patriarchy:

When you might want
to 'have it all'

Deciding whether to have children or not and balance family with your career is a bit of a clusterfuck influenced by society's expectations, tradition, patriarchal systems, familial emotional baggage, biology and our own personal desires. I don't think there's any kind of issue quite like that of prospective parenthood and fertility.

While I don't have experience of being a working mother, I *do* have personal experience of battling with my own internalized misogyny about mothers at work, and questioning not only if I *want* children, but also, if I did have them, what impact would they have on my career? I've spent a lot of time imagining what being a working mum would look like for me – could it work? Do I even want that? Does my husband want that? Can we afford that? Do we have *room* for that? Is now even a good time? What about climate change? What about Covid-19? And if we did decide to have kids, *holy shit*, don't I have twins on both sides of my family? DO I EVEN HAVE ANY EGGS LEFT?

For many women I've spoken to, beyond eggs and biology, it's the daunting challenge of balancing a child with our careers – not necessarily a lack of a romantic partner or a sperm donor – that causes so many of us to wait until we're biologically forced to decide. So, when our mid-to-late thirties come knocking, we're left with the reality that, if we do want them, no matter which route we take to having children or who we do it with, there are still some big factors to contend with.

What's more, this decision process doesn't just happen inside the walls of our homes, but while we're out in the work-force, huddled in office bathrooms and sitting exposed in open-plan offices. Our work life IS our life, and yet dealing with fertility issues or speaking openly about balancing children and work schedules – if you're a woman – is almost illicit. It's this thing that you deal with in frenzied WhatsApp conversations under your desk, in hushed phone calls in vacant meeting rooms or have coded conversations about in the canteen.

As a woman in my mid-thirties, I am involved in such conversations fairly regularly. Not necessarily intimate conversations full of emotional detail, but an eye roll and a sarcastically laden remark along the lines of, 'And, now I'm thirty-fucking-seven so I have to, ya know, DECIDE.' Or sometimes it's even as simple as, 'And I turn thirty-nine in a few months . . .' paired with a look and you immediately think, *Oof!* In that you *know* she's not mentioning it because she's worried about frown lines or even turning forty for the same reason a man might worry about turning forty, but because *her reproductive system is almost forty years old*, and her eggs, *my god*, her eggs! There are occasions at work where you know that your colleague is trying for a baby or going through IVF, but you also know what her workload is like, how busy she is, and how much you depend on her. It can cause a flash of anxiety and your bowels to twitch because, *Jesus Christ how the hell is she going to do that?* And, selfishly, *Is it going to affect you and your work?*

If you decide to have them, balancing children and your career is one of the hardest things you'll ever have to navigate in your working life. You might already be in the throes of balancing young children with work. You might be deciding whether or not you want to have children, and be weighing up your concerns about the impact it might have on your career. You might have made the decision to have children, only to find you're struggling with conceiving. You might be exploring other ways of having children in your life, whether that's through surrogacy or adoption or fostering. Or, you may have decided that you don't want children at all. In fact, you may have made that decision quite easily.

Ultimately, I don't think there's enough space given for women and people who have children to speak openly about the impact they fear children will have on their careers, and why it's so hard to be a working parent in the first place. Discussing fertility issues openly at work is practically unheard of, but we also don't talk enough about the resentment that can build up in child-free people when their colleagues with families are given extra flex and grace with their time. So this chapter is designed to hold space for these complex, uncomfortable and emotive topics that arise when we try to 'have it all'. As I don't have children, I've spoken not only with other women who are struggling to decide, but also women who have experienced coping with fertility issues at work, and other working parents on how they've found as much harmony as possible balancing their careers and their family.

The mother of all jobs ... when you already have a job

I am completely in awe of working mothers. After being fired while on maternity leave, my own mother's return to work involved a new job in a completely new industry, after being out of the workforce for nearly twelve years. She was also a newly single parent, with two school-aged daughters and little support. Those of us who had working mums, single or otherwise, know how complicated it can be, so if we're looking at becoming one ourselves, it can bring up a mix of emotions. Perhaps you know how stressful it was for your mum, but as a kid you were also frustrated that she wasn't always available when you needed her. Maybe your mum had a very successful career and also managed to coach your football team, and the pressure to live up to her standards and ways of parenting is daunting. Maybe you feel guilty for not wanting children of your own, and your mum can't see how you could possibly be fulfilled without children. Maybe you grew up without a mum.

As well as it being complicated from a personal or psychological angle, there are other factors that contribute to why being a working mother is so hard:

- Maternity leave is necessary, yet is rarely generous.
- Discrimination and prejudice against pregnant women and people who have children in the workplace very much still exists.

- Women in heterosexual couples are disproportionately responsible for time-demanding parenting duties such as school runs and nursery drop-offs and pick-ups, and other forms of emotional labour.
- There's a lack of role models who are working mothers in senior leadership roles.
- Childcare is EXPENSIVE.
- Flexible working is wonderful, but not always available or possible for some parents.
- IT'S REALLY BLOODY HARD!

Quite frankly, the way that the current working culture, maternity leave, nurseries and childcare systems are set up is wildly unfair. It's unfair to everyone involved – the children, and the parents, regardless of their gender, or how their child was brought into their lives.

A huge element of the 'great decision' is the fact that the legal rights and maternity leave policies are absolutely dreadful. The thought of taking months of unpaid leave is pretty unimaginable for so many of us, and yet, that's what women all around the world are facing.

The grim reality of maternity leave

The systems across the globe for women when it comes to maternity leave and returning to work aren't great. *Shock. Surprise.* And yet, I'm still shocked and surprised at how bad some of the world's wealthiest and 'most progressive' nations are doing, especially when compared with countries like Estonia,

Bulgaria and Croatia, where now anything from fifty-eight to sixty-two weeks of statutory leave may be offered.[1] For the best example of how atrocious things are, you need look no further than the United States.

Online magazine *The Cut* has a great explanation of just how bad it is,[2] but ultimately, the only federal law that guarantees maternity leave in the US is for unpaid leave, and that's only for some employees. There's the Family and Medical Leave Act (FMLA), which protects Americans' jobs for up to twelve weeks after giving birth or adoption, but it doesn't require that you get paid for that time. Most employers will offer around six to eight weeks' paid leave.

In December 2019 a video of Democrat representative Alexandria Ocasio-Cortez taken during the House Oversight and Reform Committee's panel on paid family and medical leave went viral. In it, she asked a panellist, 'Do we know how long puppies are allowed to stay with their mothers after a dog has given birth? Eight weeks. So, the market has decided that women and people who give birth deserve less time with their children than a dog. And I think that that, at its core, has shown that the market has failed to treat people with dignity and with basic respect.' Thankfully politicians like Ocasio-Cortez are trying to get the eight weeks bumped up to twelve – which is what she provides for her own staff. AOC for president, then!

While the gender wage gap in the UK isn't one of its best features,[3] at least its maternity leave is definitely more generous than that of the US. UK law says that 'eligible employees' can take up to fifty-two weeks of maternity leave – the first twenty-six weeks is called 'ordinary maternity leave', the last twenty-six weeks 'additional maternity leave'. You're paid differently for each phase, but companies can and often do offer more than the statutory amounts in their own maternity schemes. There's also shared parental leave, whereby couples can share up to fifty weeks of leave and up to thirty-seven weeks of pay between them. However, paternity leave remains notoriously poor, clocking in at only one or two weeks, with very few companies in the UK offering packages that match a twelve-month maternity policy (the publishers of this book being one of them).[4] The Netherlands recently increased their amount of paid paternity leave from one or two days to five days, and a new policy in July 2020 will mean fathers can take a further five weeks of paid leave during the first six months of their child's life.[5]

There is also the small issue of the motherhood penalty, which *of course* is a thing! Why wouldn't it be!

Vox have a wonderful episode in their original Netflix series *Explained* about the motherhood penalty,[6] which I highly recommend watching – it's only twenty minutes long and very comprehensive, plus it's narrated by Rachel McAdams and features commentary from Hillary Rodham Clinton. (Really, why wouldn't you watch it?) As their reporter Sarah Kliff wrote in an article titled 'The Truth About the Gender Wage Gap',[7] the line of 'women only earn seventy-nine cents to a man's dollar!' doesn't fully explain the complexity of the wage gap around the world. The complexities include the subtle way the workforce disadvantages women, and how jobs 'penalize workers who have caregiving responsibilities outside the workplace' i.e. parents, and mostly women.

In this episode of *Explained*, they clarify the motherhood penalty with a case study of two lawyers who graduate at the same time and get married. In essence, the study (and loads and loads of accompanying data and studies) shows that when a (heterosexual) couple has children, someone will have to be at home, even if they have childcare, and that usually this responsibility falls to the mother. Meanwhile, the male half of the couple sees continued success in his career and is likely to get promoted and even make partner. But the mother has had to turn down travel and some assignments owing to the need to be at home, or has scaled back her hours, changing her lifestyle to work either flexibly or part-time – which then over the course of her career means that there's now a big delta between her wages and those of her husband, despite starting off equal.*

It's a fucked-up state of affairs, right?

Maternity discrimination is alive and well

While the UK may have much better maternity and parental leave policies than most, they're still lacking on the maternity discrimination front.[8]

Pregnant Then Screwed is an employment rights organization that is 'working to end the motherhood penalty'.[9] They do everything from running a free legal advice line to a mentoring scheme for women taking legal action against an employer; they also lobby the government for legislative change. They recently helped raise awareness of how, after five years of employment, Helen Larkin was made redundant by the beauty company Liz Earle, with only two weeks' notice, when she was eight months pregnant. Larkin represented herself at an employment tribunal, where she was awarded £17,000 in damages. (Liz Earle said of the tribunal that 'it seemed that we fell short of our standards in some areas, which we sincerely

---

* Or relatively equal; a lot of men are given higher starting salaries than women in some industries.

regret', which is such a half-hearted statement it beggars belief.) The PTS website is full of terrifying statistics ('54,000 women a year are pushed out of their jobs due to pregnancy or maternity leave'; '44 per cent of working mums say they earn less than they did before they had children') and a profile in the *Guardian* with its founder Joeli Brearley explained how the full scale of maternity discrimination isn't yet clear, owing to the abuse of employers using NDAs to silence women from speaking out and, more crucially, fighting back.[10]

While none of the women I've spoken to had been made to sign an NDA or had been pushed out of their roles after telling their employers they were pregnant, one was coincidentally told her contract role was ending sooner than expected, about a week after she informed them she was expecting. And then she found out that her manager had also massively messed up her maternity leave – and had to fight to have it restored. What followed was a long, stressful few months of job searching, and eventually being hired for a much more junior role before she went on maternity leave. Thankfully, she was approached and hired by a different company while she was still on maternity leave, and they respected her desire to take a full seven months' off before starting her new role. Imagine that!

Pride and (pregnant with) prejudice

While few of us will admit it, those of us in the workforce who don't have children can be quite judgemental and unempathetic towards those who do – and it's something that we all need to work on. If you don't have children, you constantly hear 'when you're a parent, you'll understand', and I think that's true. It wasn't until I found myself thinking more and more seriously about 'could we, should we?' that I started to catch my own train of thought, and tried to be more sympathetic towards parents, both at work and in public. At times I, like so many other child-free people, can have a horrible chip on my shoulder about being made to pay for other people's life choices. Just as it's irritating to pay for expensive hen and stag weekends in Ibiza or attending seven of your friends' weddings in one summer, when it comes to colleagues with kids, it's very easy to wonder why, *just because they decided to have children, I should have to do XYZ*. And in toxic or chaotic working environments, it's even easier to think, *Oh, well, how nice that Ben gets to leave early to go get his kid from nursery, what a hero*. Or, *Sure, Carol, you're late again because of the school run. Maybe leave earlier!* It's *awful*.

'It is more socially acceptable to be late for or miss work because your train has been cancelled or your car broke down, than if your child is ill,' Nell Frizzell, journalist and author of *The Panic Years: Dates, Doubts and the Mother of All Decisions*, replied when I asked her what was the biggest thing she's learned since becoming a mum. 'Honestly, tell someone that you're going to be fifteen minutes late because the trains are all running on rail replacement buses and you'll probably get at least a sympathetic chuckle. Tell them that you're going to be fifteen minutes late because your child has been running a fever and only slept three hours last night and there will be a tiny sense that you're "not coping" as well as you should be.'

Nell's point perfectly illustrates that it's the attitudes and prejudices that so many of us have – regardless of how much our own manager let us down when she came back from mat leave, or what that pregnant lady in the office did that one time – that must be addressed. Because even if we don't feel like we can change a company's policy on flexible working, or even the maternity leave they offer, we *can* immediately and definitely change the way we treat the parents and pregnant people we work with. Plus, our own prejudices are poisoning our decisions about whether we want to have kids while trying to progress in our own careers.

And it's not just child-free colleagues who can be dicks about situations like Nell mentioned; sometimes there's a lack of empathy and understanding between parents at work due to reasons such as class, privilege and, ultimately, wealth.

'I've not seen anyone have success at the level that I'd like to have without their hours being nutty and being owned by their job,' Miranda, the forty-something from Chapter 3 who works in tech in London tells me:

> *I realized recently at work that I'm the only director without a full-time nanny, and out of all the men, none of their wives work. So, when I can't join things because of childcare issues, they can't really understand because they don't have that. I know people who have a night nanny four nights a week, so they've got a three-month old baby who sleeps through the night. If you have money, there are all these ways around it. I don't come from the kind of background where I even knew you could find someone to do that.*

While I was aware of maternity and night nurses, I once heard an older male colleague of mine whose wife just had a baby say that he'd been sleeping in the spare room at night in order to be 'fresh for work' the next day, and I was pretty shocked. It was the first time I'd ever even heard of a dad doing that – I just assumed all dads helped out, even a bit, at night and suffered through the lack of sleep like their partner would, but apparently it's a thing. (A thing for those with spare rooms and somebody with whom to co-parent, that is.)

A mother's mental load

What strikes me about the motherhood penalty, and the general attitude towards mothers at work, is that our working culture is directly affected by traditional gender stereotypes. Because women are still undertaking that 'second shift',[11] and doing the majority of unpaid domestic work and emotional labour at home, it means that their work is more greatly impacted than their male counterparts. In heterosexual relationships, as evolved as we'd like to think we've become with phrases like *co-parenting* and fathers no longer referring to looking after their own children as 'babysitting'[12] – when it comes to childcare, cooking and general housework, a recent study found that women in the UK are responsible for 60 per cent more unpaid work than men.[13] Sixty per cent!

This became even more apparent during the lockdown of 2020. The widespread closure of schools and nurseries meant that parents all over the world were suddenly having to balance full-time childcare with the additional complexity of home schooling. And those parents who were able to work from home were having to somehow do so alongside all of the above.

University researchers from Cambridge, Oxford and Zurich found that during the lockdown, 'Both employed and unemployed mothers are typically spending around six hours providing childcare and home schooling every working day. By contrast, the average father at home is only spending a little over four hours on childcare and home schooling each working day, regardless of his employment status.'[14]

Basically, regardless of salary or whatever working situation a household with school-aged children were in during the pandemic, economists found that, on average, women in heterosexual partnerships were doing more home schooling and childcare – and not because the women were working less. These stats are alarming, but for single-parent households it was even more stressful, if not altogether impossible – particularly when the UK government encouraged people who couldn't work from home to return to work.[15]

And even when there isn't a global pandemic going on, even if women are doing less dishes and laundry than their male co-parent, chances are they're still carrying a significant mental load – which we also know from Chapter 3 is a strong contributing factor to burnout. One woman I spoke to told me she has a 'scrolling mental list' she has to keep as a mother, which takes up a lot of her own headspace, previously reserved for other things. Maddie Armitage, the Chief Data and Product Officer for Dentsu Aegis Network, has two teenage children and has always worked in male-dominated industries. She says that she believes women have to work 'extra hard' to reach the same position and maintain the same level of consistency as their male colleagues, because when women turn up to do a day's work, they're already two hours into their working day:

They're getting the kids up, making breakfast, getting bags ready, sorting uniforms, checking the calendar to make sure there are no after school clubs or sport meet-ups – and all this before 8.30 a.m.! I know times have changed and couples are sharing more of these responsibilities, but women still tend to carry the lion's share. As a parent, it's impossible to switch off from that while you're at work. I guess that's why we're so good at multi-tasking.

The motherhood penalty is certainly its own kind of beast – cut off one head and another version presents itself.

Can you be it if you can't see it?

Back to tech director Miranda, who says that while she had a supportive team and employer, she knew that she couldn't do the job she was currently doing if she had a baby. She had to attend a lot of events in the evening, worked long hours and did a lot of international travel. She knew what was required of her, and she knew that having a baby in that role was neither possible nor what she wanted. She also said that she realized she didn't have any positive role models to mould her own future parenting style on, as the more senior executive women in her company all had 'two nannies each and were never at home', and it wasn't the version of success that she was hoping for.

She also told me about how her old manager – whom she had looked up to – significantly impacted how she viewed motherhood and work:

When my manager came back from maternity leave after having twins, she was really different . . . she really constrained what she did. She became a lot shorter and sharper. I had a lot less time with her. She withdrew so much. I don't know how to phrase this without being unkind to her, and while I understood it, it still felt like a bit of a let down.

When Miranda herself returned to work after having a baby, she says this was her guiding example, 'It was a massive lesson to me. I had that example in mind over the last year. I'm not sure how I could do it without upsetting her, but I'd love to ask her how much of that was a decision she took, versus it being something that just happened.'

It's also often the examples of parents who work that make

it impossible to envisage a world where we might find joy and balance in both. Of course, as mentioned earlier, there's the example of our own working parents. In popular culture, however, we're constantly teased and tempted with this idea of *having it all*, and yet it's rare we're shown anything other than a bleak, terrible future in which we're demoted, resentful, stressed, sex-starved, professionally unfulfilled and on the verge of a nervous breakdown for eighteen years or more. Or that having it all is achievable only if you're a highly paid, high-flying, powerful boss lady with a nanny, driver, cook and housekeeper who all support you in your quest to lean the fuck in – bonus points if you also have a husband who doesn't cheat on you! Extra bonus points if you're married to a powerful lesbian whose wealth is twice your own. One woman I spoke with mentioned she was currently working on a project with a male Harvard professor who makes millions a year, but from what she can tell, only works three days a week. 'Why don't I see versions of women who live like this?' she said. 'I don't see it! If you're a woman, you have to be grateful for what you've got, and hustle all the time, for *decades*!'

Our influences on whether we think having children and a career is possible for us can come from a lot of places, particularly if we don't have any positive examples of working parents in our lives. Leisel, a thirty-seven-year-old woman living in Edinburgh, says that as part of her own journey of figuring out whether to have children, over the last year she's been taking a poll of all the parents she knows, asking them if they'd do it again, 'I've not met a single woman who said, "I'd do exactly what I've done exactly this way again,"' she says. 'But every man I've asked has said yes.'

She told me about an article she'd read that had bothered her, which said that people in the US who don't have children are happier than those who do. She then listened to a podcast interview with the CEO of the Happiness Institute, Meik Wiking, who said that, while that statistic about people in the US is true, actually, people who live in Denmark and have children are happier than those without, simply because their work culture allows for it. 'That was mind-blowing for me,' she said, 'because there *are* work cultures that allow people to be more than just workers, and I started to get a bit angry that we're crap at this. We're allowing this work culture to be as it is. I also write emails at night and set deadlines without asking if that deadline is appropriate. We're all part of it, and we need to create work cultures where it's OK to have other lives without repercussions.'

It's the question of how we're all negatively contributing to this inhospitable working environment for parents that has to be brought to the forefront. Particularly as it directly impacts the capacity in which women can return to work, if at all.

Childcare and the cost of returning to work

Returning to work after you have children – whether it's full- or part-time – having to physically be at a location other than your house to make money, is complicated, time consuming and, it turns out, really fucking expensive.

As Nell Frizzell points out, it's often assumed that only very driven people want to get back to work after having children, and that it's a sign of being 'career oriented', or even somehow less maternal, or more motivated by money than by parenting. She says it's important to keep in mind that work brings social benefits, and is a huge part of most people's identity as it gives their lives both meaning and structure:

Once you have children, you will at some point want some of that other part of your identity back. You might want it part time, you might want a career change afterwards, your priorities probably will have shifted enormously, but you are likely to want to work, eventually, again. Sadly, the modern workplace seems particularly ill suited to fit the needs of returning parents.

And what is one of the most common ways that our working cultures and systems prove that they are ill suited to fit the needs of parents? CHILDCARE! As Nell says:

One of the biggest misconceptions about having children is that everyone who has a paid job can therefore afford childcare. That parents have any real 'choice' about whether or not to go to work. Thanks to the way we organize work and fund early years services in this country (i.e. badly) many parents literally cannot afford to go back to work, because their salary simply could not cover the cost of childcare while they were working. Others cannot afford not to, even if (like one friend of ours living in Preston) going back to work four days a week means that you only earn, once you took away the cost of childcare and commuting, twenty pounds a week.

The nursery bills some of my friends have told me about are, well, rather astounding. And Nell says that some useful stats to keep in mind are that in the UK the average cost of sending a child under two to nursery is £127 per week if you work part time (which is twenty-five hours) and £242 per week full time (fifty hours).[16] She goes on:

The average wage in the UK for someone working full time is £569 a week [approximately £29,600 a year]. Meaning that, once you've taken away the cost of childcare [for just one child under two] you are left with, on average, £327 a week to live on; every other bill, everything you eat, every bus ticket and student loan payment. That's 43 per cent of your income going straight to childcare.

I did a bit of research, and looking at one of the only daycare providers in my area where I live in Surrey, for a child under three years old it would cost £1,408 per month to send them to daycare four days per week – the rate for which is £82.85 per day. This is more than my mortgage repayments.

The significance of childcare in our society became crystal clear during the coronavirus pandemic, and revealed that the cracks in the system are more than just surface-level flaws, but rather deep, internal wounds that have infected the foundations of our society and culture.

A clear, safe solution hasn't been found yet, but pre-pandemic, Nell actually asked a very important question: What the fuck happened to crèches? As she writes in *The Panic Years*, the concept of twenty-four-hour, free crèches in your place of work would be 'revolutionary'. If you wanted to, you could take your kid to work with you – as Nell says, you could continue breastfeeding and spend your lunch with your child, and still get to maintain all of the parts of being employed that nourish so many of us: our work, our friendships, our identity. As Leisel found earlier in this chapter, Scandinavian and Nordic countries are doing this much better than the US and the UK[17] – whether it's on-site childcare, or simply the cost of it,[18] combined with employers giving their staff higher amounts of parental leave.

If you simply can't afford the various forms of childcare,

nurseries and nannies – or are uninterested in the emotional and physical cost of employment and school runs – and you don't happen to have retired family members who live locally and are happy to take your kids two or three days per week, other options and ways of working start to become not only more attractive, but also in a lot of cases, necessary. (And if you're in a pandemic, obligatory.)

Making it work for you

Flexible working has become a big talking point in the last couple of years, and has been championed by influencers such as 'Mother Pukka' blogger Anna Whitehouse and her Flex Appeal campaign.[19] Christine Armstrong's book *The Mother of All Jobs* is a fantastic resource for trying to parent without losing your mind (the subtitle of her book is *How to Have Children and a Career and Stay Sane(ish)*). One of her Instagram captions struck home for me; she wrote that flexible working worries her a lot, because although she believes it is a great thing, it's only great if it's *actually working*.[20] And in practice, and from the interviews with other working mothers that she conducts, it's not. She wrote that she's interviewed women who tell her they 'get paid for three days, four days or school hours but are actually connected to work full time. Or more than full time. Yet still being paid less, seen as "not committed" and missing out on pay rises and promotions.'

One of the most revealing things about the coronavirus pandemic was how swiftly so many employers were able to adjust to their entire workforce being at home, working remotely. For all the people with disabilities, mental-health problems, neurological differences, or childcare issues who were for so long told that working from home or remotely was 'impossible', this was both curious and enraging, to say the least. While having entire teams and businesses working from home permanently certainly wouldn't be practicable for every business, the myth that certain people couldn't do so permanently, or even for the majority of the time, was completely dispelled. What businesses choose to do with this revealing information is yet to be seen.

Some world leaders like Jacinda Ardern in New Zealand and Nicola Sturgeon in Scotland were quick to adapt. Early on in the pandemic recovery, Ardern suggested that New Zealand could shift to a four-day work week and encouraged business owners to consider more flexible working for their employees, as it was a good way of helping to recover the country's economy through domestic tourism, but also beneficial to people's productivity and general well-being.

While working from home in a pandemic is hardly reflective of flexible working during 'normal' times, it has certainly shifted preconceived notions about its effectiveness. As Armstrong pointed out, flexible working might not be perfect, or for everyone, but there are some forms that can be extremely effective – and now, more than ever, employers have seen that they can work. Here are a few examples of how some parents are making it work for them:

The job share

When I met Ana McLaughlin at a podcast event she mentioned that she works in a job share as a deputy publicity director, and she kindly agreed to be interviewed for this book. Ana is very enthusiastic about job sharing, but hadn't ever considered it as an option for herself until her (female) director at Hachette, the publishing house she works for, suggested it. Ana has two children, and job shares with her colleague Elizabeth. She actually started her current role as

Elizabeth's maternity cover, working four days per week. She says this would have been entirely manageable from a work-load perspective, but it was the logistics of dropping and picking up two children from different places and having a relatively long commute that made it too difficult.

'I loved the job but I had to get the kids up and dressed – as well as make myself look half human – and out of the house by 7.30 a.m. because my husband leaves for work too early to help. I then had to leave at 4.30 p.m. on the dot to get the train to make pick-up.' She says she managed it for a year, but at the end of it, both she and her kids were suffering from the constant running around, the long days and the fraught mornings, plus, she says, 'I wasn't around for homework help or, really, any quality time in those four days. Plus, on the day I wasn't paid to work, I still checked my email almost hourly and was distracted for much of the time I spent with my toddler.'

All this changed when her boss suggested a job share once Elizabeth came back from maternity leave. Now Elizabeth works Monday to Wednesday; Ana works Thursday and Friday. Ana says that logistics and organization are what make a job share work:

> The absolute key is that we share an inbox and have a
> detailed filing system for emails. We keep very detailed notes
> on each project, and we leave each other handover notes each
> week. Fortunately, Elizabeth and I naturally work in quite a
> similar way. It would be very difficult to make it work with
> someone whose style was very different to mine.

I've always been curious about job shares as my Aunt Cindy has been in one at Hewlett Packard for years, even before it became popular. I became fascinated about how exactly this arrangement worked, and whether it was something only senior executives were allowed to do. But from Ana's story, it sounds as if, in order to do a job share, you need to have in place:

- a supportive and keen manager;
- a likeminded colleague with similar approaches to working, organization and discipline as you;
- two sharers who are able to be truly collaborative, and keep their egos and envy in check; and
- a company culture that has room for creativity and flexibility about the function of the role.

The 9–5 8–4

As for parents who are able to remain in full-time, five-days-a-week, office-based employment, one of the most heartening stories I've heard came from Maggy Van Eijk, who lives in Amsterdam and has a one-year-old daughter. She works full time, and is the breadwinner in her household. When it comes to the challenge of balancing her personal life, parenting and work, she says being a 'massive introvert' works to her advantage because 'I can't be fucked to go out anyway', which speaks directly to my own, introverted heart.

She says that, while she's 'not quite sure how she's managed it', she actually feels quite guilt-free about how she balances work and time with her daughter. She says that she gets to work at around 8 a.m. and leaves at 4 p.m. so that she can pick her little girl up from nursery and spend some time with her, and that, crucially, during this time, she tries not to check email or be on her phone. She says she's 'really strict' about her schedule with work, but if she has to go to a client event or meeting in the evening, she'll just be honest that she has a young baby at home that she needs to spend time with:

I've just been really honest about it and so far it's worked. The people I feel who have made [balancing family and career] work are just really bullish about it and don't feel guilty. You end up doing more work, I end up doing more work in the day, but I'm really strict about that time of day where it's just my daughter's time and I'm not doing stuff.

Working for yourself

Outside of being in a office 9ish to 5ish, five days a week, our other working options vary, depending on the industry we work in, our level of experience, our skills and training, whether or not there's a pandemic happening and where we're based. Some of these options include proposing a new arrangement with your current employer – a job-sharing scheme, flexible working including part-time hours or working remotely from home – or a complete shift in your employment, which might include going freelance or starting up your own company.

Omidyar Network's Sarah Drinkwater tells me that many of the women she knows in her mum group have had 'shitty experiences where they get marginalized' at work, and she thinks that's why a lot of women actually start their own companies and essentially are forced into entrepreneurship. She particularly observed this while she was running Google Campus for Mums: 'We had 650 women go through this programme in six locations around the world, and I realized so many women I met had come in because their companies had marginalized them, and they were like "fuck you, I'm going to start my own thing".'

Starting your own business is a wonderful thing to do if you have the desire, aptitude and finances. On a different level, while working for yourself and going freelance isn't quite right for everyone either (financial instability; never-ending admin; constant money chasing; no colleagues), there are, of course, many benefits, too. Nell Frizzell, who was a freelance journalist even before she had her son, explains that if you're a freelancing parent, the way you view the value of your own time evolves and sharpens. She says that she used to get up at 4 a.m. and work until her son woke, and then again during his naps, and she started to be more insistent about being paid fairly, on time and well – she started only taking on work that was 'either genuinely worthwhile or well paid'. She says, 'When twenty hours of your day are spent keeping someone alive, you cannot dick around with the stuff you do during the other four hours.'

Take a crap song, and make it better

It's shocking how much emphasis is put on women and parents to just figure this stuff out on their own, without a robust infrastructure and culture to help support them. We still have this myth of the distracted, despondent dad who rarely helps and an overly capable supermum, the women who can have it all and do it all. As though men can't be capable co-parents, and if women could only figure out the secret of how the supermums do it, the rest of us could simply replicate it. What's become clear to me is that the women who have been able to remain happy in their employment (part-time, job share or otherwise) are those who are working with companies, and particularly with managers, who are willing to meet them halfway. To be supportive. To be human and humane.

While role models and representation are certainly important, beyond getting the occasional heterosexual, cis, white pregnant woman into a top position, it's still not quite enough.

The only way I can see this improving is for the onus to fix it or find that perfect balance to be taken off women and parents. And in order for that to happen, we need a relentless, multi-pronged attack. This is a vast oversimplification of what needs to happen, but essentially you need fierce and influential politicians like Jess Phillips, Jacinda Ardern and Alexandria Ocasio-Cortez in seats of power, making the legal changes. You need more parents like Candace Braithwaite, the founder of Make Motherhood Diverse,[21] to keep speaking up for what they believe in and fighting for the rights of parents.

And, crucially, when it comes to work, we need a more diverse set of women and people who have children in executive roles where they're the ones calling the shots, and making shit better for all of the people around them. Like, *properly* better. A wonderful and ballsy version of this was when the CEO of Bumble, Whitney Wolfe Herd, became pregnant, and she changed her company's (already quite generous and thoughtful) parental work policies after she realized there was more that she could do. There's a fantastic article in *Fast Company* about the changes Whitney wants to make, including onsite childcare for their new HQ building in Texas and parental stipends.[22] She said, 'There are nine months of pre-paternity or pre-maternity. Then there's everything that comes after. So I'm starting to think hard about the white space on the beforehand and afterhand of that actual leave. And making sure that once a parent does come back to work, how do we do that in a flexible way?'

Whitney is literally exemplifying the change she wants to see in the world, and she's in a powerful, visible position to do it. It just shows that it takes women to be at the top of a company to make drastic change for parental policies. But it also highlights the snake-eating-its-own-tail system of power and economic freedom and the motherhood penalty. Whitney Wolfe Herd founded Bumble, 'a female-centric [dating] app that only allows women to make the first move',[23] after enduring a shitty situation at her previous company, Tinder. She has worked extremely hard and overcome a lot to get to where she is now, but one could argue that she is where she is now because of the foundation of privilege she has as a cis, white, woman in a heterosexual marriage. And she's been able to make this important change to her company's maternity policy because power and economic freedom are both currently on her side, and she has changed the game so that she and the other people who have children on her team can stay within the realm of power and economic freedom that keeps them as insulated as possible from the motherhood penalty.

Founding a company, being a CEO, going after funding, building something giant in the world of tech bros and male VCs – it's not for everyone. But for those of you with enough power, with a foundation that contains a certain amount of privilege – will you use your economic freedom to make big changes for those who can't? We need you. What if it was you who could help build a future with in-office crèches and proper, family-oriented working systems?

To me, that is the ultimate form of sisterhood – using the privilege and power you have to create opportunities and possibilities for those less fortunate than yourself.

How on earth do we decide?

As I mentioned at the start of this chapter, at the time of writing I don't have any children, neither am I pregnant. What I do have is an ever-growing obsession with how ambitious women can have both children and satisfying, well-paid work. When I find out a woman I think is 'successful' also has small children, my inner monologue suddenly looks something like this:

How? Where does she live? How long is her commute? Does
she leave at five every day? Is she here every day? Does she just
have loads of money to pay a nanny? Does she just not mind
missing time with her kids? Is she happy? Is she constantly
miserable? Does she regret it? Is she able to work from home?
What did she do in lockdown? Does she have enough money
to buy tailored trousers and expensive eye cream? Is she
fulfilled? Is she happy? Are her kids happy or are they already
in therapy? Is she in therapy? Is her whole family in
counselling? Does she hate her nanny? Is she worried her
husband is banging the nanny? Does she want to bang the
nanny? How does she look so good? She clearly goes to Pilates
regularly whereas I can't even make it to the gym and I don't
have any kids. Fuck, fuck, FUCK.

I wish I could say the same for when I meet a man with small kids at work, but I honestly just assume the mother of his kids does most of the heavy lifting. ('BUT THAT'S REVERSE SEXISM!')

While I hate the phrase 'have it all' – it is clichéd and tired and I think most people would say *impossible* – I've had to accept that, as the three-minute exercise from the previous chapter revealed – it turns out I want it ALL. I don't just want children, I want *happy* children. I want to be able to spend as much time with them as I please – but I also want a job that pays well so that I don't have to panic about money all the time. I want to be able to easily drop off kids at nursery or school and pick them up again. I want to work from home at least two days per week. I want childcare on tap so I can still go out and get smashed with my husband, but also go and see friends alone when I need to. I want ALL OF IT.

I'm sure most working mums probably got to my second 'I want' and fell off their chair laughing because I am both naive and delusional. But I am hoping that some of you didn't. I'm hoping that there are some of you who read that and say, 'You can . . . just not all at once, and it's going to take a lot of trial and error, and it's not going to be perfection . . . but this isn't impossible.'

And it's because I want it all, and because I'm highly ambitious, that I am currently in this state of constant low-level anxiety and panic. When I'm out walking my dog in the mornings before work and see mothers rushing their children on scooters to nursery, my heart aches a bit. It's a constant battle of fear and longing. *Oh god, I want to be doing that, but fuck, do I really want to be doing that?* I see little babies with adorable knitwear and I am struck with a maternal hunger, and then imagine having to leave that cosy child at home while I shove myself onto the Northern Line, and I'm right back in that black pool of anxiety and fear: how the hell could we make it work?

From the examples in this chapter, I know that lots of women do make it work. That you find a way, just like with everything else in life. At times it can be difficult to imagine what could be when you can only see what *is*. When, at work, you're told so many things are 'urgent' and 'an emergency'. When you're made to feel bad for needing to leave work two hours early for an appointment, or take your annual leave, or – gasp! – be ill, it feels almost impossible that you could ever have enough flexibility to be a mother. And even if you did have the flexibility, what about the toll that mental load takes? The sleep deprivation? A baby is built by stealing nutrients and vitamins from your body – it literally strips the calcium from your teeth – so what of your ambition? Your creativity?

Author and critic Cyril Connolly (1903–74) famously wrote that a 'pram in the hallway' is the enemy of good art.[24] (Unsurprisingly, Virginia Woolf hated him.) There have been hundreds of articles written about this comment, arguing both in its favour and against it. It hits a nerve, particularly with women who work for themselves or work in a creative industry, because there's most certainly the fear that once you have a child, you will have neither headspace nor time to be productive, creative, or artistic. Author Maggie O'Farrell wrote for the *Guardian* in 2003 about this quote when she was six months pregnant with her first child, saying she'd suddenly wake at 3 a.m., anxious, imagining her baby 'absorbing ideas and words as it does blood sugar and then scrambling them up, like a computer virus, until they are unreadable, unrecognizable'.[25]

This is a massive subject, one complex enough for a book solely on this concept, but for the most part, what's so helpful and positive to know is that plenty of working mothers, regardless of the industry they work in, say that, basically, yes, you will be time poor, but that having children also sharpens your productivity. And from a creative perspective, those who do work in the arts say that parenting gives you a new perspective on the world, creating a new dimension to your work. Sarah Drinkwater says that when it comes to the complexities of parenthood, success and creativity, it's all ultimately a gamble: 'I feel like all of these choices that we make are gambles we take on ourselves, bets that we make on ourselves. There's a ten-year window where women are forced to choose between "Do I bet on myself creatively?" and "Do I bet on the fact that I can make money and have a family?"'

And in taking that gamble, the uncomfortable truth is that there's a possibility that the pram in the hallway will mean you have to change jobs. Or even industries. That you can't afford working or living the way you do now and have children at the same time. (Unless, perhaps, you can afford a full-time nanny, or your partner can stay at home full-time, or you're accepting of the fact that you won't be home that often.)

You may ultimately decide that children are not for you, not now, not at this stage of your career and your life. As for myself, I spent about thirty-three years thinking I did not want children – I wrote scathing blog posts about people who suggested I would one day change my mind. *How dare they? I detest children! I detest mothers! I detest the entire idea of it!* Sometimes we do change our minds. And there are plenty of times when we do not. And that is so, so OK. I envy those who know themselves well enough to decide with ease.

Fertility in the workplace

The decision about having children can be quite swiftly dampened by the biological capabilities of each of our bodies. From infertility, IVF treatment and the adoption process to miscarriage and ectopic pregnancies – there are many, many different ways that the decision and the actual journey to parenting can impact both your mental and physical health. It's actually shocking to me that most workplaces don't talk about these issues more. Personally, I've never heard an HR representative or 'people officer' address or even speak of a staff member coping with fertility issues. As I mentioned at the start of this chapter, if we decide and are actively trying to have children, this doesn't just impact us at home. Women discover they're having a miscarriage while in the loos at work. We take fistfuls of medication and vitamins with our lunches. We urinate on ovulation test kits and pregnancy test sticks between Zoom calls. We update our various fertility and menstruation apps discreetly at our desks. We have to come up with reasons for needing multiple doctor's appointments in a one-week space without making it obvious to our managers and colleagues, 'Hey! I'm trying to get pregnant and it's not going to plan and I'm devastated!'

And when it comes to the more painful side of fertility issues, one woman I spoke with pointed out that most HR systems don't even know how to categorize the time off one might take for pregnancy loss – it can damage you both mentally and physically, so is it sick leave, compassionate leave or what? It's not just one box that can be ticked.

Lily, a thirty-three-year-old based in Cornwall, shared with me her experience of having two miscarriages. She told me how she found solace and comfort online, specifically on the Miscarriage Association UK's (MAUK) Facebook group, where she found many people were discussing their concerns about dealing with their miscarriages and work.[26] One had had a miscarriage just after starting a new job; another in the same position worked in an NHS maternity ward and was looking for advice on how to cope with this particularly unfortunate set of circumstances. In both cases it was clear that the way to handle these conversations with colleagues and employers is anything but easy.

Miscarriage is one of the most common kinds of pregnancy loss, and affects around one in four pregnancies, according to MAUK.[27] The idea that so many people are suffering through this at work, in offices where people are no doubt unintentionally saying the wrong thing or handling it in insensitive ways, is so upsetting.

'The reality is that the physical side of miscarriage can be incredibly long, and difficult, and drawn out,' Lily tells me. 'Thank goodness I was working from home most of the time, because I was basically bleeding for two months and it was horrendous, a lot of pain. I had infections, I had to go to the GP a lot – and if I couldn't do that, if I had to go into the office every day, that would have been really difficult.' She says that while everyone has a completely different experience of miscarriage, some of it is 'insanely traumatic', that there are so many facets to it and that people need to start speaking about it more in the workplace.

On World Fertility Day in 2019, while I was writing this book, LinkedIn encouraged people to share stories of their own fertility struggles at work[28] (the hashtag #FertilityAt-Work if you'd like to search for it) – and it was the first time I'd actually seen people openly talking about such things, especially on a platform like LinkedIn. But how and if people do choose to speak with their employers about their fertility issues is, of course, up to them, and will be different from person to person. I think, overall, if we don't start pushing ourselves to talk about these things more openly, a shift won't ever occur. Much like how the conversations around Mental Health have seen a dramatic change over the last five years, I hope that fertility, and particularly fertility in the workplace, is given much more attention, and is addressed properly by organizations.

How to talk about it

If you're looking for a simple yet direct and transparent example of how to go about this, you might want to do something similar to what Lily did. Lily explained to me how she learned to deal with her colleagues, and even other pregnant colleagues, when she went through her miscarriages. She said that she chose to tell her immediate manager what happened, and asked her to share it with the rest of the management team she was part of so that she didn't have to have individual conversations with several people. She also spoke directly with her team, many of whom were quite young, and it was likely that they hadn't experienced anything like this before – especially the younger men on her team.

She also did two things that she found helped a great deal.

One, she sent her colleagues a PDF flier from MAUK

specifically written for employers about what she was going through,[29] and answered many of the questions they had, and also included a gentle reminder of what their legal obligations were to her during this time.

And two, she also sent various colleagues a link to a podcast from journalist Mona Chalabi about the data and silence around miscarriage – so that they could learn a bit more about what she was going through, in a medium that might be better suited to their learning.[30] Overall, Lily's approach was direct and honest: 'I just said to them, "Look, this happened, I'm quite unwell, but I'm getting better, but here's some advice if you don't know anything about it." I also said to most people, "I don't really want to talk about it, but these are some tips on things to say and what not to say." '

Another woman I spoke with, Jayne, had three miscarriages before giving birth to a healthy baby boy in 2018. Jayne and her husband both knew they wanted children for a long time, and started trying soon after they got married four years earlier. 'The first one was a shock,' she told me. 'It was the middle of the working day, I didn't really know what was happening, and you only realize post-giving birth – nobody tells you this stuff for a very good reason, because it scares the bejesus out of you, and you wouldn't do it if you knew, because it's fucking terrifying.'

Jayne says that she told her boss – mainly because she knew her manager was also going through fertility issues – after her second miscarriage. She said the hardest thing was, like Lily, managing a team of younger people who had no idea or experience of what she was going through. She told me about how, after miscarrying the third time, on her first day back in the office she got up on stage and spoke at an event that she hadn't even had a proper brief for. 'Because [my previous job] was public-facing, you're always having to wear a certain face.

It was also a very open-plan office, I had nowhere to cry some-times, so I just couldn't. I had all of these people that were looking to me. That's one of the hardest things about being a boss. There just wasn't that space to process.'

Putting on a brave face and speaking to colleagues, or choosing not to, because of your position in a company or because your office culture doesn't make it feel safe to do so – all of it is so hard.

Miscarriage and fertility issues can be absolutely devastat-ing, as well as isolating if you don't know anyone else who has had one, or if you're not feeling ready to talk to your friends or family about it. I've listed numerous resources recommended to me by people like Lily and Jayne in the back of this book. If this is something you're currently going through, I am so, so sorry.

What might parenthood look like for you?

While I can't tell you what to decide, and while I might not have the magic solution to simultaneously being an amazing parent and smashing the crap out of your career, what I per-sonally feel more confident about is that it's not impossible. The odds are against working parents. The infrastructures that exist in most countries are nowhere near good enough – which makes fucking off to Denmark to set up a new life in the suburbs of Copenhagen look rather attractive. However, from the stories of the women in this chapter, I feel we still have options. Not as many as we'd like, but they're still there.

Some good starting points for being a working parent with-out losing your mind:

- Being open with your employer about what your specific needs and expectations are as a working parent – or even with your clients.
- Doing a thorough read-through of your company's parental leave policies, and checking on your government's website what you're legally entitled to.
- If you need a more flexible working schedule and your current employer is against it, this might now be a deal-breaker for you in your current role. I know it's daunting to switch jobs, but there are more progressive companies out there that do offer flexible or remote working, and job shares. (Again, not nearly enough, but they do exist.)
- Have you considered self-employment or going freelance? Would this provide you with the flexibility you need?
- Being open with your co-parent or partner about the mental load you're carrying, and asking for help when you need it.
- If you don't have a co-parent, the infrastructure you exist in is of the utmost importance: being clear with your childcare providers and your employer is probably more important than ever. I hope that your friends and family are able to give you that extra support you need.
- If you're struggling with fertility issues at work, providing you're in a non-toxic environment or have a supportive manager, you might want to take Lily and Jayne's advice on how to handle and initiate those conversations. You don't need the added stress of covering up what's really going on.
- If you're struggling to decide, the most helpful thing I've found has been to just talk and consume as many

stories from women from as many different walks of life as possible, from podcasts to memoirs to documentaries and reality shows like *Emma Willis Delivering Babies*. If you're lacking in parenting role models or seeing pregnant women who look like you in positions of power, or you find the versions of motherhood you see on Instagram too daunting, then you might need to create your own version of what parenthood and this new chapter of your career could look like for *you*, in your own life.

I am also fully aware that, if I do end up having children, I might need to retract this entire chapter and write a completely different book. Regardless, here's to all of the working parents, prospective or otherwise, who, like me, want it all, know it's probably impossible, and are still trying anyway – whatever the circumstances.

9

Misfortune ✛ Failure:
When You Lose Your Fucking Job

Quitting a job can be liberating. It's a choice you've made, you're in control, and you probably have an exciting new opportunity waiting for you on the other side of your notice period. It can feel like the ultimate mic drop.

But involuntarily losing your job is the exact opposite. It feels out of control, like you're Alice in Wonderland – shrinking, small, insignificant – and your problems, your bills, your responsibilities are now bigger, scarier and stronger than ever. When you suddenly lose your job, your way of life, your identity, your norm and your routines all turn upside down, like viewing your life through a funhouse mirror. It's a rollercoaster of emotions, filled with odd pairings of conflicting feelings, like shame and excitement, anger and gratitude, even shock and relief.

Losing one's job, for whatever reason, is something that people usually talk about only after the fact. Years down the line. Like how most people will discuss mental health problems or depression, 'This happened, this is how I felt, this is how I addressed it, and now I'm the happiest I've ever been!' Simple. As if maintaining one's mental health is a one-off. It's not usually a struggle that's shared in real time, or that we see the messy parts of. Because it is exactly that . . . messy.

The good news is that losing your job does usually (almost always, in fact) end up being OK. But the road to the OK part is difficult; it can feel lonely, and kinda sad. It can be essentially daunting if you've lost your job in a financial crisis or in a global pandemic. It can feel very much not OK by any means when there are people all around you losing their jobs, and record unemployment figures filling the headlines. But the road to being OK is the most crucial part of the journey, no matter how unglamorous and scary it might feel.

This chapter is about the messy bits – the confusion, the anger, the grief – and how people, including myself, have got through it, and how you can (and will), too!

Redundancy vs being fired vs being furloughed

The terminology used for losing your job can get confusing, but it's important to realize that 'being made redundant' and 'being fired' are not the same thing. And until the spring of 2020, 'furloughed' wasn't a word that you heard very often, if at all.

Being made redundant means that your position, your job role, is no longer available at the company – this is commonly due to a restructure, a change in budget or the 'downsizing' of a company or department. Ultimately, it means a reduction of staff.

Being fired is when your employment has been terminated, and you've been dismissed. This can be due to performance issues, as part of disciplinary action, or if you've committed gross misconduct.

The definition of 'furlough' is technically 'leave of absence', and traditionally means a mandatory yet temporary layoff from work until you can return to your job. When you've been furloughed, you usually retain your company benefits, but aren't obliged to do any work for the company as you're not being paid. The word was generally used pretty sparingly, and pre-2020 it was only ever heard on the news during the occasional US government shutdown, but thanks to the coronavirus pandemic it has entered our everyday lexicon. The UK government introduced a job retention scheme, in which companies could furlough employees and the government would cover a percentage of the wages of the employees affected. In the early part of the pandemic, it was reported that nearly a quarter of British employees were furloughed in a fortnight, with HMRC claiming nearly 6.3 million people had been temporarily laid off by over 800,000 companies.[1]

Being furloughed, fired or made redundant are entirely separate events that occur in entirely different circumstances. Administratively, they're all handled differently as well. But the results, the financial impact, and the feelings they arouse are all very similar.

What I did after losing my job

On each of the four occasions I've lost a job – two redundancies, one company collapse, and one painful process of being managed out until I quit – I have been kicked into a new phase of my career. Despite how unlucky I may have been, it's always worked out. While extremely painful, I've found the redundancies to be amongst the most defining moments of my career. They've forced me out of whatever comfortable zone I was in and dumped me into the cold unknown. One time, it made me start my own online magazine, which transformed the next four and a half years of my life. The next time it happened, I did a panic search on the job board section of websites and companies I liked – and, lo, I applied for a job at *BuzzFeed* just months after they launched in the UK, and became their seventh employee (I followed up my application with a Twitter DM by sending them a ridiculous GIF that said 'let me love you'). And the most recent time I lost my job led to an idea for a book and, well, reader, you're reading it.

I was working at *The Pool* as its new editor-in-chief for only four months before the company collapsed. When I joined, things were a bit confusing and felt very unsettled, but I thought we were just in a rough patch, and going through a transition. I thought that once we'd got certain job roles settled, once we had our new CEO established, our sales pipeline sorted and our accountant appointed, 2019 would be our year, like we kept telling everyone it would be. Like I had been told it would be.

Instead, I got cracked open and laid bare. I found out about the immense amount of debt *The Pool* was in on the same day I had a tooth extracted and a titanium screw drilled into my skull. The next day I had to field queries from overcurious journalists and also help our temporary CEO put together an emergency financial plan that might save us – all with bloody stitches hanging out of my mouth and a cracking headache. There was so much anger, vitriol and upset being played out on social media, as so many people were owed money and explanations, and I felt very alone in trying to find the best way to respond – particularly because I didn't have the answers they were so desperate to hear.

After months of uncertainty and chaos, my employment at *The Pool* technically ended in March, with the arrival of an unceremonious letter saying that the company was insolvent and could no longer pay me. Which I kinda figured, considering myself and my colleagues hadn't been paid since the previous December. (The number of suppliers and freelance journalists who hadn't been paid, since even before December, made for a much longer list.)

Losing my dream job in such a horrid, public way was agonizingly painful. But it meant that I developed resilience I wouldn't have had otherwise. Despite being faced with people's (understandable) outrage and accusations, and being bombarded with a barrage of questions I couldn't answer, I avoided having a big public breakdown and kept calm. I didn't curse the names of those who hired me. I didn't have a spectacular Twitter meltdown. I didn't want to turn myself inside out because of some stupid decisions other people had made or because of a run of bad luck. I grieved and raged a bit in private, slowly, in little chunks, over a few months.

I felt a mixture of emotions – anger, heartbreak, confusion, grief. I knew I wasn't a failure, or the reason for the company shutting down, but ultimately, it was the shame I felt about losing my job and the risk I was suddenly forced to navigate that were the hardest to deal with. First and foremost, when you lose your job, you have to process the feelings of hurt and shame before you can do anything else.

Confronting the downside

There's no running from the fact that, whether you've been fired or made redundant, no matter how you lose your job, it can make you feel like you've failed. Really, truly, you haven't, but it can still absolutely fuck things up.

Fiona O'Grady, thirty-two, was 'stuck in a life and job rut' and moved countries to London for a fresh opportunity that seemed full of promise and potential. She even paid for her own relocation. When she started her new job, however, the direction of her role was unclear, and no matter how many times she asked for specific instructions, or a clear brief to work from, she was ignored. The company even made her feel bad for expecting them to provide her with a laptop. While on holiday, she received a text from the founder of the company asking to catch up when she returned, which she says immediately set off alarm bells. On her first day back, her manager spent the entire day ignoring her and then, as they were leaving, asked her to walk with him to his car so they could catch up:

> We stood outside the office, which is situated above a busy venue on a street which was full of commuters. My boss then turned to me and said, 'This isn't working; you aren't a lead singer. We and the partners don't think you have what it takes for this role. I'm so sad I will lose you as a friend.' All of this was standing outside on the street. After this, the conversation ended abruptly as the founder had to go to his car, so I had to go back upstairs to collect my things as I hadn't known I would get fired while going downstairs for a catch-up.

Fired on the street!

Not all firings are the same, nor do they always have the same impact. But for some, like Fiona, it can have a huge effect: 'Beforehand, I was very confident of my abilities. Afterwards, I was completely knocked out and felt symptoms of depression. This happened over a year and a half ago and I'm still working through this traumatic incident.'

The words I heard a lot when talking to women about being fired were 'ashamed', 'mortified', 'shocked'. These were then almost always followed by 'anxiety', 'depression' and/or 'trauma'.

Shame is a common consequence of being fired, and Stephanie Brown, author of *Fired: Why Losing Your Job is the Best Thing That Can Happen to You*, says she experienced it both times she was fired, 'I was surprised how ashamed I felt. In both scenarios of being fired, I did nothing wrong. The company wasn't the right fit and it was ultimately the best result for me to be let go. But I was embarrassed and ashamed.'

Alexandra Haddow, a comedian and writer who was once fired from a marketing agency says, 'Don't let it define you. I wasn't bad at the job I was fired from across the board, but in that workplace and at that time it wasn't for me. Being fired doesn't always mean you're shit, just that you might not be the right fit.' Doesn't that just sound like a beautiful couplet for the fired?

> *Being fired doesn't always mean you're shit*
> *Just that you might not be the right fit.*

Somebody embroider this on a pillow!

As well as shame, job loss introduces an element of risk that many have never experienced before. It's always inconvenient to lose your job, but some times are certainly better than others. I was once made redundant only weeks after securing a mortgage (by the skin of my teeth, might I add), and the realization that I might not be able to afford the payments, when I'd had to fight so hard to even be offered the mortgage in the first place, felt like the sky falling in. A sky that was covered in shit. And also on fire.

Personally, it's been the high level of risk I've had to endure and even embrace since losing my job at *The Pool* that's been the hardest for me to adjust to. And the shame of losing your job can easily make you want to crawl into a hole and never emerge.

It can also make you forget who you are.

You are more than a job title

One of the hardest parts of losing your job can be the loss of your identity. Whether it be your career as a whole, your job title or perhaps the company you work for, your job can create or make up part of your personal identity – for some people the proportion is greater than for others. Sometimes, it's far too great.

I'll never forget a scene from *Sex and the City* when Carrie and Miranda get in a fight about her moving to Paris, and quitting her job as a columnist:

Miranda: Carrie, you can't quit your column. It's who you are.

Carrie: No, it's not who I am, it's what I do. That's my column.

When I first saw this, I was twenty, and desperate to be a writer. The fact that Carrie would quit her sweet gig as a columnist and declare *that wasn't who she was, it was just what she did* didn't sit right with me. Now, almost fifteen years later, I understand. It's a job, not who she is.

Similarly, if you were with a big brand or a cool company that everyone loved to hear about when you mentioned you worked there – when you lose that, a job that is so associated with *you*, that takes up so much of *you*, it can be difficult to cope with.

Keira is thirty-five and lives in London. I spoke with her about what it felt like to be made redundant from the large tech company she worked at for over five years. She adored her job and worked for a brand that made people light up when they found out where she worked. She was an extremely dedicated employee and lived and breathed the brand she worked for, so much so that she regularly gave talks about the company, and why she was proud to work there.

'I was quite happy to give up parts of myself to be part of that. I was happy for that to be one of the main characteristics of my life,' Keira told me. 'But, on top of that, you just give them all your time, don't you? Because, really, that's what everybody gives to a full-time job, particularly one that's traditional working-hours based – you give them your best hours of your best days of the best years of your life, right?'

When Keira said this, it stunned me. This is precisely what we do. We dedicate our time and our attention, from some of the best years of our life. When we're young and mobile and healthy . . . we spend our days sitting in their open-plan offices, grateful to have free snacks and a loo with a bit of privacy. We give so much of ourselves to our work that I think, ultimately, we also lose a lot of ourselves if our job disappears. Which is exactly what happened when Keira was made redundant.

She went through a real crisis of identity: if she didn't tell people that she worked for X company, then who was she? 'I had been there four years, so, what do I do if I don't work here? What am I? Who am I? What are my characteristics? What do I tell people that I do? And this is very rooted in how we talk to each other as millennial people in London, we talk about our jobs. We don't say. "What do you do when you're not at work?" or, "What do you love?" '

When I was no longer able to say, 'I work at Google,' or, 'I'm the editor of *The Pool*,' I struggled badly trying to answer the 'And what do you do?' question. Because without a fancy title, people don't know how to be with you, how to rank you, or how seriously they should take you. If you're a writer, they only care if you write for a publication they're familiar with. If you say you're an author but they don't recognize your publisher or the title of your book, they're unimpressed. *Oh you write non-fiction? I only read wartime novels.*

Keira's story is one of loss, and the loss of identity is something that can pose great difficulty for those who lose their jobs. She also raises the interesting point of how millennials in particular are intensely focused on work, and how it defines them, and shapes how they relate to other people.

I suppose job loss creates a not exactly conscious uncoupling of your job title and identity, but it's what we choose to do with that separation that counts. What do we do with this opportunity, this pause in our work life, this shift in our identity?

This is where the clichéd advice 'don't put all your eggs in one basket' makes sense. If all your friends are at work, and if so much of who you are and what you are is tied up under the name of a company or brand, it sounds to me that too much of your life and identity is attached to something that is both impermanent and completely out of your control. Even worse if you've founded a company and it's taking up nearly all of your time – you're going to have your work cut out to avoid making that your entire identity. Even if it doesn't feel like it now, such identification is temporary. Even if it lasts for years, they're still temporary. They will flux and shift, die or reject you. And even if they don't, you'll have to retire one day.

That said, I don't actually think your profession, or your craft or your expertise should necessarily be entirely separate from your identity. For example, I am 'A writer'. But, I *used* to be 'Managing Editor of *BuzzFeed*'. Before that, Cate Sevilla was 'Founder and Editor of *BitchBuzz*'. The trouble was, she also thought that was *all* she was.

250

My best advice, and, I think, the only practical thing we can do for this (besides, of course, loads of therapy), is to try to think of yourself as an expert who is lending their services to a company, in exchange for money, for an extended period of time. You are not 'a Googler'. Not really. That's not a thing. You're *you*, and you happen to be working there.

That way, when that place eventually rips your heart out in some way, shape or form, you'll at least know who you are.

Keira learned a valuable lesson the evening after she was made redundant. Her friends took her to a 'wanky as fuck' food event in Soho, where she had 'one of the magic London nights' with her husband and her friends. She said she ran into people she hadn't seen in years, and was reminded of what a cool life she had, and why she'd moved to London to begin with. 'I feel like I met my real life again,' she said. She has a poster from the event hanging on the wall in her living room as a reminder. *This is your real life.*

Entering recovery mode

Recovering from being fired, or indeed being made redundant, is very much like recovering from a loss. It's grief, and it's a process. The losses and the challenges that many of us have faced as a result of losing our job are quite serious. For example, discovering you're pregnant on the same day that you've found out you're being made redundant sounds like an anxiety dream, but things like this do happen. And it's about the action that we take in spite of those emotions.

Stephanie Brown says that, while the reasonings behind firings and redundancies are different, the feelings that you're left with are the same, so there's no reason why recovering from either of them should be different:

Essentially, it's all the same. Losing your job can be similar to a grief process. If you have been 'wronged' in some way by your employer, this might be harder to handle than being made redundant as part of the process, but in the grand scheme, I don't believe there is much difference in the way it makes you feel. I have coached people who have chosen to leave a job they didn't like, struggled to find a new job and have ended up going through the same mental process as being fired or redundancy. Job loss is tough, no matter what form it takes.

She also has some helpful advice about how to approach the free time you have on your unexpected gardening leave or unemployment. Stephanie says that mindset is key when you're unemployed: 'If you believe this is a positive situation and an opportunity to grow and learn, then it will be. If you see it as negative and the worst thing that could have happened to you, this will also be true.'

She says that if you suddenly find yourself at home you should:

- keep a structure or daily routine,
- plan your days out,
- not sleep in every day.

Even if you're planning a three-hour Netflix session, she says that you should still want to keep structure to your life, 'During my unemployment, I still got up every day at 6 a.m. and went to the gym. This was important. It's a subconscious way of saying "This is my life and I'm in charge."' Although I entirely agree with Stephanie's approach to mindset and daily structure, it should be noted that if you suddenly find yourself furloughed during a national crisis, the guidance on your approach to recovery will be a bit different. Your feelings about what's happening to you personally will be either intensified or dwarfed by what's going on in the wider world. It can make things more difficult when your job loss is symptomatic of some cataclysmic event, and it's completely understandable if it takes longer than your average redundancy might to process your feelings.

Regardless of the exact circumstances surrounding your job loss, another helpful piece of advice from Fiona O'Grady is a reminder to actually let people help you, and remember that you don't have to go through all this on your own: 'It's easy to get trapped in a shame spiral about this kind of thing but actually, it isn't your fault. I found some true friends through these experiences. If you have the option and financial means, invest in therapy. I waited too long to go to a therapist, for a multitude of different reasons.'

For some of us, going to the gym at 6 a.m. (er, or at all) isn't an option – particularly as paying gym fees might not be financially viable for you after losing your job. And therapy might also not be an option for you, depending on NHS waiting times and whether or not you can afford it. It also might seem too daunting for you at this point in time. And that's OK.

Inspired by my own experience and by the women I have spoken to, here are a few things you can do to start recovering from the shock of losing your job – regardless of whether you have a gym or a therapist:

- Podcasts are your friend – they don't need to be self-help podcasts or career-focused podcasts, either. Listen to stuff that will make you laugh, if that's what you feel like doing. Without the company of my colleagues on a daily basis and suddenly being at home, I found podcasts helped curb some of the loneliness I was experiencing.

- Consume whatever you feel like – and whatever you can afford. Whether it's Netflix marathons, stuffed-crust pizza, romance novels from the local charity shop or your favourite films, whatever you need to bring you comfort, do it. For me, it was countless episodes of *The Good Place* and *The OA* (sidenote: *The OA* is so, so incredible and its star and co-writer, Brit Marling, is a genius, it's a perfect show to get lost in).
- Put it into words, even if it hurts – this might be through journalling or talking to your best friend, but either way, give what you're going through some language. This is hard and uncomfortable, but you have to release and process your feelings, not just keep them in.
- Put your energy into small acts of self-care – don't just lie on the sofa with all those negative thoughts running through your head; get moving and doing, with whatever your physical mobility will allow. This could be going for a walk, following free yoga videos on YouTube or taking a long bubble bath. Be good to yourself rather than beating yourself up.

Most importantly, while you're in this phase of recovery, do not just apply for the first available position you see on LinkedIn and rush into a new job out of panic or fear. Stephanie Brown has a brilliant blog post about this on her website 'Life After Fired',[2] but she says that in addition to just rushing into a new role, not letting go of what happened or their feelings towards their previous employer is the other big mistake people make after losing their job. Instead, she says:

Let it go. Walk away with your head held high. Holding on to anger or resentment will hurt you more than them. The truth is, once you walk out the door, they will forget about you. And you should do the same with them. Move forward, don't look back. Hanging on to anger and resentment will not serve you and will only make the process of moving on harder. Even if you have close friends from your previous job, try not to meet up with them until you have moved on. Listening to their office politics and moaning will not help set you free of this situation.

There's also no set amount of time that you should give yourself to recover; we're all different. Chances are, you will need to get back to work and start earning at some point, but so much depends on your personal situation – whether or not you have a notice period, or a severance package, or gardening leave. Or whether or not you're getting any future payments or if you've been left in the (financial) dust. I don't want to shame anyone's recovery by saying, 'You have x days to mourn and then BACK TO WORK!' but I'd generally say to give yourself at least a couple of weeks, if you can, to grieve, to move slowly, and to process.

Lily from Cornwall had been working for a global publishing company that had recently gone through a restructure: 'The morning I found out I was being made redundant, I did a pregnancy test and it was positive. And it was just like, what are the chances?' If, like Lily, time isn't exactly on your side, or if you feel like the only way you'll ever be on the road to recovery is having some sense of a future plan, there are a few things you can do. Lily says that after she had a few days of crying and confusion, she spent 'a day of looking at the budget' and then another day of 'mad hustling, meeting as many people as possible, arranging applications for jobs, brushing up my CV'. She says she felt much calmer after making things happen, and this might be the case for you too. But note that even Lily took a few days just to sit with her feelings and to let it all out.

Basically, you don't have to do any heavy lifting at this point. Rest, and when you feel that kindling of 'OK, what's next?' or a flicker of hope for the future, that's when you can start getting to work on getting to work. (See what I did there?)

You might think, while suddenly sitting at home in the middle of the day instead of jostling for an overpriced sandwich at any given café chain, that this is just your life now. You're tarnished. You'll never work again. But, you will. You just need a bit of time and some headspace to recover.

The one thing you don't want to get caught up in is comparing your pain to that of others, or yourself to the people at your company who haven't lost their jobs. It's a slippery slope – and seeing as you've already landed flat on your ass, why torture yourself with the comparison game? Unfortunately, it's hard for some to resist.

Finding the upside

In my conversations with Keira, she brought up a very interesting point about when you're one of a large number of people who have been made redundant. She says that once you move past the initial shock and worry of whether you can survive, you then start to realize the privileged position you are in compared with some who are in the same boat.

She said that she started to feel inordinately guilty because some of her colleagues weren't just losing jobs but also work visas, or their entire family's main source of income. 'Some of the people in my team who lost their jobs were also living overseas in undeveloped markets,' she explained, 'so for them, a job at the company I was working for was so incredibly lucrative, and actually not replicable in their home markets.'

In addition to privilege, and the differences between markets, there's another beast to contend with: comparison.

When whole departments or teams or, in extreme circumstances, even a firm's entire staff lose their jobs you'll inevitably start to hear comments like, 'Good job she has a husband in work,' or, 'Well, at least you don't have any kids.' I've heard from women without partners who were furious that they were facing the prospect of moving back to live with their parents as opposed to their more fortunate colleagues who did have romantic partners, or perhaps owned their own home. Not only does this completely ignore the privilege that comes with having a family that can take you in, if needed, but it also just assumes that if someone has a partner or a husband that they'll automatically be fine. As the sharp rise in calls to domestic-abuse help lines showed us during the 2020 lockdown, just because someone is living with their partner or able to be with their family during a time of financial downturn does not mean that their situation is a safe or secure one.[3]

Yes, there are some people who will be less financially affected than others. Those who have savings, wealthy parents, who don't pay rent, etc., will be less financially burdened than those who are unattached, or are single parents, or can't afford to save, or don't have any nearby family to move in with. But, when it comes to redundancies and people losing their jobs, this is a dicey if not completely insensitive game to play. When many people are experiencing a loss, particularly one with massive financial implications, it's easy to try to be the most hard done by. The *most* hurt. The *most* affected. But this helps no one, and you end up looking like an unempathetic twat.

One of the most unexpected side-effects I had to deal with

during the closure of *The Pool* was observing a weird sort of Tragedy Olympics taking place on social media – who was owed the most money? Who was the most upset? The most angry? Who had been most royally fucked over? Who was the saddest? Who had been the most affected? Who wrote the hottest of the hot takes? Who thought they knew the *real* story? It was exhausting. It was exhausting for not only a single department to have closed, but an entire business, leaving staff, freelancers and suppliers (and plenty of people who weren't talking about it on social media) all without months and months of payments. It was so odd to witness this weird situation play itself out in public, where people seemed to be competing to be the biggest loser. There was also plenty of schadenfreude and a fair amount of gleeful, ghoulish gossip happening across different Facebook and WhatsApp groups for a while, which only added to the fun. I've seen the screenshots; it wasn't great.

I'm not sure where the quote is from, but I once heard someone say that it doesn't matter if you're drowning in seven inches or seventy feet of water: if you're drowning, you're drowning. But without oversimplifying it – if you're suffering, if you're in pain, if you've lost your job and you're worried about money, that's very stressful. Do the finer details matter? No. Is it important to acknowledge that you benefit from a certain level of privilege that means the ramifications of your job loss may differ from those of your colleagues, especially if they live in a different country or culture? Absolutely.

Rather than elbowing your way to the front of the Suffering the Most queue, your energy would probably be better served thinking about the things in your life you could show gratitude for. Look at what you have, the abundance around you, rather than comparing the size of your loss to someone else's. What will it tell you, what do you expect to win, if you prove that your cup is more empty than your neighbours'?

What next?

A big question that so many folks have after they've been fired or have had a job go badly wrong is what they should tell potential employers who ask what happened in their last role.

Thirty-seven-year-old Director of Talent Atelier Jo Gilmour says that, when you feel like it's time to start applying for new jobs, don't worry too much about what your potential new employer might think about your chequered employment history: 'Generally people interviewing you don't mind if a role hasn't worked out so long as you show you've learned from your experiences and can be diplomatic about things. Don't attend interviews if you're feeling bitter about things as it shows.'

Stephanie Brown agrees:

Losing your job is nothing to be ashamed of. It is very commonplace in a modern workforce and therefore you don't need to shy away from explaining exactly what happened – as long as you didn't do anything unethical or illegal. Most people lose their job because the company was not a good fit for them, and I believe this is the best way to frame it. In the eight months I was job hunting in 2014, not one person – not a recruiter or a potential employer – spent more than two minutes discussing my recent job after I explained I'd left in my probationary period as it wasn't the right fit. If you do have someone probe deeper, I would reiterate that you believe it is important to be aligned to the company's values and culture so that you can deliver the best possible results for the company you work for. Turn it into a positive for your future employer.

As long as you're not still upset, angry, or resentful, being able to talk about what happened objectively in as little or as much detail as is appropriate for the conversation you're having will do just fine. If you're still annoyed, or come across as petty or bitter about your ex-employer, your potential new one will 100 per cent notice, and probably not exactly like what you're selling. This is a huge reason why not going after a new role until you feel ready and able is so important.

You can also treat this as an opportunity to do something new.

Look for the silver lining

Things may feel full-on awful right now if you've just lost your job, but once you've recovered a bit, and once you feel like, 'OK, what next?' then it's time to act. The 'next' might not necessarily have to be applying for a job like the one you just had. It might not even be a job at all.

Diana, thirty-eight, was given a quite generous payout when her company made her entire department redundant – and it's actually presenting her with a positive opportunity. She acknowledges that she was comfortable in her corporate job, and would never have considered a change of career otherwise. She says that she's trying to see her redundancy as a chance to try something new, and as a tremendous opportunity:

I'm thinking about training as a data scientist. I've done a course in my spare time to try to keep my skills going, so I might spend the money consolidating what I've taught myself and then try and change career into data science. It wasn't even around as a job when I graduated. But because I've got this opportunity of being redundant, it's given me a bit of a kick to something else. If you're going to get a bit of money,

why not do it now? But if I wasn't made redundant, I probably
would just stick to my current job because I like the corporate
perks. I like the salary even if my manager is awful and it's
difficult.

If you're in the position of being financially 'OK' and you've
lost your job, or if you've been given a payout – might I suggest
that you don't waste it? You might not be as OK in the future
as you are right now, so invest in yourself. If you have the
option to retrain, to start up your own business, or just to give
yourself a longer time to recover, do it. Take that opportunity.
No matter how painful it is in the beginning, don't let that
spoil what could be, the possibilities that have been born from
this loss.

And if you're not financially OK, and even if you know you
must start looking for a job in a few days or a week, I have to
re-emphasize here that you should at least give yourself those
few days off to recover, and to allow yourself to think about
what you want in your next role. Be kind. Be gentle. Sure, you
might not be able to afford to fuck off to a yoga retreat in Bali
for three weeks, or just decide that you're now an interior
design influencer and start selling tassels on Etsy, but there are
gentle and kind ways of looking after yourself (like the ones
suggested earlier in this chapter) that can help give you the
headspace to process what's happened.

'When I was recovering after being let go, my mother gave
me the age-old advice that "it all happens for a reason",' twenty-
nine-year-old Natalie told me. 'While I didn't believe her then,
I keep thinking that if I had never been fired, I wouldn't be
where I am today. I needed that big push to push myself. It
inspired me to start my own company and to work for myself.
I learned that I was more capable than I thought I was.'

Fiona, too, said that, after her relocation-gone-wrong, she

learned to trust her own gut instincts more and to listen to the advice from other people: 'I had been warned about my old boss, but the excitement of a change and the potentially exciting role made me not listen to my gut feelings about the high asks on me taking this role and what other people had said about him.' She said she also learned to negotiate a better deal for herself.

It is rare for someone to be ruined or fail to find another job after being fired or made redundant (unless they end up in jail for doing whatever they got fired for). And most people, no matter how painful the process, do find something else, learn from the experience and eventually end up on a much better path.

You will be OK

After I lost my job at *The Pool*, I didn't know what to do with my time.

At first there were days when all I could do was half-heartedly update my CV while watching endless hours of any TV show I could stomach. I made sure to walk my dog while listening to podcasts almost every day for around ninety minutes, no matter the weather. Then I gave myself time to reflect on what exactly I wanted from my new job, something I had never done before.

In the midst of recovering from all that happened, I also decided not to get another full-time job. I made my first professional website and took on editorial consultancy gigs. I decided that I wanted to write a book that would help people navigate the shitstorm I was going through. I found a literary agent, I put together a book proposal and I got a lot of rejections until, finally, I landed a book deal.

But there hasn't been a magic moment, a magic gig, a magic opportunity that has turned things around for me. I've taken risks, I've asked for help, I've worked hard at finding new opportunities and I've stuck to my vision. And that's resulted in a yes here, a yes there. I focus on the yeses now.

I've shared many other women's stories here. They've been open and gracious and kind – it's a hard thing to share your story of job loss with someone, even if you can do it from behind a different name or in disguise. My advice for anyone who has lost their job is this: Give yourself time. Give yourself space. Cry, rage, grieve. Walk your dog. Listen to a podcast. And then make a plan. Hire an accountant or master some scary spreadsheets yourself.

You are not alone – you just lost your fucking job.

You can absolutely figure this out, and you will.

10

Red Flags +
Gut Instincts:

How to avoid a nightmare job

Deciding to quit your job and to start actively looking for a new one, or to accept an offer from a new company, is one of the biggest decisions you'll make in your life. It's a nerve-wracking time, and one that's not always straightforward. The entire process of 'finding a new job' is laden with confusion and myths based on what a career counsellor or our parents once told us. It's a challenge that no amount of inspirational, pastel-coloured quotes on Instagram can help conquer.

This chapter will help steer you in the right direction when you're looking for a new job, so that you are armed with as much information as possible and don't end up with the kinds of managers and colleagues and working situations we tackled in the first two chapters.

You'll find a ton of advice for what to do when you're

interviewing for a new position – what questions to ask, things to look out for, how to achieve the salary you want – as well as a bit of advice on how to tell when it's time to quit your current one for pastures new. I've spoken with highly experienced recruitment specialists, HR managers, cracking people managers (they exist!) as well as many other women who have had varied and interesting working experiences to compile the best advice possible – all in an effort to help prevent you from taking the wrong job, selling yourself short, and getting into one of those classic 'if only I had known then what I know now' scenarios.

Personally, I've found myself in some astounding situations over the years, and I've made some really, er, interesting job choices that ended up being pretty painful. It's important to note that they weren't necessarily the *wrong* choices, but if I had known the right questions to ask from the beginning, I would have been much better prepared for the working environments I found myself in.

Despite the turmoil I've experienced (and the subsequent complaints I've made as a result), I wouldn't change any of it, no matter how painful or detrimental to my mental health or bank account some of these situations were. My only regret is that I didn't listen to my gut instincts more often, that I treated companies and management like untouchable gods and walked on eggshells in the name of being good, ignoring giant red flags because I wanted each job, each manager and each company I worked for to be my ideal situation. My dream job. I wanted them all to live up to the expectations and high hopes that I had, the fantasy I had constructed in my head, and so I didn't stand up for myself. I didn't ask uncomfortable questions. I didn't make waves for fear it would rock my THIS IS MY DREAM JOB AND EVERYTHING IS FINE boat.

The consequences of not doing this due diligence can range from 'Oh, this is a bit shit but I can live with it' to poverty and unemployment when the company goes down in a fiery blaze and you miss out on months of salary, as I and my colleagues at *The Pool* know to our cost. So, trust me when I say these red flags are important.

But you, dear reader, can learn from my mistakes, and the mistakes of the other women who have kindly added their voices and their experiences to this chapter.

Of course, it's important to note that when the economy is recovering from a global recession, the job market does change. When millions of people are suddenly out of work, it can be extremely daunting. Rather than focusing on the statistics of how many people are unemployed, how many jobs are available, or all of the other what-ifs that surround times of uncertainty – focus on you. Focus on what you want from your job. Then, take it a step at a time, and know that when the economy isn't exactly booming, such a focus becomes even more crucial. Have a clear understanding of the aspects of a role that you will – and won't – compromise on – and most importantly, identify the value you're hoping to gain from that role. Is it flexibility you're after? The skills you'll learn on the job? Or is the value in the literal monetary reward you'll receive? Knowing your 'bottom line' in a tough job market will help keep you focused and make informed decisions about your next career move.

Courting a new company

Whether you're working with a recruitment company, have been head-hunted or are scouting for new roles on your own – at one point, you will have to undergo an interview (or an 'informal chat', which is an interview held in an uncomfortable café with a coffee you're too nervous to drink), and you'll be asked 'So, do you have any questions for me?'

Now, to be clear, this chapter isn't about how to be brilliant in interviews – you can find guidance in the Resources section – but rather, how to make sure this company is the right one for you. Because the key thing to remember is that, although they are interviewing you, YOU ARE INTERVIEWING THEM AS WELL.

The recruitment process is a two-way street. Even if you aren't being head-hunted. Even if you feel like you're just lucky to be in the room. Even if this company is THE company you want to work for, and this job is THE job you want more than anything. You are interviewing them to find out if this is the best role and the best company for you to be working for at this point in your career – regardless of your excited assumptions.

This means you have to breathe, and put aside that version of you that is freaking out that you're in the building of the place you want to work at more than anywhere else. You do not take a selfie in the lobby. You act calmly, as though you have been in this building a thousand times before. You channel US soccer star Megan Rapinoe and whisper to yourself confidently, 'I deserve this.'[1] Because you do; you deserve this opportunity. The question is, do they deserve you?

In your interview, hold on to that big Rapinoe energy. Even if you desperately need that job, even if you're afraid you might vomit from nerves, you must continue to breathe, and continue to pretend that you're currently perfectly confident and content in your current role – even if you have actually just been laid off and are currently spending your days panic-crying while looking at LinkedIn in your sweatpants. They don't need to know that! You're confident and comfortable in your ability to do the job they're interviewing you for; now you just need to find out whether this place is the smartest, best move for you.

Will you flourish here? Can you develop your career here?

And crucially – does this move fit with what you want next? Because knowing what you want from your next move is so, so important when choosing a role – even if a big reason you're currently job hunting is because you just need some money to pay your damn bills.

Before you start your interview, think about exactly what you are looking for from the job. Is it . . .

- A role and company where you can grow and develop your career, and hopefully stay for the next three to five years?
- A role that will help prepare you for a very specific career milestone, such as founding your own company or becoming an executive director?
- A role you're not overly jazzed about but a stepping-stone appointment that will look good on your CV, even if you just stay a year, and so provide you with an opportunity to get the job you actually want?
- A stop-gap role where you can quickly learn a new skill and stay for a short period of time?
- An OK job but most importantly an opportunity to earn significantly more money or benefits (such as a generous maternity leave package)?
- A lower-level role that serves as a portal into a new industry or career?
- A role in which you are allowed to express your creativity in your area of expertise, and don't have to worry about managing anyone or having a ton of responsibility?
- A job that will pay your bills and nothing else? That's OK – but you just need to be honest with yourself about what you want and what you expect from a job that is just helping you stay in the black.

Knowing what you want from your next role will heavily influence the questions you ask, and the things you should be on the lookout for.

I asked Heist Studios' Cheryl Fergusson about the importance of asking the right questions in an interview, and the things to pay attention to in these conversations. She says, 'First of all, does it feel like a two way process? Because it's a good insight into what it then feels like to work there.'

Cheryl gave a brilliant list of some key questions to ask in your interviews which she says will go a long way towards revealing what the company will be like to work for.

- How do they map career pathways in their organizations?
- How do they succession plan?
- How do they work out and assess who is performing in their organization? And then how do they help them flourish and take them to the next level?
- How long do people usually stay in the organization?
- How long does it take for someone to move up a level?
- What is the overall management structure?

'That can be quite insightful,' she says. 'If it's an organization that doesn't focus on that aspect then they'll give you a generic blurb, but if it's an organization that really cares about it then you'll get an interesting answer.'

As Maddie Armitage of Dentsu Aegis Network told me:

There are questions you can ask that tease out what they're really like. 'What was your ambition when you were at this stage of your career?' 'Where did you see yourself in five years?' 'What are your main goals?' 'What are your passions?' 'What do you do in your spare time?' 'What are you looking for in a person for this role?' You know, ask lots of questions that are going to qualify how you're going to fit and how they're going to meet your needs – that's the interview process, it's a two-way street, it's not a one way. Remember, you're interviewing them, too.

Another great tip from Cheryl Fergusson is to ask to spend time with people in the organization other than just the hiring manager, or the people interviewing you:

Ask to spend some time with a representative sample of people in the organization and connect with them in a different way. Ask them to be part of the process, because at Heist, there's always like different types of people involved. We're hiring for a COO at the moment and I'm doing some 'up interviews', where people who will report into them are actually interviewing them, and it gives the candidate the opportunity to understand what all the people are like in the business and whether it's right for them, a proper 360 process.

Usually, people should be open to this '360 view', and Cheryl suggests it could be a red flag if the company isn't. However, there's also the challenge of meeting prospective team members if you currently work for a competitor, particularly if you're not even interviewing at their offices owing to the sensitivity of hiring external candidates from competitors. A few ways round this could be asking to have a breakfast or lunch meeting with some of the senior members of staff who know to keep things discreet. There's also the option of joining the team for after-work drinks or at a social event where people don't actually know you're interviewing.

I *so* wish I had known that it was OK to ask for this. Being in the office, meeting people, seeing everyone in their natural habitat, getting a feel for the office environment, sounding out how people interact – why do we leave all this for our first day? Work is a huge part of our lives; why wouldn't meeting potential colleagues, taking the temperature of the office and observing the office culture in action be part of the process? Even if you're going to be a remote employee based at home I would still ask to meet with people if possible (unless their HQ is too far away to reach easily), or at the very least, have a Zoom call or two with a few of your potential colleagues.

Root out 'deal breakers' early on

Another major benefit of asking a lot of specific questions is that 'deal breakers' won't rear their ugly heads the minute you're hired.

For example, if you're someone who has a lot of different non-work-related projects on the go, and you value having the time, energy and freedom to work on them, this is something you must consider when interviewing at a new company, particularly if the role is full-time.

Gena-mour Barrett, a twenty-seven-year-old from London, says that her independence and professional identity beyond her job title and the company she works for are of the upmost importance to her – so for Gena, a red flag would be a company putting restrictions on her own personal projects. She says that, in interviews, she always tries to ask how much she's going to be 'owned' by the company. In previous full-time jobs she's felt as though even her free time wasn't her own. She says that, now, she 'always asks what the boundaries are' so she knows whether they're going to have a problem with her freelancing or pursuing her own projects outside work.

If this type of thing is important to you, Gena is absolutely right – you have to be clear from the get-go, and ask how they feel about you attending speaking engagements, doing free-lance work for other companies, publishing poetry or being unavailable for weekend work because of other commitments – being forthright about who you are, how you spend your time, what's important to you and how that intersects with this potential new job is essential.

Along those same lines, if you have small children or will need to work flexible hours, this has to be part of your conver-sation. Helen MacBain, a thirty-eight-year-old working for a pharmaceutical company, says that for her, flexible working is a biggie: 'The obvious one for me is flexible working. If some-one says to me, "No, you have to be in the office every single day," I just think it's a massive red flag. In this day and age, why? Presenteeism?' The lockdown in the UK will have made it much harder for those companies who did have employees working from home in the pandemic to claim that it's not possible.

Helen also raises the important point of listening to your gut instincts during initial meetings and interviews. If you just don't like a person when you meet them, or if you get bad vibes from your manager-to-be – heed that feeling. Be curi-ous about how they make you feel. If it's just awkwardness, or they're kind enough but you wouldn't want to get a drink with them after work – that's fine. If they make you feel ashamed, or like they're trying to trip you up whenever you speak to them, or if the way they speak is triggering some bad feelings in you – this is no doubt what working for them will feel like.

If the interview is a nightmare, the job may be worse

The style of the interview, the way it makes you feel, the questions you are asked, all speak volumes. One of the biggest lessons I've learned with the gift of hindsight is that every successful interview process I've gone through and been hired from has perfectly reflected my subsequent experience.

Cheryl Fergusson points out that it's the style of the interview and the questions they ask you that you need to pay close attention to. She says that if it's an interview where they're putting you on the spot to see how you deal with pressure, that's exactly what they'll do to you in a job: put you under constant pressure. Is that the kind of environment you want to be in?

She also advises that if communication with you during the recruitment process has been vague or unclear, or if you're still unsure what the actual purpose of the organization is, it means that you're unlikely to receive clear direction in post, and that the company either doesn't know its mission, or doesn't know how to articulate it. Are you going to be comfortable with that level of ambiguity?

Helen Stacey, the MD and owner of Aspire Jobs, has over thirty years of experience in recruitment, and has seen all there is to see from the opposite end of the hiring spectrum. She agrees with Cheryl that a company's behaviour in the interview process accurately depicts how they are as a company overall: 'If an employer doesn't go back to a candidate who has taken the time to apply and attend interview, what does that say not only about them but also about their brand? I have had people who have attended interview directly where the interviewer has been thirty minutes late – that is disrespectful and doesn't set a good impression. Don't forget it's a candidate's marketplace at the moment with good people getting multiple job offers. If you aren't communicating with them in a timely manner they will look upon your branding unfavourably and rule you out.'

I wholeheartedly agree with what both Cheryl and Helen have said here, and it perfectly reflects the experiences I've had.

An editorial director once emailed me with an offer of a regular writing gig, and then didn't respond to my immediate reply accepting the offer and asking for next steps. I was so, so excited and then so, so worried. I couldn't imagine why he wasn't responding. Weren't they pleased to have me on board? I waited a week, followed up, and then he was like, 'Oh, sorry I totally missed your reply!' *Spoiler alert*: this company was equally chaotic and it folded a year and a half later.

On my first day at another big tech company, the team forgot I was due to start that day and I had to wait for two hours in a nearby Starbucks while they sorted out my starter kit. The first thing they did when they brought me back up to the office was to walk me into a meeting of the team senior leads and introduce me with a fancy job title I had no idea I had. *Spoiler alert*: the company undertook a massive, confusing reorganization two months later, and my entire department was made redundant.

At another company, I was interviewed by its only other female director – I was to be the second. On my first day, I noticed she wasn't there. She had left, meaning that I was now the only woman director and also the only woman in senior management, as well as being one of only three women in a company of over thirty people. *Spoiler alert*: it wasn't a female-friendly environment!

Another time, I had been verbally offered the role by the hiring manager and then ended up waiting weeks for my written offer, so I couldn't quit my current job. And the reason I wasn't being sent the offer was that the hiring manager couldn't actually get hold of the company's sole director, who was also in charge of the money and would have to sign off on my salary. He was simply having too much fun in Ibiza to reply to emails or phone in. *Spoiler alert*: this was the same guy who just stopped paying me and my staff without any notice.

But it was my experience at Google that epitomized this phenomenon.

My Google interviews: an exceptionally uncomfortable case study

The multi-stage, three-month, fourteen-interview hiring process I went through after Google approached me was, shall we say, 'interesting'. After my initial email correspondence and meeting with the recruiter who represented the team I would be working for, I had a telephone interview. This was followed up with a request to complete a task.

The task was very simple, and one that would have been better suited to a role that I had been in about three years earlier. All my conversations thus far had given the impression that the role was 'very senior', so I pointed out to the recruiter and the telephone interviewer that the task didn't reflect that. I was given many reassurances that this role was indeed senior enough for me – keeping in mind that I was then a non-executive director and shareholder at the company I was working for.

One of the most indicative (if not damning) parts of the process was a request to attend their office in London for a full day of interviews. I had to take time off of work ('Uh, I have several doctors' appointments in one day . . .') and was told I would have meetings with four people, which then quickly turned out to be six.

The round of interviews included a confusingly unfriendly session with the person who would become my manager (although I didn't know it at the time) and being sent into a meeting with a young woman who, if I got the job, would be reporting to me – which would have been (and was) fine, but neither of us had been forewarned or knew anything about the other, so it was a pretty awkward situation. I was also thrown into a last-minute video call with another team member who had zero background of who I was, why we were meeting, or what the role I was being hired for was. (Again, stressful and awkward.) I was then kicked out of the meeting room mid-conversation. (Even better!) The only good thing to emerge from this process – and no thanks to Google – was meeting someone who would later become my dear friend, and a saviour in the years I spent doing the job.

I usually leave interviews feeling confident, proud and excited. After this lot, though, I had a horrible feeling in my gut. I felt so anxious that I remember crying while sadly drinking a melted caramel Frappuccino on an overcrowded bus on my way home.

I didn't hear anything for almost two weeks, so I was convinced I hadn't got the job, and I was devastated. Finally, the recruiter called to say that, while everyone really liked me and thought I was qualified for the role, there was an HR issue because it turned out that they were hiring me on 'the wrong job ladder'. This, as ridiculous and arbitrary as it sounds, was important, because at Google you're evaluated based on the objectives and expectations set by your job ladder and job level, and when you go for a promotion, your performance is measured against that of the other people on your ladder and level. So, in order to be fair to me and my skills, they needed to move the role over to a special-content job ladder that they didn't even know existed at the time of creating the role. (Hello, bureaucracy!)

I was told that, in order to hire me, they would have to give me three more interviews alongside other candidates who were on the same job ladder as my role. 'Sure,' I said airily. 'I mean, at this point I'm an expert interviewee, what's three more?' But inside, there was lots of internal primal screaming. And a lot of panic diarrhoea.

After these three interviews were scheduled and finally finished without event, I had more phone conversations with two people I'd already spoken to at the beginning of the process. Then, after I'd received a verbal job offer, I was told what my salary package would be. That was not up for negotiation, so it wasn't a question of 'is this enough' but rather 'take it or leave it'. I was still excited about the job, and at this point, I wasn't going to argue about the salary or stay in my current role – a situation that was rapidly deteriorating.

After I accepted, I received an email a few weeks later saying that I wouldn't now be reporting to the departmental director as I had originally been told, but the person I'd had that unfriendly and awkward interview with during the first stage of the appointment procedure. I was confused and disappointed, but clearly, the decision had already been made.

Ultimately, the bad points of this whole process were reflected in the struggles I later experienced that made this role so monumentally challenging for me. Basically, this team didn't want or need someone of my level of seniority, and there was an overall misunderstanding of what my job actually was and how I would fit with the wider team.

I must admit, writing this all down makes me feel quite ashamed and embarrassed. All the signs were there, in big bold capital letters, but I was so desperate to be wanted by Google, and to get out of my current situation, that I ignored them all. I never asked myself what I wanted from my new role, I only ever thought about what I was 'good enough' for, whether I could technically be good in that role, and whether it was going to pay well. I never considered job satisfaction, or the importance of things like flexible working, or if my role would be creative or simply task based. I never thought about what I wanted, or what I needed. I was actually feeling rather broken at the time – and if Google said that they wanted me, then maybe I would finally be good enough. I would be smart enough. I would be . . . enough. Every time I walked up to their big new office in King's Cross for yet another interview, I wanted nothing more than the front doors to swish open and pull me in with open arms. I wanted to belong.

Integrity, values and risk

Your own personal integrity, your morals and the values you hold to be important must be part of this process as well.

If you care about diversity and inclusion, and when you walk into the office for the first time to find a sea of white faces, which you feel in your gut is going to be a problem – is this something that's important enough for you to create a potentially awkward situation now, rather than a more painful one later? Is it worth saying something like, 'I really loved your article in *Campaign* about how D&I is so important to this agency; what's your strategy and approach for building a more diverse and inclusive workforce here?'

If you're passionate about closing the gender pay gap and about gender balance in the workplace and you notice the company you're thinking of joining only has one woman on its board, how do you approach this? Do you say something like, 'I'm really passionate about creating gender balance in the workplace, particularly when it comes to senior management – can you tell me a bit about Platypus Associates' strategy towards creating a gender-balanced workplace?'

These conversations are uncomfortable, but how the interviewer responds to this question, and other questions like it, will no doubt tell you all you need to know. Their answer might surprise you. It could make the challenge of being one of four women in your department worthwhile, or being the only senior manager of colour even more significant – knowing that you are part of a bigger moment of change for that company. But you'll never know if you don't give them the opportunity to tell you. It's another perfect example of choosing discomfort over resentment.

That being said, there are sometimes things that you simply won't feel comfortable asking about. For example, if you're considering a gender transition, and the company seems very conservative, then how comfortable are you going to be working there? Is the risk that you'll need to constantly explain what being gender queer or trans means, and carry the burden of everyone else's ignorance – no matter how innocent or benign – worth the job?

Mental health is another factor that some of us need to consider when looking for new jobs, particularly if there are additional considerations we need in order to do our jobs to the best of our ability.

Maggy Van Eijk, the author of *Remember This When You're Sad*, says that this is a big challenge, but something that has to be addressed in one form or another before starting a new job. She says that, rather than speak directly about her mental health when she was interviewing for her current role, she emphasized how she thinks it's important that organizations value all personality types, not just alphas and extroverts. She was hired, and she was later told by her HR department that they're actively trying to diversify their teams, not just in terms of race and identity but in terms of how people work: 'There's more empathy with how different brains operate, and that's like the early work for being able to talk about mental health.'

Maggy is quite open about her mental health on social media; she's written about it for various publications and has, of course, also written a book about it. I asked if she felt nervous about this when applying for jobs:

> *Often people give potential candidates a Google or follow them, so for my new job I was interviewed by seven different people, and two of them followed me on Instagram and Twitter, where I'm constantly oversharing about mental health, so I felt on that occasion, I didn't need to say it because they probably knew already. That is a privileged position to be in, it meant that I didn't need to do the talking. It means that I can kind of chicken out, when I shouldn't, really.*

I disagree with Maggy that this is chickening out – I think this is actually a fine example of how social media can be a positive tool when looking for a new job. It can have conversations for us or communicate on our behalf so we aren't necessarily forced to. And if a company is accurately vetting candidates and learns about someone's mental health struggles, again, it says a lot about what a company chooses to do with that information. If they don't want to hire you because they're afraid you might go off sick with depression or anxiety – that's not a place you want to be working anyway.

It's also worth remembering that what you put on social media is easily findable by prospective clients, hiring managers and the people you might yourself be hiring. (If that made your blood run cold, this might be a good time to lock down your Instagram account . . .)

Do your research

Another factor that should go into your job hunt, is doing a bit of research on the company you're potentially joining and lending your name and reputation to.

A few things to check out beforehand:

- Run the company's name through Google News, Twitter and sites like Glassdoor, and see what comes up. (This might seem obvious, but is something I haven't always done.)
  - Has there been an HR scandal that made the news?
  - If they're a large company, have they released their gender and ethnicity wage gap information?
  - Is their team just a sea of white faces on Google Images?
- Do the same for the hiring manager and CEO of the company.
- If you're joining a start-up or a small company, have a look at their details on the Company's House website.
  - Are their accounts up-to-date?
  - How many directors and board members have they had join and leave over the last few years?
  - Does it seem like a lot of turnover?
- If there's something about the company's business model that seems confusing or you don't understand, ask!

Talking about money

Talking about money is everyone's least favourite thing. In fact, I think I would be more confident asking someone why they don't have any women on their senior leadership team than I would for £10k more in my salary package.

This is an area where I feel there are unspoken rules and myths that women pass around amongst each other. I've heard many, and disagreed with many, and have probably passed along some dumb rules myself, when I was younger.

I've spoken to many women, HR professionals and recruiters about this.

Here's what I've learned:

1) Your current salary does not dictate your next salary.

Cheryl Fergusson says:

> *It's irrelevant what you earned in your last role. Do you know what the role you're going for is worth in the market? It's not difficult to find out, there are resources like Glassdoor, etc., that will map them. So many people default to thinking their previous salary has to be disclosed or is the most relevant thing in the room, and it's irrelevant! What's the market value of the role? It's very rare to be able to check, no one will ever check your P45, they're only going to pay what they're willing to pay or have budget to pay.*

So, next time you are asked, 'What are your salary expectations? What are you currently on?' you can say, 'The market rate for this role is around an average of £60k. Considering my significant experience in this area, I would expect no less than £65–70k for this position.'

If they ask what you're currently on, you don't actually have to tell them. You could respond by saying something like: 'It's a very different role, and the company sizes are fairly different, so the two are not comparable.'

But, when I have had to answer, I've sometimes upped the number by £10k or more. If the person you're talking to doesn't understand market rate, or thinks that's the way salaries or someone's value are decided, being honest that you currently make £15k less than the role is being advertised for isn't going to do you any favours.

I appreciate, however, that this is hard for a lot of people, particularly women.

A twenty-nine-year-old journalist I discussed salaries with explained her anxiety around the matter: 'Whenever I'm asked for salary expectations I'll say "Well, this is what I'm on now, so I'd like it matched." I know it isn't good, I just feel like if I overprice myself they'll say no. I know that sounds silly, but that's how I feel.'

I know the exact feeling she's describing and, ultimately, it's the fear of retaliation. The fear that a hiring manager will find us disgusting for thinking we are worth so much. And they will be so disgusted with us, with our female arrogance and our ambitious greed, that they'll revoke their offer altogether. *Spoiler alert*: this doesn't happen. At least, I've never heard of this happening. And if it does . . . is that really the kind of place you want to be working? Take it as a sign from the gods and run for the fucking hills.

2) *Market research is everything*

The perfect antidote to the fear of retaliation described above is to go into these negotiations armed with knowledge. And that knowledge is your buddy market research. Now, 'market research' sounds pretty intimidating, and to be honest I wasn't even sure how to go about this other than to Google 'how to do market research', so I spoke to Kate Pljaskovova, co-founder of She Wins[2] – an organization that aims to help women better negotiate their salaries – about how best women can approach negotiating their pay, in both job offers and in jobs they're already in. Here's her advice:

Search online

Before you start – create a spreadsheet, set criteria for your search (e.g. position, location, industry, years of experience, company size etc.) and gather a lot of data points, thirty can be a good number. There are many websites that allow you to compare compensation, bonuses and other benefits against others in similar positions within similar industries, locations etc.

Speak to recruiters and HR specialists

There are tens of thousands of recruiters out there and most of them would be happy to talk to you about the new role you're considering. They will be happy to compare their notes about similar jobs. If you decide to talk to them, always talk to more than one, from three to five would be an appropriate sample. You can also ask a friendly HR person from a different company if you have one accessible to you.

Kate suggests asking them questions such as:

- 'What do you think would be an appropriate salary for a person like me performing this job? Any idea about bonuses and benefits I should I ask for?'
- 'Do you know the approximate salary range for a job like this with my skill set?'
- 'How much experience and what skill set would a person need to have to get XXX salary in this industry?'

Speak to men in similar roles

Sacré bleu! Speak to men about money? But, honestly, it makes sense. Kate says a good way to approach this is by reaching out to friends doing similar work, finding people in comparable jobs on LinkedIn, or contacting a manager in your chosen field to get an idea of what his team members earn. You will get better answers if you approach them as experts rather than asking specific questions, i.e.: 'In your experience, approximately what sort of salary package could I expect for a job like this?' not 'How much does XXX pay?'

3) Bring up salary in a practical, timely way (not in the first interview!)

If you're working with a recruiter, I think they should ask you about your salary expectations, and tell you specifically what the company's budget is for the role, quite early on in the process. But this isn't always the case.

When should this conversation happen?
If you're dealing with an employer directly, the consensus I've heard in the UK is to wait until it's brought up, take their lead, but certainly don't wait until they offer you the job to have that first conversation. What happens if your expectation massively exceeds their budget, and you've both gone through this entire process for no reason? Cheryl Fergusson advises:

> *I wouldn't necessarily say to introduce it if it's not been introduced to you. Once you feel like you've hooked them a little bit on yourself, then I would open the door to the conversation, and very much frame it as, 'On a practical level I just want to make sure that we're really aligned here,' and, 'Is your budget aligned with the market rate for this kind of role? Can we talk about that?' and just have the information. Have five key roles that have been advertised recently and that are similar to the role that you're going for, and know what those salaries are, and talk about the impact that role will have in their business, the benefit it will bring, or why it's worth that amount or more.*

This can be particularly sensitive, depending on the country and culture you work in. Although Maggy lives in the Netherlands, she has worked both there and in the UK. She says that the way they approach money is very different where she is:

> *The problem in Holland is that before you had started the interview process, if you mention it or ask what the salary would be, they would find it really weird. First you go in and you'd have to go through the whole process and then wait to find out what the salary was. I think people in the UK are getting a bit better about telling you the salary up front, but in Holland, not at all, that would be seen like a really weird thing. The Dutch are more straightforward on loads of different aspects, but for some reason when it comes to money, no, let's just not talk about it.*

This is definitely something to keep in mind if you're interviewing for roles abroad or in a culture you're not used to working in. If you're interviewing in a culture that's not the one you grew up in or have lived in before, you'll absolutely want to do a bit of research on their working practices, and their attitudes towards money. If you're working with a recruiter, they should be able to help you with this; otherwise there's the good ol' internet and resources like the Hofstede Index, which lets you compare countries and their values.[3]

9) Negotiate your salary in a way that's natural, and authentic to you

I've been on the receiving end of some negotiation tactics that were less than stellar. It's a really awkward situation to be in, when someone is adamantly arguing for something that you simply can't give them. Or that is undeserved. Or doesn't make sense. Negotiating is difficult for all parties involved, but the thing that makes it worse is when people start to behave and speak like they're criminal defence lawyers in a courtroom drama, or as if they're an MP speaking on behalf of their constituents in the House of Commons. 'The right honourable lady will refrain from any further acts of labour until the required compensation and increase of declared monies owed is released henceforth!'

This doesn't help anyone, and if you start to speak and write emails like someone who's just read *Salary Negotiation for Dummies* or, for example, have your friend who happens to be an employment lawyer write your email for you using language only a judge would understand, you're really not doing yourself any favours. As Cheryl says:

> *It's more difficult for women. It's just, that kind of aggressive negotiation thing that, stereotypically in a lot of people's minds, isn't aligned with women. And so women sometimes do push a bit aggressively in a way that doesn't always then seem authentic to them, and can cause a bit of friction, so it's about using different strategies to have those conversations that are more aligned with your personal style. Personally, I always go with a business case. I love good, thorough research analysis and to present the business case. I'll write it and present it and go down that route of proving myself and my value and why I'm asking for this salary, rather than just going 'GIVE ME ONE HUNDRED GRAND!' because that wouldn't be very me. And I think women need to develop their own strategy for it, in a way that resonates with them, because without that authenticity, it doesn't work.*

If you're self-employed

If you're self-employed, one of the hardest things to know is whether you're charging enough for your day rate. While I can't give you specific guidance on that without knowing your experience level or which industry you work in, this is where Google (and social media) really is your friend. If you know other freelancers in your industry, talk to them about it. Get their advice, because, as you've no doubt heard before, if you're not asking for enough because you're afraid prospective employers will reject you as 'too expensive', you're actually undercutting your other peers who are asking what they're worth. We all lower the standard if we don't ask for enough.

It's also worth noting that, even though my anxiety has convinced me this will one day happen, I've never had anyone respond to my day rate by saying, 'Absolutely not! We'll take our business elsewhere.' Sometimes they'll request a discount, and sometimes I'll agree. There is always room for negotiation.

Some other things to keep in mind:

- Always ask and agree the day rate before you accept a job. (I recently failed to do this, and ended up working for around 20 per cent of my usual rate. It was both my fault and the fault of the person who hired me, and we each left that situation feeling awkward AF.)
- Always confirm payment terms (thirty days, forty-five days, ninety days?) up front and investigate what the invoicing process and frequency is like – if you're working somewhere on a full-time contract but won't get paid until you've been there for two months (invoicing at the end of the month, then thirty days before you're paid), it's worth asking for a deposit or if

you can invoice weekly or fortnightly, even if just for the first month.

- If you're contracting somewhere for a regular period of time, it's also worth asking about equipment (laptop, desk, monitor), expenses and any other allowances that might impact your work and ability to perform your job.
- Get an accountant, save your receipts. Trust me, it's worth it.

How to know when it's time to quit

When you find yourself in a less than stellar employment situation, the best thing to do is move on, but getting the timing right can be difficult.

Various conditions can be in play here. Sometimes, of course, the choice is made for us: we're made redundant, or we're fired. Sometimes, life springs a surprise: we're head-hunted and presented out of the blue with an amazing opportunity we can't refuse. Other times, we need to go because we're feeling just plain miserable, unhappy or stuck.

I asked a therapist in London about this:

Honestly, a lot of my clients, there's this part of me that really wants to say, 'Get the fuck out of there!' And I want to rescue them, I really feel for them. People have different levels of toleration, and it's about figuring out what's important. And that means a lot of different things for different people, and that's why having the space to discuss this [in therapy] is good, because it makes you think about your priorities.

There's many different factors to look at, if somebody was severely burnt out and depressed and hated going to work every day and there wasn't anything they were getting out of that place, I would encourage them to think about leaving.

Personally, I think when your mental health is starting to suffer from a work situation then that's when you probably need to make a move.

It's also important not to confuse workplace anxiety with situational stress or other naturally occurring phenomena that can have an impact on your mental health. Knowing what's situational and normal for you will make it easier to recognize when there are prolonged symptoms and evidence that your current working situation is having a negative or even severe effect on your mental well-being.

Before you quit, though, make sure that:

- You've given the role enough time – this doesn't mean a specific length of time (one year, or six months) but rather that you've given yourself longer than a couple of days to decide whether or not you like it. Basically, have you been in the role long enough to know that you've given it a proper chance?
- You've had the big, difficult conversations with the necessary people at your company, whether that's a difficult boss, a colleague, or even taking your concerns to HR or other members of senior management.
- You've set the necessary boundaries for yourself at work to try to protect your mental well-being, but it hasn't had the desired effect.
- You've reached out to co-workers, or employee resource groups for advice or assistance.

- You've been totally honest with your mentor or your career coach about what's going on and why you want to leave. Have they given you honest feedback and advice on what to do next?
- You've thought about changing roles within your company. Could you transfer to a different office? Is there a sponsor at work who could help with this?
- You know what you want from your next role, and your next company. What would make leaving better for you?

Essentially, I advise making sure you've tried everything you can do to rectify your current problem. If you've done all of the above, if you've sat with the discomfort for a bit and you know you're unhappy; that your mental health is prejudiced by working in these conditions; that you just need to fucking go, then go. Fly! You are released!

Important sidenote: if you're being harassed, abused or bullied – this checklist doesn't apply. Keep yourself safe, make the necessary HR and legal complaints, and get the fuck out of there pronto.

A work wife isn't a reason to stay in a job (and neither are free snacks)

One of the main reasons people decide to stay in a job for longer than they maybe should, is the relationships they make at work. If you have a best friend or a work wife (or husband) in the office, it makes it so much harder even to consider leaving, because, well, can you imagine working somewhere without them? But then, more often than not, our work partner leaves us first. And that can be just as hard.

In her book *The Sisterhood*, Daisy Buchanan writes about her 'work wife' Zoe, with whom she worked at *Bliss* magazine. Both Daisy and Zoe overcame their initial, envious preconceived notions about each other and subsequently became very good friends. But then, Zoe left, leaving Daisy to figure out what she wanted from her career on her own. I asked Daisy about this relationship and how Zoe leaving actually allowed her to blossom:

> *We were both in our mid twenties, and at that point where our ambition outstripped our abilities and experience, our mutual restlessness brewed and we just had fun – we were very lucky to work in a place where there was so much fun to be had. I think that when Zoe moved she proved that moving was possible. Our office was a cosy house, and she'd pushed a wall down and shown me that the outside world was cold and scary, but enormous.*

Did she think that the comfort of being able to 'brew' in their 'mutual restlessness' was a negative, rather than a positive aspect of their friendship? Daisy said she thinks that sharing dissatisfactions with people at work is bonding and comforting in the short term but that it can eventually be dangerous and destructive. 'If someone's lack of ambition is keeping you in your comfort zone, and if you know that you like talking about how unhappy you are, but deep down you're worried that you're not prepared to do anything about it, it's a red flag.'

The other difficult side to this is that the friendships at work that seem so vital to your daily happiness rarely continue to feel that way once either of you leaves. If all you have to talk about is your bitch of a boss, and the only things in common concern work, you're probably going to struggle to maintain this friendship out in the real world.

'The people are great' is also not a reason to stay. While having an amazing group of colleagues is wonderful, 'great' people are everywhere, and if they're so great and you are so truly close, you will still see them when you no longer work together. The great thing about social media is that you can still follow what these people are doing. It's not like you or they drop off the face of the earth when you leave a job. I still talk to many of my ex-colleagues on Twitter and Instagram. And considering most of us are communicating on Slack at work rather than talking in person anyway, what's so bad about just talking to them on social, but without the bullshit of the job that you all hate?

Just like the people, the benefits of a job shouldn't be keeping you in a job, either. I've worked in places where there are FULL SPIN STUDIOS in the building. Complete with heavily discounted deep tissue massages, three free meals a day, plus free fancy coffees made by our very own baristas. Other places I've worked have boasted cool T-shirts, wonderful pay, celebrity founders and free beer and pizza once a week. And did I mention the Christmas parties and the bagels we got given on Fridays?

It's great if the company you work for has a wellness centre and a doctor in house, but here's a hint: if you're constantly having to visit the wellness centre at work, what is it exactly that is making you unwell?

There are plenty of reasons why you might need to stay in a job for health benefits, or salary, if your personal circumstances render this necessary. But if you don't have those constraints, there is no mentor, no boss, no free snack or work wife that is a good enough reason for you to stay in a job if you're unhappy, or overly stressed, or burnt out. A toxic working environment cannot be saved by the one nice person there. Your time and energy and sanity are worth more than the free snacks.

Before you quit, make a financial plan

I don't advise just quitting without planning how you're going to manage moneywise. Even if you're lucky enough to have savings, you don't necessarily want to spend them on rent and keeping yourself fed. That's not what savings are for.

Finding a new job is always, always, so much easier when you're already in one. It means that desperation and the pure drive for money aren't clouding your ability to identify a role that is right for you. It also allows you the time to research roles properly, to understand the industry you're moving into and so on. Sometimes, this stuff takes time, and when you're out of work, time is never on your side.

Learning when it's time to leave any situation – whether it's a romantic relationship, a friendship, or a job – really is an art form. And it's nearly impossible to get it just right. If you're going through the 'do I stay or do I go?' battle with yourself, I hope you find the points and stories and advice in this chapter useful.

So, here's to you deciding to quit your job – or not. And here's to those of you going into your new jobs, armed to the teeth with information and market research. Informed decisions are the absolute best kind of decisions, and I truly hope that the ridiculously uninformed decisions I've made in my career will help you make better ones.

Conclusion

Work for women today is pretty mad. We should be girlbosses, but still likeable. We should achieve our dreams, but in a tidy way that's inspiring and aspirational without being messy or intimidating. Our struggle has to seem *relatable* – preferably in a very stylish outfit in highly curated surroundings. Perhaps at a women's co-working club where you pay to work in a meeting room named after an inspiring heroine from days of yore who probably wouldn't have been able to afford a membership there . . .

It's hard to challenge systems and fight the good fight when we're exhausted, stressed-the-fuck out or caught up in some psychological battle with our manager. But we *can* do it! While so many things in our career are out of our control, there are a lot of areas that *are* in our power.

We can control how we spend our time, the boundaries we set, and stressful relational issues. We can choose to be the grown-up in the room, to initiate difficult conversations. We can ask for what we need – whether that's help, more flexible hours or next Friday off so you can spend the day mooching around a museum and eating lunch at Shake Shack. The better we know ourselves, our own desires and what fuels our ambition, the better we'll be able to manage our energy – investing time where it's truly needed, not just where it's demanded.

Ultimately, the answer to how to work without losing our mind is in the *doing*. It's in the daily actions we take. It's in our interactions, how we choose to respond to challenges big or small, and what we allow to take up our time, energy and headspace. It's in the time we take to rest, too.

How do you work without losing your mind? We've covered a lot of ground trying to answer that question, but here are a few key points that I hope will serve as an aide-memoire:

- Learn how to have difficult conversations and ask difficult questions as a way to defuse fraught relational issues with managers and colleagues and to make things less stressful.
- Learn how to stand up for yourself by identifying and stating your needs in both your current and future roles. This includes the creation and reinforcement of boundaries on both your time and your energy.
- Accept what is in your control, and what is not. This is about knowing you've done all you can to try to mend a rocky relationship with your manager, for example, or figuring out that you're having a hard time getting on with a colleague because you're envious. It's about knowing what's your shit and what's their shit, and either sitting in the discomfort of that or finding an alternative place to sit.
- Understand your own psychological make-up. What insecurities or vulnerabilities might be colouring our written or verbal interactions with our clients,

colleagues and managers? What are our feelings of envy trying to tell us? Are we bringing our own unresolved emotional trauma to work or acting out familial psychodramas there?

- Reflect on what you want from your career and remember that you are not your job, or your job title.
- Tend to the relationship and connection between your body and mind. This is really important, and is individual to everyone, but learning how to listen to your body, and understanding when it's stressed because your mind is stressed, is priceless.

Let go of that super-manic-crazy-busy-working-lady life

As we all were harshly reminded in 2020, there are very few things in life that we can fully control. But the way you look after yourself and the way you engage with your work, are two of them. Even when things get stressful and it feels like everyone in the world wants something from you, you must remember to stand up and have a drink or a loo break every hour or so. What is not fine is making yourself physically uncomfortable or potentially unwell simply because you're 'too busy' to take basic care of yourself. You don't need a pandemic as an excuse to finally take a day or two off. The fact that a breather or a five-minute break here and there seems radical is at the heart of why just working at a perfectly reasonable pace feels like underperforming. We're not allowed to be just average, we must be *excellent*. No breaks for me, thanks! *Gosh, I've been so flat out all day I forgot to eat lunch! I've just been so busy* excelling . . .

You have to remember to leave on time, and to book extra hours or time off in lieu if you've had to work over here and there.

I urge you to monitor your reactions, to examine what your stress triggers are, to give everyone the benefit of the doubt, and to *chill the fuck out*. Yes, you might feel like you can't take a lunch break because you have six urgent emails from your manager and some PR incident kicking off . . . but the world won't stop turning if you take twenty minutes to clear your head by listening to the latest episode of the 'Thirst Aid Kit'* podcast. And you have to start somewhere.

Try to remember what your true desires are, and what is fuelling your ambition. It's so easy to forget that quite often when we're overworking ourselves, we are filling a void. We are spinning the hamster wheel like crazy to mask something else going on in our lives. To prove that we can indeed control the entire space–time continuum using just willpower and an iPhone. To prove our competency to ourselves. Maybe we're chasing some goal we think might *finally* impress Mum, or perhaps you think that once you update your social media bios with some impressive-sounding job title, your online nemesis will see it, and it will ruin her whole fucking day. Like *that*'s the thing that might finally fill that wild emptiness inside you. Trust me – it's not!

For example, just the other night I made the mistake of checking my emails right before switching off the bedside lamp. When I read the subject line, I knew immediately that the message would for *sure* piss me off. That it would raise

---

* Shout out to Bim and Nichole!

both my blood pressure and my anxiety level, and that the subsequent adrenaline rush would prevent me from sleeping. I also knew that once I read it, I'd need to formulate a clever and cunning reply, which would take at least twenty minutes. I also knew that all this would keep my husband awake, and that he had an early flight to catch the next morning. So I just didn't read it. I waited until the morning. I left it unread for over eight hours and, you know what? NOBODY DIED. Nothing happened. It was fine. I tweeted about my tiny act of rebellion and had a fair amount of responses that were all like, 'OMG how???'

It was a small decision but it made a big difference to both my sleep and my husband's, and the next day I felt both more rested and better able to respond, and managed to move on with my day without stress. I'm still learning about all this myself, but what would happen if we all made little adjustments like this on a daily basis?

'Young Hearts, Run (stress) Free'

I wrote this book so that it could help you survive the hell of the modern workplace – whether that's an open-plan office or your kitchen table. Even if you extract only one or two nuggets of information that might change how you interact with your manager, or can help ease the extreme stress you're experiencing in a no-win situation, I'll be happy.

If, like I've done in the past, you've spent parts of your working day hiding in corners trying to breathe normally, or crying in various spots around your workplace, I hope that *How to Work Without Losing Your Mind* has helped you dig below the surface feelings of anger and frustration at your job, and to find what's at the root of what's going on for you at work.

Accepting that the perfect working environment probably doesn't exist can be difficult. Things being average is hard to sit with sometimes. Understanding that in order to have a healthier relationship with work you'll have to be uncomfortable more than you'd like to be for a while isn't exactly thrilling. I get it! We have become conditioned to expect excellence from ourselves at all times, so realizing that, actually, giving 75 per cent at work so that you can preserve some energy for your side projects or have more emotional capacity available for your kids might take some getting used to.

I fervently believe that work doesn't have to take up our entire lives, steal our identity and our joy. Just like the character Jenna sings in *Waitress: The Musical* about how the diner she works at and the people she serves as a waitress have both taken more than she gave them, work takes more than you give it. And when you realize that's happening, the onus to do something about it is on you. It won't be easy. Like Gloria Steinem once said, 'The truth will set you free, but first, it will piss you off.' And it will. But after you've cooled down a bit, what *will* you do about it?

Personally, I'm excited to see what you do next, and if this book has helped you make a change, please let me know on social media – I've listed my accounts for you in Resources. I can't wait for you to learn and discover your own power, and the control you can exert over your career. You deserve to feel *good* and to find satisfaction in work that you enjoy, that pays you well and that doesn't take you to the brink of insanity. I want this for everyone. I truly believe it would change the world – especially now that the world of work has been irrevocably altered, and we've all had a glimpse of what flexible working is like, and the positive impact empathetic leaders can have.

Thank you for buying and reading this book. Thank you for holding space for my ideas about working, and how we can make it better. It's made all of my challenging work experiences feel purposeful, rather than just crap luck.

So, here's to us, dear reader, and finding ways to work without losing our damn minds.

Resources

General resources

Organizations

ACAS: www.acas.org.uk/

Citizens Advice: www.citizensadvice.org.uk/work/problems-at-work/

Equality and Human Rights Commission: www.equalityhuman rights.com/en

Mind: How to find a therapist: www.mind.org.uk/information-support/drugs-and-treatments/talking-therapy-and-counselling/how-to-find-a-therapist/

Online resources

How's Work with Esther Perel: https://howswork.estherperel.com/

Publications

Brené Brown, *Dare to Lead* (audiobook) (Random House Audiobooks, 2018)

Brené Brown, *The Power of Vulnerability: Teachings of Authenticity, Connection, and Courage* (audiobook) (Sounds True, 2012)

Alison Grade, *The Freelance Bible: Everything You Need to Go Solo in Any Industry* (Portfolio Penguin, 2020)

Viv Groskop, *How to Own the Room: Women and the Art of Brilliant Speaking* (Bantam Press, 2018)

Jennifer Romolini, *Weird in a World That's Not: A Career Guide for Misfits, F*ckups, and Failures* (HarperBusiness, 2017)

Get in Touch with Cate

Instagram: @CateSevilla

Twitter: @CateSevilla

LinkedIn: linkedin.com/in/CateSevilla

Email: catesevilla.com/contact

1 Power + Authority

ACAS on discrimination, bullying and harassment: www.acas.org.uk/discrimination-bullying-and-harassment

Forbes, 'How To Deal With A Bullying Boss' (includes Gary Namie's 25 most common tactics adopted by workplace bullies): www.forbes.com/sites/jacquelynsmith/2013/09/20/how-to-deal-with-a-bullying-boss/#a3f25783d378

Lean In: www.leanin.org

National Bullying Helpline: www.nationalbullyinghelpline.co.uk/employees.html

Search Inside Yourself Leadership Institute, 'SBNRR – Stop, Breathe, Notice, Reflect, Respond': https://siyli.org/downloads/SIY_Handouts_2Day_SBNRR.pdf

Douglas Stone, with Bruce Patton and Shelia Heen, *Difficult Conversations: How to Discuss What Matters Most* (Penguin Random House USA, 2010)

TUC on bullying: www.tuc.org.uk/resource/bullying-work

UK Government advice on your legal rights: www.gov.uk/workplace-bullying-and-harassment

The Workplace Bullying Institute: www.workplacebullying.org/

2 Envy + Jealousy

Daisy Buchanan, *The Sisterhood: A Love Letter to the Women Who Have Shaped Us* (Headline, 2020)

Viv Groskop, *Lift as You Climb: Women and the Art of Ambition* (Bantam Press, 2020)

Lucy Sheridan, *The Comparison Cure: How to be Less 'Them' and More You* (Orion Spring, 2019)

3 Success + Sanity

'Armchair Expert' podcast: https://armchairexpertpod.com/

BuzzFeed, 'How Millennials Became the Burnout Generation': www.buzzfeednews.com/article/annehelenpetersen/millennials-burnout-generation-debt-work

The Cut, 'The Ambition Collision': www.thecut.com/2017/09/what-happens-to-ambition-in-your-30s.html

The Energy Project: https://theenergyproject.com

How To Academy, *Elizabeth Gilbert on Life and Love* (video): www.howtoacademy.com/videos/elizabeth-gilbert-on-life-and-love/

Lean In, 'The "Broken Rung" ': https://leanin.org/women-in-the-workplace-2019

Lenny, 'The Psychic Stress of Being the Only Black Woman at Work': www.lennyletter.com/story/the-stress-of-being-the-only-black-woman-at-work

New York Times, 'You Accomplished Something Great. So Now What' (arrival fallacy): www.nytimes.com/2019/05/28/smarter-living/you-accomplished-something-great-so-now-what.html

No Bad Days Notepad: https://shopwitanddelight.com/no-bad-days-checklist-notepad/

Refinery29, 'Let 2020 be the Year We Get Rid of Girlboss Culture for Good': www.refinery29.com/en-gb/2020/01/9044921/girlboss-culture-women-work

Workaholics Anonymous UK: www.wa-uk.org/

4 Boundaries + Egos

Leil Lowndes, *How to Talk to Anyone: 92 Little Tricks for Big Success in Relationships* (HarperElement, 2014)

5 Leadership + Responsibility

Earwolf, *Getting Curious with Jonathan Van Ness*: www.earwolf.com/show/getting-curious-with-jonathan-van-ness/

Reni Eddo-Lodge, *Why I'm No Longer Talking to White People About Race* (Bloomsbury, 2018)

Amy Edmondson, *Building a Psychologically Safe Workplace* (TEDx talk): www.youtube.com/watch?v=LhoLuui9gX8

'Nancy' podcast: www.wnycstudios.org/podcasts/nancy

Franchesca Ramsay's YouTube channel: www.youtube.com/user/chescaleigh/

6 Authenticity + Mental Health

Back to Work After: http://backtoworkafter.co.uk

'Fresh to Death' podcast: www.bbc.co.uk/programmes/po81q47x

Glaad, 'A Beginner's Guide to Being an Ally to Trans People': www.glaad.org/amp/beginners-guide-being-ally-to-trans-people

Glaad, 'Tips for Allies of Transgender People': www.glaad.org/transgender/allies

'Griefcast' podcast: https://cariadlloyd.com/griefcast

Huffington Post, 'What's the Difference Between Mental Health and Mental Illness?': www.huffingtonpost.co.uk/entry/whats-the-difference-between-mental-health-and-mental-illness_uk_5d399 1fae4b02ocd994f55ee?guccounter=1

Nora McInerny: www.noraborealis.com/

Mental Health at Work: www.mhaw.uk.com/

Mental Health First Aid Training: https://mhfaengland.org/

Mental Health Foundation: www.mentalhealth.org.uk/

PinkNews, 'How to Support a Trans Person at Work': www.pinknews.co.uk/2018/05/04/how-to-support-a-trans-person-at-work/

Psychology Today, 'Re-Enacting Family Dynamics in the Workplace': www.psychologytoday.com/us/blog/credit-and-blame-work/201104/re-enacting-family-dynamics-in-the-workplace

'Terrible, Thanks for Asking' podcast: www.ttfa.org/

TUC: 'How to be a Good Trans Ally at Work': www.tuc.org.uk/resource/how-be-good-trans-ally-work

Maggy Van Eijk, *Remember This When You're Sad: Lessons Learned on the Road from Self-Harm to Self-Care* (Lagom, 2018)

7 Desire + Planning

Brené Brown, *The Call to Courage* (documentary): www.netflix.com/title/81010166

Roz Savage, 'The Obituary Exercise': www.rozsavage.com/the-obituary-exercise/

Search Inside Yourself Leadership Institute: https://siyli.org/

8 Parenthood + Patriarchy

Christine Armstrong, *The Mother of All Jobs: How to Have Children and a Career and Stay Sane(ish)* (Green Tree, 2018)

Fast Company, 'Pregnancy is Making Bumble CEO Whitney Wolfe Herd Rethink Parental Work Policies': www.fastcompany.com/90365442/pregnancy-is-making-bumble-ceo-whitney-wolfe-herd-rethink-parental-work-policies

Nell Frizzell, *The Panic Years* (Bantam Press, 2020)

Guardian, 'Is the Pram in the Hallway Still the Enemy of Good Art?': www.theguardian.com/world/2003/mar/17/gender.uk

Linkedin Blog, 'We Need To Talk About Fertility at Work': https://blog.linkedin.com/2019/october/29/we-need-to-talk-about-fertility-at-work

Make Motherhood Diverse: www.instagram.com/MAKEMOTHERHOODDIVERSE/

Miscarriage Association: www.miscarriageassociation.org.uk/

Miscarriage Association, 'Miscarriage and the Workplace': www.miscarriageassociation.org.uk/wp-content/uploads/2016/10/Miscarriage-and-the-Workplace.pdf

Mother Pukka, 'Flex Appeal': www.motherpukka.co.uk/flex/

Pregnant Then Screwed: https://pregnantthenscrewed.com/

'Strange Bird' podcast – 'Miscarriage': https://podcasts.apple.com/gb/podcast/strange-bird/id1348332336?i=1000402489110&mt=2

UK Government policies on maternity pay and leave: www.gov.uk/maternity-pay-leave

Vox, 'Pay Discrimination Only Explains Part of the Gender Wage Gap': www.vox.com/2018/9/7/17828964/gender-wage-gap-explained-netflix

9 *Misfortune + Failure*

Brené Brown, *Rising Strong* (Vermilion, 2015)

Stephanie Brown, *Fired: Why Losing Your Job is the Best Thing That Can Happen to You* (independently published, 2017): https://lifeafterfired.com/

Stephanie Brown, 'The Single Biggest Mistake Most People Make After Losing Their Job': https://lifeafterfired.com/recently-fired/single-biggest-mistake-people-make-losing-job/

Elizabeth Day, *How To Fail: Everything I've Ever Learned from Things Going Wrong* (Fourth Estate, 2019)

10 Red Flags + Gut Instincts

Lucy Clayton and Steven Haines, *How to Go to Work: The Honest Advice No One Ever Tells You at the Start of Your Career* (Portfolio Penguin, 2020)

Companies House search: https://beta.companieshouse.gov.uk/

Glassdoor: www.glassdoor.co.uk/index.htm

Viv Groskop, *How to Own the Room: Women and the Art of Brilliant Speaking* (Bantam Press, 2018)

Hofstede Insights Compare Countries tool: www.hofstede-insights.com/product/compare-countries/

Leil Lowndes, *How to Talk to Anyone at Work: 72 Little Tricks for Big Success Communicating on the Job* (McGraw-Hill Education, 2018)

She Wins Workshop Events: https://shewins.co/for-women

She Wins: https://shewins.co/

UK Government: Redundancies, dismissals and disciplinarians: www.gov.uk/browse/working/redundancies-dismissals

Acknowledgements

This feels like the Oscar acceptance speech I never expected to give, but have also been prepared for my entire life. I can't wait to cry my entire way through writing this.

Firstly, thank you to Charlie Viney, my superb and very charming agent. I never thought in my life I'd have an agent of any kind, so it makes me feel very glamorous and fortunate to have been signed by you. Thank you for believing in me and in this project. Also, a big thank you to the endlessly talented Hannah Jewell for recommending me to Charlie, I am for ever grateful.

Next I must say the biggest, soppiest thank you to my wonderful editor, Lydia Yadi. Thank you for going above and beyond to get this project green lit. Thank you for understanding my sense of humour and not being put off by my copious F-bombs and terrifying grammar. You have been a dream to work with, and I am so proud to have you as my editor.

My glorious team at Penguin Business – Matt Crossey, Leo Donlan (I'm still sorry for that time I confused you with the tall, blonde intern), the mighty Celia Buzuk, Martina O'Sullivan, Kayla Fuller, Ellie Smith and Charlotte Faber – THANK YOU. A huge thank you to Holly Ovenden for designing such a bold and beautiful cover, I love it. Thank you to Trevor Horwood for being such a patient copy-editor! I am so proud and it's such an honour to be a Penguin author.

Thank you so much to the people who provided quotes and their expertise for this book – to name a few: Nell Frizzell, Kimberlie Walker, Tara Jane O'Reilly, Stephanie Brown, Helen Stacey, Ana McLaughlin, Hilda Burke, Kate Hogan, Cheryl Fergusson and Kate Pljaskovova.

To the women who kindly spent hours talking with me about their personal work experiences, who opened up to me about some of their most private and painful memories, this book would not be what it is without your insight, your openness and honesty, thank you for trusting me with your stories. To Marianne and the women I've named Virginia, Lily, Lucy, Jane and Aisling along with so many others – thank you, thank you, thank you.

For all the heartache *The Pool* inflicted upon us all in the end, I am so thankful to have been close to such a wonderful network of intelligent, bright, fierce individuals. Zoe Beaty, Iesha Thomas, Tory Frost and Emily Baker, thank you for all the pints. To Kat Lister and Vic Parsons, THANK YOU for being part of this book and trusting me with your stories. Daisy Buchanan, thank you for your quotes and your friendship. Viv Groskop, thank you for being so supportive and for your quotes for this book. Sali Hughes, your kindness, openness and generosity helped me so much in the last year, thank you. Lauren Laverne, I will never cease to be impressed by your warmth, kindness and work ethic, thank you for your support.

To my Google mates who gave me solace and friendship during one of the hardest periods of my career, Jenni Armstrong and Jen Harvey, thank you. (Special shout-out to Sylvie and Horatio.) Kate Lauterbach, your friendship, kindness and our eleventh-floor coffees saved me in so many ways, I'm so happy we found each other. Leonie Shinn-Morris, Hollie Jones and Rebecca Fulleylove – thank you for being such a solid editorial crew. You were the best part of my job.

Sarah Drinkwater, your guidance, insight and support has meant so much to me. Thank you for being part of this book.

Jessica Elvidge, thank fuck you are in my life! You are so special to me and I'm so glad you are my friend. Thank you for your constant support.

To Tina Walsberger, I am so thankful for our serendipitous meeting and that we've become friends. Thank you for being part of this book.

Gena-mour Barrett, thank you for our talks and for your support and for always making me laugh. Maggy Van Eijk, thank you for your quotes and for your openness and insight. You are like sunshine.

To Hayley Campbell, thank you for the years of being my work wife, and for all the cornbread.

To Amelia and Samm and my Dove Crew at R29, it's been such a pleasure to relearn how wonderful colleagues can be.

To Maddie Armitage, thank you for being part of this book and for being my unofficial mentor. You are so inspiring and I am so honoured to have you as a friend. (Shout out to Cool Matt, Tommy, Milo and Alfie.)

Before I go into thanking my family, and I start crying even more, I'd also like to thank Dario Marianelli for all of the wonderful soundtracks he's composed that have helped me write. Thank you to Stacey Halls for the Diptyque candles, I swear they increase word count.

To Mick and Jean Green, thank you for all you've done to help support me, you've made my life here possible and wonderful. Thank you for welcoming me into your family with such warmth and kindness.

Thank you, Uncle Mark, for introducing me to so many

books and encouraging my love of reading from such a young age. Thank you, Uncle David and Aunt Malai for being both my family and my friends; you have both taught me so much.

To my wider Gion family all over the world, I love you all. To Pauline and Dick, I miss you every day. Thank you for encouraging my imagination, and teaching me about unconditional love and support.

To Dad, thank you for being so unabashedly supportive and loving, and for all of the music you've brought to my life.

To Mom, thank you for showing me what hard work and doing what is necessary and important and being 'Ain't Skeerd' looks like. Thank you for all of the books, and bringing the Ingalls into my world.

To my sister Meg, thank you for your companionship and friendship, even though we're thousands of miles away. I love you and I'm so proud of you.

To Lynn Dowdell, aka Ms Zentner, thank you for encouraging me to write and to be a journalist, and for being such a source of comfort and guidance when I needed it most.

To Michelle H, I never would have been able to write this book if we hadn't started working together. You've changed my life, thank you.

To my husband, Iain – you're my constant. My best friend, my cheerleader, my conscience. Thank you for believing in me, for taking risks with me and never making me feel ashamed for the depths of my ambition or the height of my goals. I love you.

To my dog Barbara 'Bobbi' Louise, you can't read, but I love you, too.

Notes

Introduction

1. www.independent.co.uk/news/at-last-a-degree-of-honour-for-900-cambridge-women-1157056.html
2. www.bbc.co.uk/news/magazine-36662872
3. www.fastcompany.com/3050109/the-state-of-women-owned-businesses-in-the-us
4. www.americanprogress.org/issues/women/reports/2016/12/19/295203/breadwinning-mothers-are-increasingly-the-u-s-norm/
5. www.indiewire.com/2019/12/little-women-greta-gerwig-screenplay-1202199536/
6. www.nytimes.com/2020/04/18/us/coronavirus-women-essential-workers.html

1 Power + Authority

1. www.psychologytoday.com/us/blog/finding-new-home/201809/workplace-bullying-causes-effects-and-prevention
2. You can check out the specific numbers online. A 2017 Gallup poll of more than 1 million employed US workers concluded that the No. 1 reason people quit their jobs is a bad boss or immediate supervisor: www.linkedin.com/pulse/employees-dont-leave-companies-managers-brigette-hyacinth/
3. www.forbes.com/sites/jacquelynsmith/2013/09/20/how-to-deal-with-a-bullying-boss/#a3f25783d378

4. http://www.oprah.com/spirit/how-to-set-boundaries-brene-browns-advice
5. www.psychologytoday.com/gb/blog/in-the-workplace/201910/your-boss-is-jerk-theres-still-hope

2 Envy + Jealousy

1. www.psychologytoday.com/gb/blog/joy-and-pain/201401/what-is-the-difference-between-envy-and-jealousy
2. www.psychologytoday.com/gb/basics/jealousy
3. https://royalsocietypublishing.org/doi/full/10.1098/rstb.2013.0080
4. www.forbes.com/sites/bonniemarcus/2016/01/13/the-dark-side-of-female-rivalry-in-the-workplace-and-what-to-do-about-it/#b211d1c52551

3 Success + Sanity

1. www.lennyletter.com/story/the-stress-of-being-the-only-black-woman-at-work
2. https://leanin.org/women-in-the-workplace-2019?utm_source=newsletter&utm_medium=email&utm_campaign=wiw
3. www.who.int/mental_health/evidence/burn-out/en/
4. www.bbc.co.uk/news/business-51032631
5. http://banbossy.com/
6. www.thecut.com/2014/05/sophia-amoruso-nasty-gal-millennial-advice.html
7. https://about.americanexpress.com/files/doc_library/file/2018-state-of-women-owned-businesses-report.pdf
8. www.theguardian.com/world/2019/oct/18/the-wing-how-an-exclusive-womens-club-sparked-a-thousand-arguments
9. www.refinery29.com/en-gb/2020/01/9044921/girlboss-culture-women-work
10. www.theguardian.com/money/2018/nov/17/klarna-buy-now-pay-later-system-that-is-seducing-millennials
11. www.bbc.co.uk/news/uk-england-london-51014040

12. www.buzzfeednews.com/article/annehelenpetersen/millennials-burnout-generation-debt-work
13. www.thecut.com/2017/09/what-happens-to-ambition-in-your-30s.html
14. https://hbr.org/2015/05/companies-drain-womens-ambition-after-only-2-years
15. www.girlboss.com/work/millennial-women-work-anxiety
16. www.independent.co.uk/life-style/work-burnout-men-women-positions-power-self-esteem-family-balance-study-montreal-a8377096.html
17. https://theenergyproject.com/team/approach/
18. https://shopwitanddelight.com/no-bad-days-checklist-notepad/

4 Boundaries + Egos

1. www.reddit.com/r/AmItheAsshole/
2. https://nypost.com/2018/03/22/slack-will-allow-employers-to-read-your-private-messages/
3. www.bbc.co.uk/programmes/m000bxpd
4. www.nationalgeographic.com/science/2020/04/coronavirus-zoom-fatigue-is-taxing-the-brain-here-is-why-that-happens/
5. www.linkedin.com/pulse/20140313205730-5711504-the-science-behind-ted-s-18-minute-rule
6. www.refinery29.com/en-gb/zoom-houseparty-how-to
7. https://cyberpsychology.eu/article/view/6757/6215

5 Leadership + Responsibility

1. www.iacmr.org/Conferences/WS2011/Submission_XM/Participant/Readings/Lecture9B_Jing/Edmondson,%20ASQ%201999.pdf
2. https://rework.withgoogle.com/blog/five-keys-to-a-successful-google-team/

6 Authenticity + Mental Health

1. www.huffingtonpost.co.uk/entry/whats-the-difference-between-mental-health-and-mental-illness_uk_5d3991fae4b020cd994f55ee
2. www.bitc.org.uk/wp-content/uploads/2019/10/bitc-wellbeing-report-mentalhealthatworkreport2018execsummary-oct2018.pdf
3. www.basw.co.uk/system/files/resources/basw_50944-9_0.pdf
4. www.psychologytoday.com/us/blog/credit-and-blame-work/201104/re-enacting-family-dynamics-in-the-workplace
5. Ibid.
6. https://psychology.wikia.org/wiki/Psychological_containment
7. www.headspace.com/blog/2017/07/18/noting-technique-take-advantage/
8. www.mprnews.org/story/2016/06/28/books-nora-mcinerny-purmort-its-okay-to-laugh-crying-is-cool-too
9. https://cariadlloyd.com/griefcast
10. www.bbc.co.uk/programmes/p081q47x
11. http://backtoworkafter.co.uk/about/

7 Desire + Planning

1. https://siyli.org/
2. www.rozsavage.com/the-obituary-exercise/
3. www.bbc.co.uk/programmes/articles/1nFR2NSPbzG3hDhpW2MTG5c/12-things-we-learned-about-daniel-radcliffe-from-his-desert-island-discs

8 Parenthood + Patriarchy

1. https://workplaceinsight.net/are-these-the-best-countries-for-parental-leave-worldwide/
2. www.thecut.com/article/maternity-leave-usa.html
3. www.ons.gov.uk/employmentandlabourmarket/peopleinwork/earningsandworkinghours/bulletins/genderpaygapintheuk/2019

4. www.thebookseller.com/news/prh-publishes-gender-pay-gap-9-months-early-company-wide-offer-years-patental-leave-1045551
5. www.mercer.com/our-thinking/law-and-policy-group/dutch-government-increases-paid-paternity-adoption-leave.html
6. www.vox.com/2018/9/7/17828964/gender-wage-gap-explained-netflix
7. www.vox.com/2017/9/8/16268362/gender-wage-gap-explained
8. www.government.nl/latest/news/2016/09/09/longer-paternity-leave-for-partners
9. https://pregnantthenscrewed.com/
10. www.theguardian.com/lifeandstyle/2019/jan/22/the-public-would-be-shocked-if-they-knew-how-gagging-contracts-cover-up-maternity-discrimination?CMP=Share_AndroidApp_Tweet
11. www.icpsr.umich.edu/icpsrweb/instructors/biblio/resources/111143
12. www.bbc.co.uk/news/blogs-trending-36144487
13. www.ons.gov.uk/employmentandlabourmarket/peopleinwork/earningsandworkinghours/articles/womenshouldertheresponsibilityofunpaidwork/2016-11-10
14. www.theguardian.com/world/2020/may/03/i-feel-like-a-1950s-housewife-how-lockdown-has-exposed-the-gender-divide
15. www.huffingtonpost.co.uk/entry/single-parents-work-lockdown-coronavirus_uk_5ebc0a25c5b63d4159524312
16. www.moneyadviceservice.org.uk/en/articles/childcare-costs
17. www.weforum.org/agenda/2019/03/nordic-nations-best-places-for-parents-children/
18. www.irishtimes.com/life-and-style/abroad/childcare-around-the-world-how-other-countries-do-it-better-1.3626710
19. www.motherpukka.co.uk/flex/
20. www.instagram.com/p/B63K87FFCos/
21. www.instagram.com/MAKEMOTHERHOODDIVERSE/
22. www.fastcompany.com/90365442/pregnancy-is-making-bumble-ceo-whitney-wolfe-herd-rethink-parental-work-policies
23. Ibid.
24. https://en.wikiquote.org/wiki/Cyril_Connolly

25. www.theguardian.com/world/2003/mar/17/gender.uk
26. www.miscarriageassociation.org.uk/
27. www.miscarriageassociation.org.uk/information/miscarriage/
28. https://blog.linkedin.com/2019/october/29/we-need-to-talk-about-fertility-at-work
29. www.miscarriageassociation.org.uk/wp-content/uploads/2016/10/Miscarriage-and-the-Workplace.pdf
30. https://podcasts.apple.com/gb/podcast/strange-bird/id1348332336?i=1000402489110&mt=2

9 Misfortune + Failure

1. www.theguardian.com/business/2020/may/04/over-a-fifth-of-british-employees-furloughed-in-last-fortnight
2. https://lifeafterfired.com/recently-fired/single-biggest-mistake-people-make-losing-job/
3. www.bbc.co.uk/news/uk-52433520

10 Red Flags + Gut Instincts

1. www.huffingtonpost.co.uk/entry/megan-rapinoe-i-deserve-this-ashlyn-harris-womens-soccer_n_5d26016de4b0583e482a870a?ri18n=true
2. https://shewins.co/
3. www.hofstede-insights.com/product/compare-countries/